GODDESSES

GODDESSES

MYSTERIES OF THE FEMININE DIVINE

Joseph Campbell

EDITED BY SAFRON ROSSI, PhD

JOSEPH CAMPBELL™
FOUNDATION

New World Library
Novato, California

New World Library
14 Pamaron Way
Novato, California 94949
www.newworldlibrary.com
(800) 972-6657

Text design by Tona Pearce Myers

Library of Congress Cataloging-in-Publication Data
Campbell, Joseph, 1904–1987, author.
Goddesses : mysteries of the feminine divine / Joseph Campbell ; edited by Safron Rossi, Ph.D.
    pages   cm
Includes bibliographical references and index.
ISBN 978-1-60868-182-2 (hardcover : alk. paper)
1. Goddesses. 2. Mythology, Greek. 3. Greece—Religion. 4. Egypt—Religion.
5. Middle East—Religion. 6. Goddesses in literature. I. Rossi, Safron. II. Title.
BL473.5.C36 2013
202'.114—dc23   2013030964

First printing, December 2013
ISBN 978-1-60868-182-2
Printed in Canada on 100% postconsumer-waste recycled paper

10 9 8 7 6 5

CONTENTS

ABOUT THE COLLECTED WORKS OF
JOSEPH CAMPBELL

━━━━━━━●━━━━━━━

AT HIS DEATH in 1987, Joseph Campbell left a significant body of published work that explored his lifelong passion, the complex of universal myths and symbols that he called "Mankind's one great story." He also left, however, a large volume of unreleased work: uncollected articles, notes, letters, and diaries, as well as audio- and videotape-recorded lectures.

The Joseph Campbell Foundation—founded in 1990 to preserve, protect, and perpetuate Campbell's work—has undertaken to create a digital archive of his papers and recordings and to publish *The Collected Works of Joseph Campbell.*

THE COLLECTED WORKS OF JOSEPH CAMPBELL
Robert Walter, Executive Editor
David Kudler, Managing Editor

EDITOR'S FOREWORD

Das Ewig-Weibliche, / Zieht uns hinan
"The eternal feminine / Draws us on."

—GOETHE, *Faust*

GOETHE'S WORDS from *Faust* are the golden thread of the volume you hold in your hands. Between 1972 and 1986 Campbell gave over twenty lectures and workshops on goddesses, exploring the figures, functions, symbols, and themes of the feminine divine, following them through their transformations as though he were Theseus guided by Ariadne's thread in the labyrinth of culture and time. This volume shows how Campbell traces the blossoming from one Great Goddess to the many goddesses of the mythic imagination, and follows the feminine divine from Marija Gimbutas's studies of Neolithic Old Europe into Sumerian and Egyptian mythology, through Homer's epic *Odyssey*, the Greek Eleusinian Mystery cult, Arthurian legends of the Middle Ages, and into the Neoplatonic Renaissance.

In approaching this material I was presented with the challenge of Campbell's deep commitment to certain motifs and themes, which in some cases appear in greater detail elsewhere. One of his favorite themes is the transformation and endurance of the archetypal symbolic powers of the feminine divine despite the past two thousand years of patriarchal and monotheistic religious traditions that have attempted to exclude them. I was blessed to have access to the lectures in which he most clearly provided the narrative structure by which he explored the bones and imaginations of the great goddesses. These lectures are investigations of the symbolic, mythological, and archetypal themes of the feminine divine in and of herself, and for Campbell her main themes are *initiation* into the mysteries of immanence experienced through time and space and the eternal; *transformation* of life and death; and the *energy consciousness* that informs and enlivens all life.

The goddess lectures that make up this book sprang from Campbell's work on the *Historical Atlas of World Mythology*. Campbell sought in this multivolume opus (first begun in 1974) to weave the various ethnic and cultural threads of myth and sacred tradition into a tapestry that shows the interplay of the universal and archetypal roots of psyche in specific cultural manifestations. During his research, he came upon the brilliant and pioneering work of Marija Gimbutas on the Great Goddess of the Neolithic world of Old Europe (7500–3500 B.C.). Gimbutas's work convinced Campbell even more deeply of what he was sensing, namely, that the Great Goddess was the central divine figure in the earliest mythological conception of the world, and that the powers outlined by Gimbutas were the roots of those that he saw in the goddesses of later mythologies and sacred traditions. The goddesses of the Paleolithic period provided a critical point in the beginning of his *Historical Atlas*. Campbell contextualizes Gimbutas's work in the scope of the development and manifestation of the mythic imagination. He weaves Gimbutas's profound insights and deep work on the Great Goddess and the oldest roots of mythology and culture into the larger and still unfolding story of the development of the human imagination.

The exploration and study of goddess mythology has progressed significantly since Campbell presented these lectures over three decades ago. It is my hope that this volume holds the counterpoint to the idea that Campbell was focused solely on the hero and was not sensitive to or did not find of interest goddesses, their mythologies, or the questions and concerns of women who seek to understand themselves in relation to these stories. The mid-twentieth-century conversation from which this volume springs is representative of elements that have only been deepened in terms of how we see and understand ourselves individually and collectively. These lectures show his sensitivity to the uniqueness of the feminine form in mythology, and what that could mean to women. Further, Campbell understood and honored the vital importance of the female spirit and its creative potential to birth the meaning of women's experiences into mythic and creative form. He saw this as the gift and challenge of our age and honored women in their visioning and forming of the journey.

In structuring this work, I chose to follow the sweep of the historical narrative as it unfolds in his lectures. It is illustrated with the images Campbell used, many of which can be found in his other published works, therefore showing how integral goddess images and mythologies are to the entire body of Campbell's work. The method I used for compiling this source material included relying on the scholars whose work Campbell himself used, including Jane Ellen Harrison, Marija Gimbutas, and Carl Kerényi. I made use of captions in two ways, as cross-citations to those scholars whose work Campbell relied upon and for inclusion of post-Campbellian scholars who have gone further with the mythological, religious, and cultural material in the decades since Campbell's death. The suggested source reading list includes scholars whose work is key to this field and is highly suggested for a deeper orientation to the material. This was intended to allow us to see the conversation as it has continued beyond the early 1980s and Campbell's work of integrating the tradition of the feminine divine into the larger—and now known to be younger—mythological systems.

This book has been created in honor of the legacies that Joseph Campbell and Marija Gimbutas left for us, and by which they continue to both inspire and challenge us. This book would not have come to be without Robert Walter, president of the Joseph Campbell Foundation, who gave me this project in the same spirit in which Campbell was given Heinrich Zimmer's posthumous work—thank you. Lastly, this volume is dedicated to the feminine divine who in all her names and graces draws us on.

Safron Rossi
Santa Barbara, California
May 24, 2013

FIGURE I. Thetis and Peleus (red-figure kylix, Classical, Greece, fifth century B.C.)

———•———

On the Great Goddess[1]

MANY OF THE DIFFICULTIES that women face today follow from the fact that they are moving into a field of action in the world that was formerly reserved for the male and for which there are no female mythological models. The woman finds herself, consequently, in a competitive relationship with the male, and in this may lose the sense of her own nature. She is something in her own right, and tradition-ally (for some four million years) the relationship of that something to the male has been experienced and represented, not as directly com-petitive, but as cooperative in the shared ordeal of continuing and sup-porting life. Her biologically assigned role was to give birth to and to rear children. The male role was to support and protect. Both roles are biologically and psychologically archetypical. But what has happened now—as a result of the masculine invention of the vacuum cleaner—is that women have been relieved, in some measure, of their traditional bondage to the household. They are moving into the field and jungle of individual quest, achievement, and self-realization, for which there are no *female* models. Moreover, in pursuing their distinct careers they are emerging progressively as differentiated personalities, leaving behind the old archetypal accent on the biological role—to which, however, their psyches are still constitutionally bound. The grim prayer of Lady Macbeth before her deed, "unsex me here!"[2] must be the unspoken, deeply felt cry of many a new contender in this masculine jungle.

There is no such need, however. The challenge of the moment—and there are many who are meeting it, accepting it, and responding to it, in the way not of men but of women—the challenge is to flower as individuals, neither as biological archetypes nor as personalities imitative of the male. And, to repeat, there are no models in our mythology for an individual woman's quest. Nor is there any model for the male in marriage to an individuated female. We are in this thing together and have to work it out together, not with passion (which is always archetypal) but with *com*passion, in patient fostering of each other's growth.

I have read somewhere of an old Chinese curse: "May you be born in an interesting time!" This is a *very* interesting time: there are no models for *anything* that is going on. Everything is changing, even the law of the masculine jungle. It is a period of free fall into the future, and each has to make his or her own way. The old models are not working; the new have not yet appeared. In fact, it is we who are even now shaping the new in the shaping of our interesting lives. And that is the whole sense (in mythological terms) of the present challenge: we are the "ancestors" of an age to come, the unwitting generators of its supporting myths, the mythic models that will inspire its lives. In a very real sense, therefore, this is a moment of creation; for, as has been said: "No one puts new wine into old wineskins; if he does, the wine will burst the skins and the wine is lost, and so are the skins; but new wine is for fresh skins" (Mark 2:22). We are to become the preparers, that is to say, of the fresh wineskins for a new and heady wine—of which we are already having the first taste.

The Goddess in the Old Stone Age

In the art of the Old Stone Age, from the period of the painted Paleo-lithic caves of southern France and northern Spain, about 30,000 to 10,000 B.C., the female is represented in those now well-known little "Venus" figurines, as simply naked. Her body is her magic: it both invokes the male and is the vessel of all human life. Woman's magic is thus primary, and of nature. The male, in contrast, is always rep-resented in a role of some kind, performing a function, doing some-thing. (And indeed, even today, we address and regard the woman in terms of her beauty but the male in terms of what he can do, what he has done, what his job is.)

The life in those times was of hunting and foraging tribes, the women gathering roots, berries, and small game and the men engaged in the dangerous great hunt, as well as defending their wives and daugh-ters from marauders—for women, you must know, are valuable, as well as interesting, booty. The bow and arrow had not yet been invented.

Hunting and fighting encounters were at close hand. And the animals were enormous: wooly mammoths and rhinoceroses, huge bears, cattle herds, and lions. Under such circumstances—and these circumstances had already prevailed for hundreds of thousands of years; indeed, it was under those conditions that the bodies that we inhabit today evolved and became established in their functions—there developed and was maintained a radical split between the worlds and interests of women and men. There was not only a biological selection to function but also a social training in two totally different directions.

The little female figurines have been found, not in the great painted caves, which were of the men's rites, but in the actual shelters where the families lived. No one ever *lived* in the deep, dark, dank, and dangerous caves. Those were reserved for the rituals of a male magic: converting boys into courageous men and instructing them in the rites of the hunt, and by means of those rites appeasing the beasts, thanking them for having given their lives, and magically returning their lives to the womb of the mother of us all, this Earth, the dark, deep, awesome womb of the great cave itself, for rebirth. The beautiful animal forms on the rock walls of these earliest temples of humankind (wombs of the goddess Earth, as later the cathedrals were to be of Mother Church) are the seed forms of the animal herds above, on the surface of the upper-world animal plains. It is amazing, how, when one is down in those caves, in the absolute dark, with all sense of direction lost, the light world above is but a memory and, curiously, but a shadow world. The reality is down here. The herds and all the lives up there are secondary: it is from there that they derive, and to here that they will return. In several of the greatest of these caves we have the portraits of the ceremonial masters—shamans, wizards, or whatever they might have been. And they are not shown simply standing naked, like the little Venus figurines, but in costume, masked, doing something. The great example is the so-called Sorcerer of the cave known as Les Trois Frères. But there are others. And they are always masked in semi-animal forms, doing something as magicians of the great hunt.

FEMALE AND MALE MAGIC: IN CONFLICT AND ACCORD

There is some evidence that between the two magics of the female and male sides of the primitive hunting and gathering stages of life there was not only a tension but also, at times, an outbreak of physical violence. In the mythologies of a number of very primitive societies (the Pygmies of the Congo, the Ona of Tierra del Fuego, etc.), we find a legend of the following kind: Originally all magical power resided with the women. The men then murdered them all, keeping alive only the youngest girls, who were never taught what their mothers had known, the men having taken the knowledge for themselves. And, in fact, in one of the big dwelling shelters of the Paleolithic age in the south of France (at Laussel) there were found a number of female figurines lying broken, the suggestion being that they might have been at some time deliberately destroyed.

Generally, where there is a men's legend of this kind and a male society of secret rites, the women are seriously intimidated by a pantheon of deliberately invented spooks that appear (in masks) when the male rites are enacted. However—and here is the big surprise— as Colin Turnbull tells us,[3] there may also take place, on rare and most holy occasions, male-rite ceremonials in which the women fully participate, and the secret truth then appears, that the women really know all about the men's rites and are themselves recognized, still, as the possessors of the greater and essential power. The other belief system is secondary, not of nature, but of the social order, and is assented to by the members of both sexes in a sophisticated, socially useful game of make-believe.

THE GODDESS OF THE EARLY PLANTERS

Very late in the history of human life on this Earth the arts of plant and animal domestication were developed, and with these a shift of authority followed from the male to the female side of the biological equation. No longer hunting and slaughtering, but planting and fostering, became the high concerns; and since the Earth's magic and women's are the same—giving both life and its nourishment—not only did the role of the Goddess become the central interest of mythology, but the prestige of women in the villages became enlarged as well. If there was ever anything like a matriarchy (which I doubt), it would have to have been in one or another of the early planting centers—of which there now seem to have been originally three:[4]

1. in Southeast Asia (Thailand, etc.), about 10,000 B.C., or
   perhaps earlier
2. in Southeast Europe and the Near East, also about 10,000
   B.C.
3. in Middle America and Peru, some four or five thousand
   years later

The large question of possible influences from one domain to another has not been settled. But in any case, there is a myth widely disseminated throughout Southeast Asia, the Pacific Isles, and the Americas that appears to have been basic to many of the earliest planting cultures.

The plants domesticated in the Southeast Asia area, from where this myth seems to have originated, such as the yam, taro, and the sago palm, are reproduced not by seed but by slips and cuttings. The animals were the pig, the dog, and barnyard fowl, familiars of the household. The episodes of the myth take place in a timeless mythological age, the Age of the Ancestors, when there was no distinction between female and male, or even between human beings and beasts. It flowed on, an undifferentiated, dreamlike epoch, until at a certain moment—the end moment—a murder was enacted. In some of the myths the whole group slew the victim. In others the act was of one individual against another. In all, the body is cut up, the pieces are buried, and out of those buried parts grow the food plants by which human life in this world is now supported. We are living, that is to say, on the substance of the body of the sacrificed god. Moreover, at the moment of sacrifice, when death came into the world and with it the flow of time, there occurred also a separation of the sexes; so that with death there came also the possibility of procreation and birth.

The pairs of opposites, thus, of male and female, of death and birth (possibly, also, the knowledge of good and evil, as in the biblical version of this widespread myth), came into the world, together with food, at the end of the Mythological Age, by way of the mythological act of a murder, after which there evolved the world of time and differentiation. And the high rites by which this world of time is kept in being, the sacramental rites, are normally observances of a sacrifice in reenactment of that Mythological Act. Indeed, symbolically interpreted, even the sacrifice on the cross of him whose "flesh is meat indeed" and whose "blood is drink indeed" (John 6:55) was a mystery in the sense (spiritualized) of this mythological theme. The cross as the astronomical sign of Earth (⊕). Christ on the cross, Christ on his mother's knees in the image of the Pietà, and the buried sacrifice in the womb of the mother-goddess Earth are equivalent signs.

Now, the moon dies into the sun once a month, to be born from it again, just as the body of the first sacrifice died into the earth, to be born again as food. In this early, goddess-centered mythology, therefore, the sun, like the Earth, is female. Or, according to another image, the male moon begets itself in the sun: the creative fire of the sun and creative fire of the womb and of menstrual blood being then the same. Equivalent, as well, is the fire of a sacrificial altar.

Our earliest images of the Great Goddess of the planting-culture mythologies are not from the Southeast Asian matrix but from Europe and the Near East, and they are of a period from about 7000 to 5000 B.C. Among them is a little figure in a stone from a village site known as Çatal Hüyük, in southern Anatolia (southern Turkey, as it is known today), which perfectly illustrates the mythic role of the female in this context. She is shown back-to-back with herself, in one aspect embracing an adult male and in the other, holding a child. She is the transformer. She receives the seed of the past and through the magic of her body transmutes it into the future, the male representing the energy so transformed. A male child thus carries forward the life—or as India would say, the *dharma*, the duty and law—of his father. And the mother is the vessel through which the miracle comes to pass.

The animal generally symbolic of the power of the sun is the lion; that of the moon is the bull, whose shining horns suggest the crescent form. Again from Çatal Hüyük we have a ceramic figurine showing the Goddess enthroned, giving birth, flanked and supported by lions; and from Rome, six millennia later, we have a marble image of the same Anatolian goddess (now named Cybele), also enthroned and flanked by lions. In still another image from Çatal Hüyük (a bas-relief on a chapel wall) we again see the Goddess giving birth, not to a human infant, this time, but to a bull. The moon dies into the sun: the bull is pounced upon by the lion. The moon is the celestial sign of the sacrifice: the bull is the animal sacrificed on Earth in the altar

fire, the earthly counterpart of the sun, as well as of the fire of the
womb. Analogously, the bodies of the dead are in sacrifice either in-
terred in the womb of the Earth or committed to the funeral pyre,
for rebirth.

In one of the early Indian Upaniṣads dating from about 700 B.C.,
there is an account of the two possible spiritual ways to be followed
in death by those whose bodies are burned on the funeral pyre: the
way of the smoke and the way of the flame.[5] The first carries one to
the moon, the sphere of the Fathers, for rebirth, but the second carries one to the sun, the golden sun-door to eternity and disengagement from the bounds of time, released and never to return. Thus the
Great Goddess in the form of the sun, who pours into the phenomenal world the energy and light that brought it into being and sustain
it, may also become, for those who (as the scriptures say) have yielded
all to the fire of her consuming love, at once the messenger and the
golden portal of the Perfection of Wisdom.

And so it is told that when the prince Gautama Śākyamuni, in the
thirtieth year of his age, was seated on the Immovable Spot, beneath
the Bo Tree of Enlightenment, he was approached by the Lord of the
Illusion of Life, whose magic moves the world and whose name is
Kāma (Desire), Māra (Death: the Fear of Death), and Dharma (Duty
and the Law). As Kāma he displayed the forms of his three voluptuous
daughters, but Gautama was unmoved. As Māra he flung at the prince
all the weaponry of his demonic host, but Gautama was unmoved.
Then as Dharma he challenged the one there absorbed in meditation
to prove his right to the Immovable Spot; whereupon the yogi simply touched the Earth with the fingers of his right hand, calling the
Great Goddess to witness his right, and with a sound as of thunder, a
universe of thunder, with a hundred, a thousand, a hundred thousand
roars, a voice testified, and the elephant upon which Dharma rode
bowed in reverence to the Buddha.

Then the Cosmic Serpent, Mucalinda, who lived beneath the
Bo Tree in a vast hollow among the roots, came up to worship. And
when a prodigious thunderstorm arose with a freezing gale and terrible darkness, to protect the one there sitting in absorption, the great
serpent wrapped his coils seven times around the body, spreading his
giant cobra hood above the head, and for seven days so remained, until
the sky had cleared. Then he relaxed his coils, assumed the form of a
gentle youth, bowed in worship of the Blessed One, and returned to
his place.

Her Golden Age

The first high period of the kingdoms and the power and the glory
of the Goddess was that of the dawn of civilization in the valleys of
the Tigris-Euphrates and the Nile. In both areas her earliest images
(fourth to third millennium B.C.) show a mother standing with her
infant in her arms; and in the mythologies she appears in many forms
and roles representing her universality as both the facilitator of transformations and the enclosing, protecting, and embracing governess of
the process.

In Egypt she appears early as the cow-faced goddess of the enclosing horizon, Hathor, the "House (*hat*) of Horus (*hor*)." She is the Wild
Cow whose four legs are the pillars of the heavens, her belly spangled
with stars. Or she is the overarching sky-goddess Nut, whose head and
arms are at the western horizon, legs and feet at the eastern. Her spouse
in this mythology is the Earth—the Earth-god Geb or Keb.

In the Tigris-Euphrates area these cosmic positions are reversed:
the male is above, as heaven, and the female below, as the Earth. In
the beginning, as we there learn, from the depths of the primeval sea a
cosmic mountain emerged. The name of the sea was that of a goddess,
Nammu, and the name of the mountain, An-ki, "Heaven and Earth."
An (above) begot on Ki (below) the air-god Enlil, who tore the two
apart and pressed the sky, his father, on high. We know the similar tale
from Hesiod (*Theogony* 153 ff.), of Ouranos, Heaven, separated from
the Earth-goddess Gaia by their son, Kronos. And from the Maori of
New Zealand (in the sphere of the Southeast Asian agricultural matrix)
we have the story again: of how the heaven-father, Rangi, lay so closely
upon Papa, the Earth, that their children, the gods, could not leave
their mother's womb, until Tane-mahuta, the forest-god, lay on his
back upon his mother and with his feet thrust his father high above.
In Egypt the separating god was not the child but the male parent of
the cosmic couple: Shu, the air-god, consort of Tefnut, a lion-headed
goddess sometimes identified with the likewise lion-headed Sekhmet,
who typifies the fierce, destructive power of the sun, but is the consort
of Ptah, the god-mummy of the dark night of the moon.

It is within the bounds and embrace of such female personifications
of aspects of the being of the universe that all the life and action of
both humankind and the gods took place throughout the centuries of
the earliest civilizations. The pharaohs of the first dynasties, revered

as incarnations of Osiris, who "fills the horizon," wore in token of this sovereignty a belt ornamented before, behind, and at the sides with the medallions of the cowlike face of Hathor of the Horizon, while hanging from the belt behind was the tail of the moon-bull, her spouse, who begets himself. The hawk-headed son of Osiris, Horus, who was identified with the solar disk, crossed the heavens in a daily passage along the belly of the goddess Nut, at sundown entering her mouth in the west and at dawn being born from her womb in the east, self-begotten as it were, of a virgin birth.

And not only all-embracing: the goddesses were equally the agents of all transformations. In the fundamental legend of the death and resurrection of Osiris, it was because of his seduction by Nephthys, the wife of his brother Set, that the first great pharaoh was slain, clapped in a coffin, and thrown into the Nile. And it was then by virtue of the loyalty of his own wife, Isis, that he was sought for and resurrected, to reign now forever in the underworld as Judge and Lord of the Dead. It is a long and fantastic tale, but in brief: When she found the body of her spouse, Isis lay upon it in grief and conceived of it the god Horus, who then assumed the role of pharaoh in the world of the living. Osiris's throne in the underworld is attended and protected by Nephthys and Isis together; that of Horus, the living pharaoh, is the very body of Isis herself. Like Mary, she is the Mother of God, with the Savior enthroned on her knee. Indeed, the pharaohs are even represented nursing at her breast.

The Degradation of the Goddess

Whereas throughout the nuclear Fertile Crescent and across Asia Minor into the Balkans, the villages, towns, and civilizations of the Great Goddess were maintained chiefly by agriculture, in the neighboring great regions to the south and to the north—the Syro-Arabian desert in the south, European and West Asian grassland in the north—tough tribes of cattle nomads ranged: to the south, Semitic sheep and goat herders, who, in time, mastered the camel; and in the north, the various scattered Indo-European races, battle-ax people and cattle herders, who in the fourth millennium B.C. acquired weapons of bronze, in the third mastered the horse and later invented the war chariot, in the second acquired iron, and by the end of the first millennium B.C. were dominant across Europe and western Asia,

from the Irish Sea to Ceylon. These warrior tribes were not patient tillers of the soil, but nomadic raiders, and their chief patron gods were
thunder-hurlers, very like themselves: among the Semites we find
Marduk, Ashshur, and Yahweh, for example, and among the Indo-
Europeans, Zeus, Thor, Jove, and Indra.

Now, the tendency on the part of the Indo-European deities
when they would come in with the warrior folk would be for the male
deities to marry the local female goddesses. This is one reason why
Zeus had so many adventures; that's all right when he's in this valley
marrying a goddess, and in another valley marrying another goddess,
but after the culture begins to unify all these areas he has developed
quite a lively history of love affairs. That's all an accident, you might
say, in mythological history.

The other system is that of the Semites. They come raiding up
from the Syro-Arabian desert into Canaan and Mesopotamia, again in
waves, and at about the same time as the Indo-Europeans were pressing in from the north. There's a very interesting and strange parallel-
ism and synchronicity when we compare the mythological traditions
that come out of the Indo-Europeans and those that come out of the
Semites. The Semites, however, were considerably more ruthless than
the Indo-Europeans in putting down local goddesses.

The earliest of the great Semitic kings in Mesopotamia was Sargon
of Akkad, about 2350 B.C., the famous legend of whose lowly birth
in secrecy by a mother who placed him in a basket of rushes, sealed
it with bitumen, and set it in the river became, about a millennium
and a half later, a model for the legend of the birth and exposure of
Moses (Exodus 2:1–3). "The river bore me up," the account of Sargon
reads; "and it carried me to Akku, the irrigator, who took me from the
river, raised me as his son, made of me a gardener: and while I was a
gardener, the goddess Ishtar loved me. Then I ruled the kingdom."[6]

Hammurabi of Babylon (c. 1750 B.C.) was the second of these most
illustrious Semitic warrior-kings. It has been suggested that he may
have been the monarch remembered in Genesis 10:8–12 as Nimrod,
"a mighty hunter before the Lord." It was from the period of his reign
that the Babylonian epic of the sun god Marduk dates, whose victory
over Tiamat, the old goddess of the primeval sea, marks the moment

of a decisive transfer of loyalty in that quarter of the world from the universal goddess of nature to an assortment of politically established tribal gods.

Marduk was the patron god of Babylon, which city Hammurabi had made great. The older gods of the earlier pantheon were sitting in abject fear of the approaching great-great-grandmother of them all, when the brand-new young hero-god, incomprehensible and difficult to look upon (he had four eyes and as many ears, and when his lips moved, fire blazed forth), went against her. Tiamat, uttering wild, piercing screams, trembling, shaking to the roots of her limbs, pronounced an incantation as she advanced. But Lord Marduk spread out his battle net to enmesh her, and when she opened her mouth to the full, let fly into it an evil wind that poured into her belly. He shot into her an arrow that tore her inward parts and pierced her heart, and she was undone.

Then with his merciless mace he smashed her skull, and with his scimitar split her like a shellfish. He set one half above, as a heavenly roof, that the waters above should not escape, placed the other half over the abyssal Deep, and when that work of world creation was done, assigned the gods to their places, variously, in Heaven, Earth, and the Abyss. Finally, then, he shaped Man to serve the gods, so that all should be free to repose at ease.[7]

How interesting! In the older view the goddess Universe was alive, herself organically the Earth, the horizon, and the heavens. Now she is dead, and the universe is not an organism, but a building, with gods at rest in it in luxury: not as personifications of the energies in their manners of operation, but as luxury tenants, requiring service. And Man, accordingly, is not as a child born to flower in the knowledge of his own eternal portion but as a robot fashioned to serve.

The full spiritual import of this total victory of the male over the female principle becomes evident in the second great Babylonian epic of Hammurabi's time, the legend of the hero-king Gilgamesh, who, when struck with the fear of death, set forth to gain immortality. After certain adventures, he learned of a plant of eternal life at the bottom of the primeval sea, dove for it, and obtained it but was so fatigued by the adventure that, when he came ashore, he fell asleep with the plant, uneaten, beside him. A passing serpent consumed it. And that is why snakes can now cast their skins—as the moon its shadow—to be born again, whereas Man must die.

Sargon I was beloved of the Goddess. By Hammurabi's Marduk she was slain. In the next major chronicle of these desert-born warrior-kings, she is cursed.

For, as we have heard: When the Lord God discovered that the man fashioned to work in his garden had been lured by his wife and a serpent into eating the fruit of the tree of knowledge, which he had reserved for himself, he cursed the serpent to crawl on its belly, the woman to give birth in pain, and his disobedient gardener to toil "in the sweat of his face" on an Earth of dust cursed to bring forth thorns and thistles. And then, as we read: "lest he put forth his hand and take also of the tree of life and live forever—therefore Yahweh sent them forth from the garden…and at the east of the garden of Eden placed the cherubim and a flaming sword which turned every way, to guard the way to the tree of life" (Genesis 3).

It is surely clear (and can be shown) that the two trees in question are aspects of the one Bo Tree of Enlightenment and Eternal Life under which Prince Gautama sat, where the cosmic serpent Mucalinda lived, and the Goddess (here in reduced form as the serpent's messenger, Eve) testified to the right of Man to come to the knowledge of the now forbidden Light.

HER RETURN

One is moved to ask why the Hebrews, of all the peoples on the beautiful Earth, turned their backs so resolutely on the goddess and her glorious world. The earth of which Adam was fashioned is dust ("You are dust, and to dust you shall return," Genesis 3:19). The goddess of the neighboring Canaanites is called the "Abomination" (2 Kings 23:13). Indeed, "there is no God in all the earth but in Israel" (2 Kings 5:15), and that God, of course, is this local tribal Yahweh—alone: "Our God is one!"

A completely contrary understanding and attitude is presented in the mythological systems of the other great complex of warrior tribes that in those brutal centuries were overrunning the settled agricultural towns and cities of the fourth to first millennium B.C. Like the bedouins of the desert, they too were patriarchal herding folk and their leading tribal gods were gods of war—finally subject, however, to the larger powers of nature and, beyond these, the round or rhythm of Destiny, Moira, "Fate," a goddess to whom even Zeus was subject.

When the Indo-European tribes came with their gods into fresh territories, it was not their custom to generally wipe out the gods and cults of the local shrines, but to recognize that as nature gods and goddesses these divinities took other names and forms of their own. The Indo-European style was to let their gods take over the local shrines, marry the resident goddesses, and even assume the names and roles of the deities formerly in charge. By this means the comparatively barbarous, warlike thunder-hurlers of the original invading pantheons became progressively tamed and tempered to the domestic manners of an agriculturally based, proper civilization.

Freud asks in *Moses and Monotheism* why it was that just when all the other peoples of the eastern Mediterranean were learning to read their myths poetically, the Jews became more confirmed than ever in the concretistic (Freud calls it "religious") way of interpreting their idea of God.[8] The obvious reason, I would say, is that both they and their tribal deity failed to realize that the waters of the Deep (*tehom*) over which Elohim was brooding and blowing in the first two verses of Genesis 1 was not just water, but the old Babylonian goddess of the primeval sea herself, Tiamat (*ti'amat*), and that his failure to appreciate the poetry of her presence there was the beginning of his whole misunderstanding even of himself. It was to her, his cosmological wife, that he should have turned to listen, occasionally, when moved to throw the Book at their disobedient children.

It is wonderful the way in which, both in India and in Greece, the presence and power of the goddesses came gradually back to authority following the devastating ravages in both regions of the Indo-European invasions (mid-second millennium B.C.). By the eighth century B.C. in Greece we have *The Odyssey*—which Samuel Butler believed might have been written by a woman—where it is told how the nymph Circe of the Braided Locks, who could turn men into swine and back again, introduced the warrior Odysseus to the mysteries, not only of her own bed, but also of, first, the world of the dead, and then, the Island of the Sun, her father. From India of the same date, we have the important Kena Upaniṣad, where the goddess Uma, daughter of the Snowy Peak, Himalaya, introduces three of the chief gods of the Indo-European, Vedic pantheon (Agni, Vayu, and Indra) to the transcendent-immanent mystery, *brahman*, of which they were themselves but the ignorant agents.

In Greece, at Eleusis, the ancient temple of the mysteries of Demeter and Persephone became a classical shrine of enormous influence; the oracle at Delphi, of the Pythoness, equally great. And in India, progressively, the worship of the numerous names and forms of the cosmic goddess Kālī (Black Time) became the leading and most characteristic religion of the land.

In the year 327 B.C. Alexander the Great entered the Punjab, and the gates where opened between East and West. He had already conquered the whole of the Near East, and the cults and mysteries of Egypt, Greece, Anatolia, and Iran were running together in a vast movement of syncretistic insights. By about 100 B.C. the Old Silk Road (as it has been called) was in use between Syria, India, and China, and by 49 B.C. Julius Caesar had conquered Gaul. So that, by the time of the birth of Christ there was an exchange, not only of goods, but also of ideas and beliefs, throughout the civilized world.

The principal shrine of the Goddess at that time in the whole of the Near East was at Ephesus, now in Turkey, where her name and form were of Artemis; and it was there, in that city, in the Year of our Lord 431, that Mary was declared to be what the Goddess had been from before the first tick of time: *Theotokos* (Mother of God).

ENVOY

And is it likely, do you think, after all her years and millennia of changing forms and conditions, that she is now unable to let her daughters know who they are?

GODDESSES

Figure 2. Venus of Lespugue (carved ivory, southwestern France, c. 25,000 B.C.)

CHAPTER I

Myth and the Feminine Divine[1]

THE GODDESS IN PALEOLITHIC CULTURES

In the mythologies that I'm going to focus on to begin with, the goddesses are prime—and why not? The simplest manifestation of the Goddess in the early Neolithic planting traditions is as Mother Earth. The Earth brings forth life, and the Earth nourishes life, and so is analogous to the powers of the woman.

There are, however, two major orders of primal mythology. One is that of planting agricultural people, and it is with this order that the Goddess is primarily associated; the other is that of the masculine gods, who are usually associated with herding nomadic people. In early societies, the women are generally associated with the world of the plant. In very early hunting and collecting traditions, the women are the ones who typically collect the plant food and the small game, while men are associated with the major hunting. So the male becomes associated with killing, and the female with the bringing forth of life. That's a typical A-B-C association in primal mythologies.

Before the invention of food domestication, before early planting, horticulture, and the domestication of animals, all the human populations of the world were simply foraging and hunting people. The areas of the great hunt spread from the European plains across to Lake Baikal in Siberia. Later these hunting people spread up along the Arctic. Then they migrated into North Africa—as the Sahara at that time was a grazing plain—and when the Sahara dried up, they went down into southern Africa.

Along the equatorial zone, however, the principal food is vegetable, and this leads to two entirely different kinds of people, two
entirely different kinds of cultural accent.

In the hunt the food is brought in by the males at great risk.
Before 1500 B.C. they didn't even have bows and arrows; they had
to go charging these enormous animals—woolly rhinoceroses, mammoths, and so on. In hunting tribes, then, there is a masculine accent
on action, on courage, on celebration of the individual who had the
ability to bring the food in.

Along the equatorial zone, however, well, *anybody* can pick a ba-
nana, so that the celebration of individual achievement is way down.
Furthermore, since the biological functions of a woman orient and
associate her in a mythological way with the Earth itself, bringing forth
life and nourishment, her magic is the magic that is particularly powerful in the tropical zone.

In general, then, where you have the hunt accent you have a male-
orientated mythology, and where you have the plant accent you have
the female orientation.

Now, the earlier type of society is of course that of the ranging
hunters. The earliest examples we have of their masculine-oriented
mythology comes from the art of the old Aurignacian caves, dating to
about 40,000 B.C. And the earliest theme of art that we know is that of
the naked Goddess figurines that are known as the Paleolithic Venuses.

In these hunting societies the principal flattery goes to the male
because it does make a difference if a chap is a good shot or not, and it
does make a difference whether he can slay the enemy, which is normally ruthless animals at this time, but also members of neighboring
tribes who are hunting the same herds that his little group is hunting.
So everything is done to flatter the male psyche.

In these cultures, the male hunter is supported by the female.
This comes out in a rather interesting rite that the ethnologist Leo
Frobenius[2] observed in Africa. He was on an expedition in the Congo,
and his company had been joined by three Pygmies, two men and a
woman. The Pygmies are very good hunters, and so when he needed
more meat for his company on the safari he asked the three Pygmies
to get him a gazelle. Well, they were shocked to think that they should
bring the meat in that day—they had to perform a ritual first. And
Frobenius followed and watched them in this rite.

First, they went up on a hill and cleared off the grass on the top,
and then they drew on this cleared ground the picture of the gazelle

that they were going to kill. The next morning, precisely at sunrise, when the sun's rays struck that picture-gazelle, one of the little warriors drew his arrow and let the arrow fly—along the sunbeam as it were—to hit the image, and the woman raised her hand and gave kind of a cry. Then they went and killed a gazelle and struck it right at the same point where the arrow had struck the picture. Then the next morning they brought some of the blood and hair of the slaughtered gazelle and put it on the picture, and when the sun struck it again they erased the picture.

This is a basic point in mythology: that the individual is performing an act not out of his own impulse, but in accord with the order of the universe. The sun always represents the killing, drying, desiccating principle and so the killer is always associated with the solar power. Here the arrow comes on the sunbeam and the man is simply enacting the rite of nature, and the role of the female is indicated by that cry.

Now, what does that mean?

From the Paleolithic era, going back thirty thousand years or more, we already find evidence of the woman viewed mythologically both as the guardian of the hearth and as the mother of the individual's maturity, the individual's spiritual life.

In the Paleolithic wall art of North Africa there is a very striking picture of a woman in just exactly that posture (Fig. 3), with the navel cord coming from her body and connecting to the navel of the warrior or hunter, who has his bow and arrow and is shooting at an ostrich. In other words, it is her power that is supporting him, the power of Mother Nature, along with the power of the solar shaft.

The little standing Venus figurines are found in the shelters where Paleolithic people actually lived. In contrast, men's initiation rites were held in the deep caves, and there we see very little of the female.[3] No one lived in those caves. They're chilly, they're dangerous, they're dark, they're awesome, they're deep. Some of them contain miles and miles of dark corridor. We see on those walls masculine shamans among multitudes of animals, images that have to do with the rites inviting the animals to be killed. This is the fundamental theme in the hunting people: that the animals are willing victims and are offering themselves with the understanding that certain rituals—returning their blood to the soil, for example—will be enacted to return their life to the Mother Source.[4] The cult of the Goddess goes right back to those early caves. There, She is the cave itself, so that initiates who

FIGURE 3. A woman connected to a hunter by an umbilicus (carved rock, Paleolithic, Algiers, date unknown)

passed through the rites deep under the earth were returning to and reborn from Her womb.

Here is a principal mythological role of the feminine principle: She gives birth to us physically, but She is the mother too of our second birth—our birth as spiritual entities. This is the basic meaning of the motif of the virgin birth, that our bodies are born naturally, but at a certain time there awakens in us our spiritual nature, which is the higher human nature, not that which simply duplicates the world of the animal urges, of erotic and power drives and sleep. Instead, there awakens in us the notion of a spiritual aim, a spiritual life: an essentially human, mystical life to be lived above the level of food, of sex, of economics, politics, and sociology. In this sphere of the mystery dimension the woman represents the awakener, the giver of birth in that sense. In these caves where the boys went to be initiated, to be transformed from the children of their physical mothers into the children of the cosmic Mother, in the womb of the Earth, they experienced symbolic rebirth.

This is represented very vividly in a cave in the Pyrenees known as Les Trois Frères, where there is a long flume through which water had been running during the Würm glacial period, opening a kind of pipe through the rock that runs for fifty yards but is hardly two feet high. Through this one has to wriggle to enter into a great chamber. The boys were sent through that canal in a symbolic rebirth—coming to birth not from their personal mothers but from the transpersonal universal Mother who brings each of us into maturity.

FIGURE 4. Venus of Peterfels (amulet sculpted from jet, Upper Magdalenian, southwest Germany, c. 15,000 B.C.)

Among the earliest explicit images we have of the Goddess are the so-called Venuses, female figurines from the Magdalenian period at the end of the Stone Age, scattered all the way from the west of France across to Lake Baikal on the borders of China. The accent in these figurines is on the procreative mystery of the loins and the mystery of the breasts, the reproductive and nourishing aspect of the woman. Nature has given to woman this power so she becomes, as it were, a manifestation, the signification of the mystery of nature itself. Woman is then the first worshipped being in the human world.

These were the first plastic, three-dimensional figures, the first *idols*, as we say in the history of art, and what they represented was the standard female muse, the power of the female body as a transformer into life. These figurines appear not in the caves of the men's hunting rites, but in the dwelling places, in the rock shelters where people lived. One of the characteristics of these figures is that there is typically no face with specific features, so highlighting the mystery aspect—not the personality but the raw Woman as the carrier of nature into manifestation. The feet are always missing from these figures, which suggests that they were made to stand up in little shrines and in the ground.

FIGURE 5. Pregnant Goddess (carved stone, Neolithic, Greece, c. 5800 B.C.)

"Although a great deal of emphasis has been placed on the 'Earth Mother' of prehistoric religion, she is but one—albeit an important one—of the aspects of this early Divine Feminine principle. One reason for this emphasis may be that, in the agricultural communities throughout Europe, she survives to the present day. Another is the fact, long accepted by ethnologists, that pre-industrial agricultural rites show a definite mystical connection between the fertility of the soil and the creative force of woman. In all Europan languages, the Earth is feminine. The Old European Pregnant Goddess is the likely prototype of the Grain Goddess, young and old, such as Demeter, and of the Earth Mother of all European folklore. As an Earth Mother she is also the Mother of the Dead. How old is she, this symbol of the nutrient earth, fullness, and the cornucopia of the fruitful womb?"   —Marija Gimbutas[5]

The Venus of Laussel (Fig. 6), from a shelf in the Pyrenees, is a very important and suggestive figure. She is holding in her right hand, elevated, a bison horn with thirteen vertical strokes[6] that is the number of nights between the first crescent and the full moon. The other hand is on the belly, and what this suggests—we don't have any writing from this period—is a recognition of the equivalence of the menstrual and the lunar cycles. This would be the first inkling we have of the recognition of a connection between the celestial and earthly rhythms of life.

FIGURE 6. The Venus of Laussel (limestone relief, Aurignacian, southwestern France, c. 25,000 B.C.)

The accent here is on the pregnancy, the miracle! Women, by bringing forth life, take on the quality of the inexhaustible vessel of life itself. They are the first worshipped objects outside the animals, which represent the other powers of nature, the vessels of the power of nature rather than nature itself.

FIGURE 7. Goddess with labyrinth design (terra-cotta, Neolithic, Romania, c. 5500 B.C.)

The Goddess in this figurine displays a labyrinth design all over her, and rather important is the center. Her navel is the world navel, and the world is the rectangle radiating from that point: north, south, east, and west. According to Marija Gimbutas, the lozenge design is an ideogram related to the square, "the perennial symbol of earthbound matter."[7]

The thing to note is that all these female figurines are simply naked, whereas the male figures in all the caves are represented in some kind of garment, dressed as shamans. The implication is that in embodying the divine, the female operates in her own character, simply in her nature, while the male magic functions not from the nature of the men's bodies but from the nature of their roles in the society.

This brings out a very important point for the whole history of the female in mythology: She represents the nature principle. We are born from her physically. The male, on the other hand, represents the social principle and social roles—and this comes out in the psycho-analytic theories of Freud, for example, where the father represents the initiator of the child into his or her adult role.

For the first years of a child's life, the father is simply mother's hairy helper. There comes a moment, then, somewhere around the third or fourth year, when the child registers the difference between male and female, and at that point the little boy must know that he is a man and is related to the role of his father, and the little girl realizes that she is a woman and her main reference now is not to be mother but to be Woman. The father is the initiator into society and the meaning of life, whereas the mother represents the principle of life itself. She represents that principle in both its beneficent and its hor-rendous roles: the Earth gives birth, and she gives nourishment, but she also takes us back. She is the mother of death as well, and the night sleep back to which we go.

From the hunting tradition of the Blackfoot tribe of Montana comes a story that seems to tell very vividly of the mythological role of the woman in these hunting cultures that were principally masculine in their mythological orientation.[8]

There was a time in the fall of the year when these people had to build up their meat supply for the winter. And they used to do this by driving a buffalo herd over a precipice so the animals would fall down, break their backs, and be easily killed at the foot of the precipice.

Well, in this particular case the buffalo simply would not go over the buffalo fall, and so it looked as though the people were going to have a very tough winter.

Early one morning, a young woman gets up to draw the water for her family for the day and she comes out and she sees up above the precipice this herd of buffalo. And in that moment of just spontane-ous delight, she says, "Oh, if you would only come over and fall over the precipice, I would marry one of you." Big offering. And was she surprised—they *did* come over! The whole buffalo herd comes tum-bling down, breaking their backs.

But then a great big bull buffalo comes up and says, "Okay, girlie."

And she says, "Oh, no!"

He says, "Oh, yes. Look what happened here: You made a promise and we did our part and now you're backing away? Come on!" And so he takes her away.

Well, her family wakes up presently and everybody is amazed to find all the buffalo there ready to be butchered, and they just love it. And after the hurry and scurry of doing the job, they realize that the young woman isn't around.

Reading the footprints, the daddy sees that his daughter has gone off with a buffalo. So he puts on his walking moccasins, gets his bow and arrow, and goes off up the cliff and follows along. Finally, after walking some distance, he comes to a wallow—a place where buffalo like to roll around and get the fleas off and where there is always water nearby—and he sits down to think.

And then a magpie comes along. Now, the magpie is a very clever bird, and particularly clever animals (like foxes, magpies, ravens, and so forth), are shaman animals. So when the magpie comes down, the man says to him, "Beautiful bird, have you seen my daughter anywhere around here? She ran off with a buffalo."

And the magpie says, "Well, there's a young woman over there with a buffalo right now."

And the father says, "Well, could you just go tell her that her daddy's here?"

And the magpie flies over to where she is sitting—I suppose weaving or something like that—and all the buffalo are asleep roundabout, while beside her is this great, big old boy. The magpie comes picking around and gradually approaches her and says, "Your daddy is over at the wallow and he wants you."

"You tell him to wait and I'll be coming."

So, presently Big Buffalo wakes up and he says, "Go get me some water." So, *pluck*, she takes one of his horns and goes over to get the water where Daddy is.

Daddy says, "You come along home."

And she says, "No, no, no, it's very dangerous. Wait until he goes to sleep again and then I'll be able to come. They're just waking up from their nap."

"Well," he says, "all right, I'll be waiting here."

Then she goes back with the water, but the buffalo sniffs and says, "Fe, fi, fo, fum, I smell the blood of an Indian!"

And she says, "Oh, no!"

And Big Buffalo says, "Oh, yes!" He gets up and he roars and stamps around and all the buffalo get up and then, what do you know? They go over to the wallow and they trample poor Daddy to death. They trample and trample and trample until there's nothing visible left of him.

The girl's crying, "Oh, Daddy!"

And Big Buffalo says, "Yes, you're crying, you've lost your daddy. But what about us? Look at us. Our fathers, our mothers, our children, our wives, everybody—all gone."

Still, all she keeps saying is, "But Daddy!"

Then he says, "Well, okay. If you can bring your daddy back to life, I'll let you go."

So here's what she does. She says to the magpie, "Pick around and see if you can find some little bit of Daddy somewhere."

And the magpie goes to work on this and he comes up with a little bit of the father's backbone.

She puts the backbone down, puts her blanket over it, and starts singing a magical song. Well, presently it's clear that under the blanket is a man. So she lifts it up and it's Daddy, all right. He's not alive yet, however, so she puts the blanket back and sings some more, and finally he gets up.

The buffalo are amazed. Big Buffalo says, "Well, if you can do this for your daddy why don't you do it for *us*? We'll show you our dance, and you dance our dance and revive the buffalo that you killed and then we'll have a pact with you, a covenant."

This is the basic pact of an ancient hunting people between the animals and the hunters, consecrated through rites of worship, and it comes from the act of that young woman. She is the link between the two worlds; there are hundreds of myths of this kind, of the wife of the animal who is a member of the tribe and becomes then the link between the two worlds and the supplier finally of the food, which the men go out to get.

And that, of course, is, as Frobenius realized, the sense of the Pygmy woman giving her cry: it is her power that gives the animals the confidence to come, to be killed, and to be revived. She is the principle of birth and rebirth all the way down the line.

The Goddess as Nature

In most mythologies, whether primal or from the high civilizations, deities are personifications of the energies of nature. The energies are primary, while the deities are secondary.

Now, the energies of nature are present in the outer world, but also inside ourselves, because we are particles of nature. So when you are meditating on a deity, you are meditating on powers of your own spirit and psyche, and on powers that are also *out there*. One finds in practically all the religious traditions of the world (with a few exceptions) that the aim is for the individual to put himself into accord with nature, with his nature, and that's both physical and psychological health. These are what in our traditions are called the nature religions, and the deities are not final terms; they are references to spiritual energies. So when mythology is properly understood, the object that is revered and venerated is not a final term; the object venerated is a personification of an energy that dwells within the individual, and the reference of mythology has two modes—that of consciousness and that of the spiritual potentials within the individual.

If a mythology doesn't have that accent, what's it all about? The way to misunderstand mythology is to think that the image is the final term. And of course this is one of the problems in what we call the monotheistic systems. God is not transparent—he's a final term. And when the deity is a final term and is not transparent to transcendence, then the worshipper is the final term also and is not transparent to transcendence, and what you have then is a religion of a relationship of the individual to the god. But as soon as you open the god and realize that he's a personification of a power, then you yourself open as another personification and vehicle of that power. In such a system, you can have such a saying as comes from the Chāndogya Upaniṣad: *Tat tvam asi* (Thou art that).[9] That is heresy when the god is closed.

Since we're going to be talking about the pagans, we children of the biblical traditions have to realize that *they* are not idolaters; in a real way, it's we who are the idolaters, because we mistake the symbol for the reference. I think that deep inside us all we know that that's idolatry, and that's why we go around calling everybody else idolaters and insist that they believe the way that we do so that we can reconfirm and reassure ourselves that we're okay in terms of our own mythology.

My definition of *mythology* is "other people's religion," which suggests that ours must be something else. My definition of *religion*, then, is "misunderstood mythology"—and the misunderstanding consists in mistaking the symbol for the reference. So all the historic events that are so important to us in our tradition should not be important to us in any way except as symbols of powers within ourselves.

When you go into a church, you often see the stations of the cross around you, and there is meant to be no doubt that this represents

what actually did happen to Jesus of Nazareth on the day of his crucifixion: first Jesus's condemnation by Pilate, then Jesus taking up
the cross, then Jesus stumbling, and so forth, on up to his being laid
in his tomb. The station that would come after the one showing the
burial—the station that *isn't* shown as part of the series—would be
the Resurrection. And finally after *that* would come still another one,
the ascension to heaven.

Now, if all that is taken literally, then you're in trouble. Read a
modern book of physics, and you'll wonder where he went—even
going at the speed of light, he would not be out of the galaxy yet.
Then we find there's no literal place for the literal body to go, so we
say, "This is untrue." We lose our religion; we lose our symbols.

When the symbol is interpreted concretely that way, you've lost
the message. The symbol that should be introducing us to our own
deep, inward life is lost and we have no vehicle for connection. So the
popular way of interpreting the word *myth* is "falsehood," whereas
myths, in the sense that I'm speaking of them, are the final terms of
wisdom—that is the wisdom of the deep mysteries of life. That's what
I'm going to be talking about here: not only the history of the Goddess, but through that into something of our own mystery.

Herding mythologies have their own traditions and their own
integrity, so there is a deity that represents the tribal energy, the mythology of that particular people. Different tribes have different characters;
we're not supposed to think that anymore, but they have. Generally
the patron deity of the tribe is secondary to the great nature deities.

With the Semites and the faiths they left us, the patron deity of
the tribe is the top god—the *only* god. I've tried to figure out why this
should be, and I came to a little conclusion as I was reading an earlier
edition of a very good book about archaic thinking: *Before Philosophy*
by Henri Frankfort and others.[10] In a final chapter, Frankfort suggested that life in the desert doesn't leave you feeling terribly grateful
toward the Mother Goddess; your whole dependency is on the tribe,
and the tribal god then becomes the dominant figure.

A very strange problem comes from this: When the powers that
we are giving our primary attention to are the powers of nature, we
can go from Greece to India and we can say in India, "He whom you
call Indra, we call Zeus." Alexander's soldiers immediately understood
who these Indian gods were and those who remained in Bactria as
governors and rulers adopted the Indian deities without any violence
done to their reverence to their own gods because these are the same
gods with other names. In the sixth book of *The Gallic Wars*, Caesar

discusses the local religion of the conquered Celtic Gauls, but he uses the Roman names for the gods, so we don't know what Celtic gods he is talking about.¹¹ This is known as *syncretism*, and it is the mode of most of the religions of the world. Hindus are enormous syncretists, and Buddhists had no problem with this either. The Egyptian priests were such syncretists that when the little villages along the Nile finally were incorporated into one great empire, the two realms of northern and southern Egypt, they could combine those local mythologies easily. So the great big mythology of Isis and Nephthys and Osiris are combined mythologies, but they cohere properly in mythological terms.

However, imagine an ancient Hebrew saying, "He whom you call Assur, we call Yahweh." That doesn't work! So when your local god is your top god, that brings with it exclusivism. Read the Old Testament: the gods of other people are not *gods*; they're *demons*. Read also the story of the Christian Spaniards conquering America: they actually called the deities of the Native Americans *devils*. Using the word *devil* is a strange thing; let's use the word *dīmon*. For the Greek, the *dīmon* was the energy of your life, and the energy of your life doesn't obey the rules necessarily that your head puts on it. So the *dīmon* becomes a danger—a demon—for people who are stuck with their head trip, and consequently those people call such powers *devils*.

What we're looking at in these mythologies is a world of dīmonic powers, and these dīmonic powers are the powers of our own lives.

When the Semites moved in as conquerors, then, they dislodged deities to make way for their own, and the Hebrews are the most extreme in turning against the Goddess, who represents the powers of the Earth. In the Old Testament, the local goddesses of Canaan are called the Abomination, and this hangs on in our Christian tradition.

One of the worst things Protestants say about Catholics is that they worship the Virgin. Catholics are very sure to make clear they don't worship the Virgin—they *venerate* the Virgin. There's a difference. When you recite the litany, you ask the Virgin, "Have mercy on us," you say, "Pray for us." So she is an intermediary; we're keeping women in their place.

The powers that we're talking about when we're talking about the Goddess are the powers that live in every woman in the world. I remember that when I was in India, I learned that all women are divinities. The three great crimes in India are killing a cow, killing a brahmin, and killing a woman, because they all represent the sacred powers. Of course when you go to India you realize you can be very, very sacred and yet be in a rather inferior social position, but that's the incongruity of life—a mystery.

The earliest form of the Goddess, we will see, is simply as the goddess Mother Earth, but when we come to Egypt, the great goddess Nut represents the overarching heavens. In the civilized traditions that are devoted not simply to the soil and the Earth but to the planets that sail through the constellations in regular rhythmic or mathematically controllable movements, the Goddess becomes the whole sphere within which we dwell. We are as it were within the womb of the Goddess, and within that womb dwell all beings that have form and that have names, and this includes the gods. So when Mary is called the Mother of God, she's promoted, and in the old tradition it means not only the mother of the incarnation but the Mother of the Universe, and of all the powers that operate within the universe and are given names and forms, whether they are concrete or mythological. In these traditions, the gods exist within the field of the Goddess; they are all merely manifestations of aspects of Her.

Now, a very interesting thing happened at the end of the eighteenth century, when Hindu texts began to be translated into the European languages. Just before the time of those translations, European philosophy took an immense step forward with the work of Immanuel Kant. There are two kinds of philosophers in the world: those who have understood Kant, and those who have not. Kant worked on the problem that had already been announced by Locke: How do we know that what we experience through our senses is really what is there? Do our senses distort? Kant begins with what he calls the *a priori* categories of logic. We can't even think of anything except in terms of subject and object, right and wrong—pairs of opposites, logical categories. Without those categories, there's nothing to discuss. Kant then brings up the point that what our senses do is put time and space around us, and everything comes to us through the *a priori* forms of time and space. But suppose there was not time or space; then there would be no separateness. We're separate in space, we're separate in time—otherwise we'd be one with the people who sat where we are sitting a year ago, or a century ago, or on the other side of the world. Taken together, time and space are what Nietzsche calls the *principium individuationis*—the individuating principle that makes us separate creatures.

It was Schopenhauer who realized that Kant's *a priori* forms of sensibility and the *a priori* categories of logic were simply equivalent to the Hindu idea of Māyā. So these two philosophies—European rationalism and Indian mysticism—flow together marvelously in the work of the nineteenth-century German Romantics. Schopenhauer asks in a beautiful paper of his called "The Foundations of Morality" how it is that a human being can so experience the pain and danger of another that, forgetting his own self-protection, he moves spontaneously to the other's rescue?[12] You see a little child about to be run over and *you'll* probably be the one who's run over. How is it that what we think of as the first law of nature, the law of protecting this separate entity, is suddenly dispelled and a new law takes precedence: that of what Schopenhauer calls *Mitleid* ("compassion"; literally translated as "suffering with")? Schopenhauer says the reason is that in truth a metaphysical realization has come to you and has broken through the veil of separateness—you realize that you and that other are one. You are, together, the one life that is showing itself in various forms. That's the breakthrough to where the gods are; a god is simply a mythological representation of these mysteries transcendent of separateness.

St. Paul wrote, "I live; yet not I, but Christ liveth in me."[13] What did he mean? Jesus of Nazareth, the separate incarnation, had already ascended to the galaxies. Did Paul think that Jesus had come back to live in him? Of course not. You have two aspects in this figure—one is the temporal incarnation Jesus, and the other is the eternal principle Christ, the second person of the blessed trinity, transcendent of time, who is present and true yesterday, today, and tomorrow. One characteristic bit of dogma of the Christian tradition is that Jesus is the only living being who was identical to Christ. Now, the great Buddhist idea is that we are all Buddha beings, only we don't know it, or don't act as though we are. So when Paul says, "I live; yet not I, but Christ liveth in me," what he's really saying is what every Buddhist says.

There's a wonderful little story that I ran into in one of the writings of Daisetz Suzuki, the Zen philosopher: a Zen student said to his master, "Am I in possession of the Buddha nature?"

And the master said, "No."

The student said, "But I've heard that all beings are in possession of the Buddha nature: the stones, flowers, birds, people."

"You're right," said the Zen master, "all beings are in possession of the Buddha nature: stones, flowers, birds, animals, people, but not you."

"Not me, why not me?"

"Because you're asking this silly question."[14] So he's identifying with his mind, and what his mind sees around him in the world is out of sync with his own inward truth. The function of myth is to put us in sync—with ourselves, with our social group, and with the environment in which we live.

One of the most interesting and simple ways to get this message is from the mythologies of the Navaho. Every single detail of the desert in which they live has been deified, and the land has become a holy land because it is revelatory of mythological entities. When you recognize the mythological aspect of Mother Nature, you have turned nature itself into an icon, into a holy picture, so that wherever you go, you're getting the message that the divine power is working for you.

Modern culture has desanctified our landscape and we think that to go to the holy land we have to go to Jerusalem. The Navaho would say, "*This* is it, and *you're* it." I'm talking now in terms of mythologies; this isn't heresy because I don't believe these things to be literally, concretely, true. I had a very strange experience when I was invited to lecture at a seminary in Long Island where priests are trained. The priest who wrote and invited me said he was very eager to have me come because I had in my writings introduced him to the inward life. So I go there and find these men studying Zen. I was stunned because I was brought up a Catholic and I would have received nothing like this kind of reception forty years ago. Meditation has to do with finding the Christ in you, finding the energy in you. Well, that is what sitting *zazen* is all about, too: realizing one's own Buddha nature.

You know what inspired this for me now, all of this? I teach in all sorts of places these days. Often, I come into a church to speak, and I realize I'm going to talk about all these pagan gods that the early Christians spent their time smashing. When you go to the Mediterranean, or to Egypt, or to Greece, there are smashed images all over the place, and here I am bringing them back in this environment. So I'm trying really to work this out and harmonize myself with the landscape.

On the simplest level, then, the Goddess is the Earth. On the next, archaic, level she is the surrounding sky. On the philosophical level, she is Māyā, the forms of sensibility, the limitations of the senses that enclose us so that all of our thinking takes place within Her bounds—she is *IT*. The Goddess is the ultimate boundary of consciousness in the world of time and space.

FIGURE 8. Enthroned goddess giving birth (terra-cotta, Neolithic, Turkey, 6000–5800 B.C.)

---●---

CHAPTER 2

Goddess-Mother Creator

NEOLITHIC AND EARLY BRONZE AGE[1]

STONE TO COPPER: ANATOLIA AND OLD EUROPE

In approaching mythology in general, the first big division we have to make is between what might be called the nonliterate, oral folk traditions and the literate societies and cultures. The invention of writing wrought a great transformation upon human life, thought, and spiritual experience, and the rise of what we call the high cultures.

The recorded history of the Goddess belongs primarily to the planting cultures that derived their primary sustenance from the plant world. There the female is associated with the Goddess Earth, who gives forth the fruits of Earth, and gives life and nourishment to the world. According to that thinking the powers of women in that biological sense give them a magical power that makes it particularly possible for them to activate and be in accord with these powers. And so we find that wherever the planting world has become the main source for the sustenance of people, the Goddess and the female are dominant. There are three main centers in the world of the origins of planting cultures: Southeast Asia at about 10,000 B.C. or perhaps earlier; Southeast Europe and the Near East, also about 10,000 B.C.; and Middle America.[2] The areas of Southeast Asia and Southeast Europe will be the two centers of focus for this discussion of the goddess traditions in the Neolithic age.

The picture of southeastern Europe and southwestern Asia has since the 1970s acquired a whole new look. The carbon-14 system of dating gives quite firm dates to materials for which we have no other sort of documentation to help determine their ages. Scientists realized that the cosmic rays entering the atmosphere of the Earth differed from year to year and that these altered the carbon-14 readings, and so the determinations of these changes were made on the basis of tree ring analysis. As a result, some of the European dating got pushed back a thousand to fifteen hundred years, and this has placed the early dating for the goddess cults in Europe as far back as 7000 B.C. We don't find any comparable social organization or culture magnitude in India until about 2500 B.C. So Europe turns out to be about five thousand years ahead, and this shifts some of the thinking of the world, you might say.

It's in this light that I want to explore the very earliest appearance of the Goddess. In the Roman Empire, during the golden era of Apuleius in the second century A.D., the Goddess was celebrated as the Goddess of Many Names. In Classical myths, she appears as Aphrodite, Artemis, Demeter, Persephone, Athena, Hera, Hecate, the Three Graces, the Nine Muses, the Furies, and so on. In Egypt she appears as Isis, in old Babylon as Ishtar, in Sumer as Inanna; among the western Semites she's Astarte. It's the same goddess, and the first thing to realize is that she is a total goddess and as such has associations over the whole field of the culture system. In later periods these different associations became specified and separated off into various specialized goddesses.

Now, the two areas in the Old World where plant domestication and animal domestication first emerged are Southeast Asia, on the one hand, and Southwest Asia and Asia Minor, on the other, and the first cities emerged in Mesopotamia and in Egypt. For years there has been great argument as to whether Southeast or Southwest Asia was the first center of plant and animal domestication. As early as the end of the nineteenth century, Leo Frobenius insisted that Southeast Asia must have been the first; Carl Sauer, an anthropologist at the University of California, Berkeley, supported this view in his *Agricultural Origins and Dispersals.*[3] It seems now that the dates for agriculture, horticulture, and animal domestication along the river valleys that run down through Thailand, Cambodia, and Vietnam go back to 11,000 B.C. and perhaps even earlier—the exact date is a matter of some dispute. These were fishing people; apparently the women of these populations were the first to cultivate plants. Now, the plants cultivated there are reproduced not by seeds but by propagating slips and cuttings. These include such crops as sago palm, taro, and sweet potatoes. The animals domesticated were the dog, the pig, and chickens—familiars of the household.

Socrates, just before taking the hemlock, said to his friends, "I owe a cock to Asclepius," meaning he wanted them to bring an offering to Asclepius, god of medicine, in the form of a rooster. Well, the cock comes from down there, from Southeast Asia. I've always said that where a cock can be transported, an idea can be transported also.

Following the agricultural diffusion up into the area of South China, into the Abyssinian and the Near Eastern and European zones, we have a transition from that kind of agriculture to seed agriculture, and the use of the plow to furrow the earth for planting. In the first kind of planting, the work is women's and digging sticks are used: a little hole is made in the earth, and the slips are put in. With the coming of seed planting and the plow, however, the obvious analogy to the sexual act is recognized, and the act of planting is turned over to the males. In fact, the early plows in Mesopotamia seeded while they furrowed—a restatement in a sort of cosmic way, as it were, of the human act of procreation.

The animals domesticated in this zone were primarily the sheep and the goat, and later the great cattle herds that finally became dominant. These were first cultivated in the mountain areas of northern Iraq, Iran, southern Anatolia (Turkey), and Syria.

Carl Sauer pointed out that the lice on European domesticated pigs are from Southeast Asia. This is among other bits of evidence that suggest an influence from Southeast Asia into Europe.

Now, the contrast between these two systems, both in types of planting and in the domestic animals, will play a pivotal role in relation to the Goddess.

In southern Turkey, which in ancient times was known as Anatolia, there is a plain where a team led by James Mellaart excavated an ancient city called Çatal Hüyük.[4] One of the very early agricultural communities in the Near East or indeed in the world, it looks something like a Southwest American pueblo. Houses are built right on top of each other, and entrance and exit are by ladders through the roof. You can't have a settlement of that size without agriculture or horticulture, and the plants they grew were an early kind of wheat. In this area the principal animals were the pig, the dog, and cattle.

Çatal Hüyük became tremendously important when Mellaart discovered the earliest ceramic pottery in this part of the world, from 6000 B.C. Where you have ceramic ware you immediately have images of the Goddess.

A little town like Çatal Hüyük is rather difficult to capture; you have to tear it down to take it. But around the fourth millennium B.C., towns of this kind began to have walls built around them, and so we know that the invaders were coming in. The Semites of the south came in as raiders from the deserts, and that's when wars of conquest began. The first real conquistador was Sargon I, in 2350 B.C., and we have the texts of celebration of his victories:

"I took the city of this man and I killed everybody in it. I took the city of that man and I killed everybody in it, and I took the city of this next one and killed everybody in it, then I washed my weapons in the sea."[5]

FIGURE 9. Double goddess (carved schist, Turkey, 6000–5800 B.C.)

And that statement, "I washed my weapons in the sea," becomes a horrible refrain. The best places to get a notion of what this type of warfare was like are the Book of Joshua and the Book of Judges.

From Çatal Hüyük (c. 5800 B.C.) comes a green schist stone (Fig. 9) with the image of the Goddess in her two roles. She is presented back-to-back with herself, on the left embracing an adult male, and on the right holding a child in her arms. It's the key to the whole mythology of the Goddess-as-transformer. She is the transforming medium that transforms semen into life. She receives the seed of the past and, through the miracle of her body, transmutes it into the life of the future. She is woman as the transformer, while the male is that which is transformed; she is the intermediator between child and father.

The idea that the child is a rebirth of the Father energy brings the notion of the child having begotten himself. When you read in Dante's *Divine Comedy* St. Bernard's prayer to the Virgin, the same role is assigned to her, and her son is the Father, the one God in two persons. We're here at the beginning of the whole story of the Goddess.

> *Virgin mother, daughter of your Son,*
> *More humble and sublime than any creature,*
> *Fixed goal decreed from all eternity,*
> *You are the one who gave to human nature*
> *So much nobility that its Creator*
> *Did not disdain His being made its creature.*
> *That love whose warmth allowed this flower to bloom*
> *Within the everlasting peace was love*
> *Rekindled in your womb; for us above,*
> *You are the noonday torch of charity,*
> *And there below, on earth among the mortals,*
> *You are a living spring of hope. Lady,*
> *You are so high, you can so intercede,*
> *That he who would have grace but does not seek*
> *Your aid, may long to fly but has no wings.*
> *Your loving-kindness does not only answer*
> *The one who asks, but it is often ready*
> *To answer freely long before the asking.*
> *In you compassion is, in you is pity,*
> *In you is generosity, in you*
> *Is every goodness found in any creature.*[6]

FIGURE 10. Enthroned
goddess giving birth
(terra-cotta, Neolithic,
Turkey, 6000–5800 B.C.)

This ceramic piece of the Goddess giving birth (Fig. 10) was found
in a grain bin, so we know she is the mother not only of children but
also of the plants. She is the one to whom we pray for prosperous
crops. She is seated on a throne flanked by two feline animals, possibly panthers or lionesses. This association of the feline—the lion, the
panther, the tiger, and the leopard—with the Goddess is continuous
and it comes down even to the later tradition of the witch, who always
has a black cat.

Six thousand years later, Cybele, the Anatolian goddess in Rome
(Fig. 11), is in exactly the same position. At the time of the Carthag-
inian wars, circa the second century B.C., the worship of Cybele was
brought from Asia Minor into Rome and became an extremely popular cult. On her head is the crown that is the city, so she is the goddess
of the city. The city is the mother city, and its walls are symbolic of
the walls of time and the walls of space that enclose us. So the city is a
microcosm, a small cosmos. In her hand is the solar disc—symbol of
the round of rebirth and the cycle of the solar door through which the
soul passes into infinity—and she is flanked by two lions. This shows
the association of the lion with the sun, and the association of the goddess with the sun, and the moon in this tradition is male.[7]

Meditation on a deity opens up in all directions to the various
manifestations of the power that that deity personifies. In one of the
little chapels devoted to this goddess in Çatal Hüyük are two leopards,
the male and the female leopard facing each other. We would have

FIGURE II. Cybele, Mother of the Gods (carved marble, late Roman, c. third century A.D.)

The great Phrygian goddess Cybele, mother of the slain and resurrected young Phrygian deity Attis. Her cult was early introduced to Greece, where she was identified with Rhea. Known generally as Mountain Mother as well as Mother of the Gods, her sanctuaries were on mountains, frequently in caves, her animals were lions, and her attendants Corybantes, half-human, demonic beings. Her priests, the Galli, were self-emasculated eunuchs, attired in female garb and wearing long hair, fragrant with ointment.[8]

to go between them to get to the Goddess, so they are the threshold guardians. What does this mean, this pair of opposites facing each other? They represent the threshold of passage from the field of secular thinking, where "I" and "you" are separate from each other in an Aristotelian sense—that is, *a* is not *not-a*—to a world transcendent of that kind of bipolar thinking, more in the way of a dream logic, where the dreamer and the dream, although they seem to be two, are actually one. These are the pairs of opposites between which you must pass when you pass through this active door, called in another context the clashing rocks, the Symplegades.

The ultimate mystery of the universe is transcendence of the phenomenal world, which is made up of pairs of opposites, Kant's *a priori* categories of thought. When Adam and Eve fell, the first thing they experienced was the knowledge of good and evil—that is to say, the knowledge of pairs of opposites. Before that they didn't know any distinctions. We are kept out of the garden by our knowledge of the pairs of opposites. Leaving that behind, going back to the place of innocence—beyond the rational discrimination of this from that—going back to that transcendent realm is the passage past the clashing rocks, beyond the guardianship of the threshold guardians of the temple.

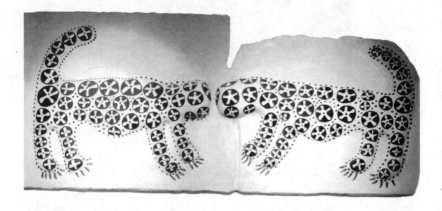

FIGURE 12. Leopards with trefoil spots (terra-cotta relief, Neolithic, Turkey, 6000–5800 B.C.)

Here are our leopards again. The felines' pelts are represented with spots that have trefoils in them, three little leaf forms. It is fascinating that this principle of three keeps coming up with respect to the field of time and space, which we have to pass in order to get to the transcendent, to the realm of the mother light: the Goddess who is transcendent of, gives birth to, and takes back from the world of time. The number three, representing past, present, and future, appears in one way or another in many mythologies.

When you go to Japan and approach temples, there are all kinds of guardians. One will have the mouth open and the other the mouth closed.[9] They typically represent the male and female, but in the Buddhist sphere they also represent the two emotions that bind us to life:

the emotion of fear and the emotion of desire. The notion is that if you're going to pass through to the experience of immortality, which is within the shrine, you must leave behind those two emotions.

In India, it is said that the divine energy of *brahman* manifests itself in time as Māyā, and the energy has three functions or qualities, called *guṇas*: the function of energy, the function of inertia, and the function of harmony. *Rajas guṇa* is the quality of energy, *tamas guṇa* is the quality of pressure and inertia against which the energy plays, and *sattva guṇa* is the harmonization of the two. In Chinese philosophy there is yin and yang. The yang energy is analogous to *rajas guṇa*, or the thrust, and yin energy is *tamas guṇa*, or inertia, and one has to have a balance between them and that's the *sattva guṇa*. When you look at that Chinese sign of the revolving yin and yang, you have energy, mass and harmonious movement. We have this in Einstein's formula of $E = MC^2$. Energy is E, mass is M, the C is the speed of light. When you realize that those leopards represent the guardians, they can be read as the forms of sensibility, the categories of logic through which we have to penetrate to get to what Kant called the *Ding an sich*, the "thing in itself," and what the Indians call *brahman*, that which is the one life consciousness of which we are all manifestations.

In Çatal Hüyük is a ceramic figure of the Goddess with her arms and legs lifted in what has been called the birth-giving posture, and the child she is delivering is a bucranium, a bull's head. Where we saw her before she'd given birth to a child, and now she gives birth to a symbolic form of the moon bull. These are alternate personifications of the same power. The bull's horns facing the Goddess, or acolytes, are in an attitude of reverence to the event—they appear to be in adoration. With the idea of the deity you have the devotee, and the devotee is the one who just has a couple of clues about the fact that he really is one with the deity. Now, the horns of the bull represent the crescent moon, that celestial sphere that dies and is resurrected. The moon carries within itself its own death in the form of its increasing shadow, as we all do. It has, however, the power to throw off that shadow and be reborn. So the moon represents to us the promise of rebirth, of the power of life engaged in the field of time and space to throw off death and be reborn. That's the sense of these representations—that in procreation death has been thrown off and the seed has gone to rebirth through the miracle of the woman's body, which the navel represents.

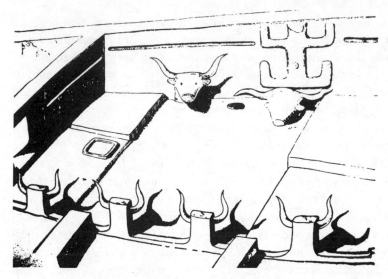

FIGURE 13. Goddess birthing a bull's head (artist's reconstruction of plaster and wood, Neolithic, Turkey, 6000–5800 B.C.)

The accent on the navel highlights the connection with the mother, with Mother Earth, and with the world navel. The omphalos at the temple at Delphi, for example, was the world axis for the Greeks, the sacred principle, and the sacred place of any cult is mythologically thought of as the navel.

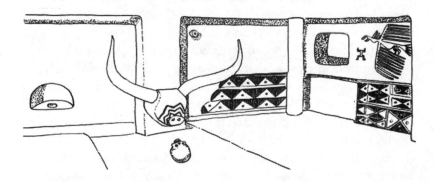

FIGURE 14. Bull's head and vulture (artist's reconstruction of plaster and wood, Neolithic, Turkey, 6000–5800 B.C.)

The next phase of this miracle from the mythological point of view is illustrated in another Çatal Hüyük shrine by a bull's head and underneath it a human skull. In these shrines actual skulls were found under the *bucrania*, each representing the head of the bull that died and was resurrected. On the wall is a representation of a vulture pouncing on a beheaded body. That would be the corpse from which the head comes, and the corpse is to be eaten back by the agent of the Goddess. The vulture becomes the agent of the Goddess eating back bodies for recycling, and that's the role she plays right down into Egypt under the name of Nekhbet, the vulture goddess. In the late Lotus Sūtra, the Buddha is talking to his Bodhisattvas on the mountaintop—as Jesus talks to his disciples on the Mount of Olives—and the name of the mountain on which the Buddha is talking is Griddhraj Parvat (Vulture Peak), where the body is eaten back.

Gimbutas observes, "The human legs of the vulture...imply that it is not simply a bird but rather the Goddess in the guise of a vulture. She is Death—She Who Takes Away Life, maleficent twin of She Who Gives Life—ominous in flight on great, outspread wings. Despite the incarnate presence of Death, the vulture scenes of Çatal Hüyük do not convey death's mournful triumph over life. Rather, they symbolize that death and resurrection are inseparably linked."[10]

The head as the focal center of consciousness becomes representative of that which is to be reincarnated and is placed here under the bull's head. If one were to write a prayer for that which is symbolized in that shrine it would say, "May I whose body goes back to the Mother obtain rebirth as the moon bull is reborn." So, here we have an evident doctrine of rebirth and reincarnation, with the moon symbolic of that which dies and is resurrected. All of the dead and resurrected gods of the Mediterranean area are associated with the moon: Osiris, Attis, Adonis, and Jesus. The moon mythologically is three nights dark, just as Jesus was three nights in the tomb with the dark rock over the door.

In Çatal Hüyük and Southeast Europe we are at the root of this whole mythology of the Goddess in her two aspects as She who takes the seed and transmutes it into life, and She who eats back the body and brings it forth renewed.

The Indian Taittirīya Upaniṣad tells us:

Oh, wonderful! Oh, wonderful! Oh, wonderful!
I am food! I am food! I am food!
I am a food-eater! I am a food-eater! I am a food-eater!
He who knows this, has a brilliantly shining light.
Such is the mystic doctrine!
And anyone who withholds the food that he is from the world is a hoarder.
    It is a question of yielding this body to the process.[11]

FIGURE 15. Bulls'-head shrine (artist's reconstruction of plaster and wood, Neolithic, Turkey, 6000–5800 B.C.)

The bull's head dominates another Çatal Hüyük shrine. Below the three bulls' heads are breasts and within them, covered in plaster, are boars' jaws.

Within these breasts where the nipple is open Mellaart found the skulls of vultures, so that the beak was positioned where the nipple would have been. "She who feeds, eats back," the image says. Here, the death totem is not the head of a vulture but the lower jaw of a boar—the pig eats back too and is the agent of the Goddess through this aspect of consuming.

The pig is associated with the goddess of death in all the mythologies of Southeast Asia. In the myths from the Malekula in the New Hebrides, on Ceram just north of New Guinea, we find the boar's tusk as the lunar crescent and the boar's head as the dark night.

Men's secret societies are very important in these early planting societies. Women are the ones who are raising the children, raising the crops, building the houses—what have the men to do? They become neurotic and they gather together for psychological protection: men's secret societies. In the men's secret society in Malekula they raise male pigs and they turn them into sacred animals. The spiritual exercise consists of knocking out the canine teeth of the pigs, which allows for a very interesting tusk to grow in a complete circle, some in three rings. With the pig's own tusk going back to his jaw the pig is in considerable pain, so it doesn't get fat; rather, it's a *spiritual* pig. And every stage of the development of that tusk requires a sacrifice of other pigs. The idea of sacrifice in these societies is that the power, the energy, of the sacrificed animals flows into the owner's pig, so that by the time he's got a pig with three rings, it's become a powerful pig. Furthermore, the owner of the pig becomes of higher rank spiritually and his name is changed. With this enterprise one learns the labyrinth pattern that leads to the underworld; one is learning the secret of the immortal life:

A man dies and goes on the death way to the volcano in the fires of which the immortals dance. And on the way stands a goddess— her name in this culture is Sevsev—and she's there to eat him. She's Mother Universe. As he approaches she draws the labyrinth on the ground and erases half of it; and to pass her he has to know how to draw that other half, and the only place he can have learned would have been in this secret society. If he can draw that labyrinth again, he gives her his pig to consume and he goes by.

So there's a big mystery associated with the knowledge of this cult: it saves you from the jaws of the goddess of mortality.

Now, there's another use of the pig that is described in a wonderful book by John Layard called *The Stone Men of Malekula*, one of the major studies of this whole system. In a society like Malekula, where the presence of the women is immediate and very strong, a little boy has a hard time disengaging his libido from his mother. One of the problems of the male is to become a willing, active agent. He cannot become a willing, active agent until he has disengaged his libido from Mother, and it is his father who takes over that concern. He gives the little boy a pig to love so the boy finds something else besides the mother. When he is quite in love with the pig, the father helps him sacrifice the pig so he learns how to sacrifice that which he loves. So the pig actually is the boy's guide to his manhood and means of disengagement from the personal mother. Then he's given another pig and it is also sacrificed. This is an interesting psychological operation, as there comes a time in a man's life when the erotic principle is not necessarily the dominant one, but rather the aggressive one. Then there comes this competition in the raising of pigs and the building of the three-loop tusk, which helps you to get past Mother Death. As the boy is released from bondage to the mother of his life, man is released from the jaws of Mother Earth–as-death.

One must realize that part of the accent of the cult of the Goddess is achieving release from Her, insofar as She represents bondage to time, bondage to death. Now, in this devotion to the pig, the pig is understood to represent a divine male power, and the individual identifying himself with his own private pig is in a relationship to the vicarious offering and the vicarious salvation through that sacrifice, which is identical with the essence of one's own being. Here we are at the root of a whole mythology that goes along with the agricultural civilization and in this context is related to the cult of the Goddess.

In the later period, when the bull and cattle culture comes into Southwest Asia and Southeast Europe, the bull takes over the role of the pig, but as we'll see, the pig keeps its connection to the underworld cult. The pig's tusks turn down and the bull's horns point up, and as Jane Harrison points out, there are two main cult lines in Classical Greece. One is that of the *chthonic*, the underworld reference, and the other is that of the *ouranic*, or the heavenly reference,[12] and we're going to see that split.

MAP I. Old Europe

Marija Gimbutas, in her splendid book *Gods and Goddesses of Old Europe*, shows the earliest constellation of the images of the Goddess. Old Europe, Gimbutas's term for the geographic area from the Neolithic period, includes Crete and Malta, both powerful areas for the old Neolithic goddess cult, the northern Balkans, Czechoslovakia, Yugoslavia, Hungary, Romania, and Bulgaria. Says Gimbutas:

> Villages depending upon domesticated plants and animals had appeared in southeastern Europe as early as the seventh millennium B.C., and the spiritual forces accompanying this change in the economic and social organization are manifested in the emergent artistic tradition of the Neolithic.... Between c. 7000 and c. 3500 B.C., the inhabitants of this region developed a much more complex social organization than their western and northern neighbors, forming settlements which often amounted to small townships, inevitably involving craft specialization and the creation of religious and governmental institutions.[13]

Beginning around 4000 B.C., however, the first influx of Indo-European tribes swept over the Rivers Don and Volga from the grasslands of the sub-Russian steppes. A masculine, war-oriented mythology brought by descendants of the old plains hunters (now herders of cattle) came smashing in and the whole culture field changed. Nonetheless, the cult of the Goddess survived in the Aegean and so we have worship of the Goddess continuing until around 1500 B.C.

Figure 16 shows one of the earliest images of our Goddess, with three important elements. The first element to observe is the breasts,

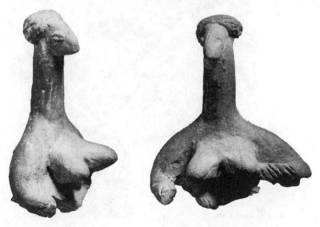

FIGURE 16. Long-necked goddesses (ceramic, Neolithic, Greece, 5900–5700 B.C.)

which make it very clear that it's a female and also with human qualities; second is the bird's head, and third the long pillar neck. The Goddess is the *axis mundi*, the world axis, the pillar of the universe. She represents the energy that supports the whole cycle of the universe. In its flight, the bird is free from the bonds of the world and represents the spiritual life.

People often think of the Goddess as a fertility deity only. Not at all—she's the muse. She's the inspirer of poetry. She's the inspirer of the spirit. So, she has three functions: one, to give us life; two, to be the one who receives us in death; and three, to inspire our spiritual, poetic realization.

FIGURE 17. Figure carrying a sickle (terra-cotta and copper, Chalcolithic, Hungary, c. 5000 B.C.)

In the early traditions the deities are part human and part animal. Then, as the humanization becomes more emphatic and people become more aware of a distinction between the human mode and the animal mode, the animal becomes a vehicle or a companion of the Goddess. The energy of that third, spiritual, function of the Goddess is represented as avian—the dove remains the principal bird of Aphrodite, and the peacock of Hera. These avian forms provide a metaphor for bringing the animal aspect of the body into accord with the human aspect. This is pictorial script, writing through images.

In Figure 17, we see a male figure wearing a mask. The mask motif indicates that the person you see is two people. He's the one wearing the mask and he is the mask that's worn—that is, the mask of the role. The sickle dates from 5000 B.C. and is made of copper, which is one of the oldest examples of metal use anywhere in the world. Related to harvesting, the reaping of grass indicates we are in the field of agricultural life. All other copper implements found from this complex and period are tools for tilling the soil, and none of them weapons. This period before the male-oriented Indo-Europeans came in was one of basically peaceful communities; Marija Gimbutas makes this point strongly:

> The Goddess-centered art with its striking absence of images of warfare and male domination, reflects a social order in which women as heads of clans or queen-priestesses played a central part. Old Europe and Anatolia, as well as Minoan Crete, were a gylany.[14] A balanced, non-patriarchal and non-matriachal social system is reflected by religion, mythologies, and folklore, by studies of the social structure of Old European and Minoan cultures, and is supported by the continuity of the elements of a matrilineal system in ancient Greece, Rome, Basque and other countries of Europe.[15]

The accent in these pieces is on aesthetic stylization. In *The Transformation of Nature in Art*, A. T. Coomeraswamy says that the transformation of nature has to do with indicating its mystic dimension, and nature just naturally is out there, so what! You see it in pictures, you go out in the fields and you see it again. But what the artist does by his organization is so to render a rhythmic statement that something of the mystery dimension comes radiantly through and touches us. Cézanne had a saying, "Art is a harmony parallel to nature,"[16] and the harmony that is stated in art is of the nature that is both the nature of our own lives and the nature out there. So we get an "Aha!" a sense that, "Ah, yes, I've known that all the time."

FIGURE 18. The "Thinker" of Hamangia (terra-cotta, Chalcolithic, Romania, c. 5000 B.C.)

FIGURE 19. Fish goddess (carved sandstone, late Neolithic, Serbia, sixth millennium B.C.)

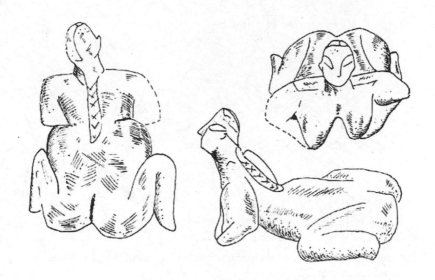

FIGURE 20. Toad goddess (ceramic, late Neolithic, Turkey, sixth millennium B.C.)

We've seen the divine feminine expressed in avian form, but you find them in piscine form as well. Fish goddesses become nymphs and the fish represent the powers that later are going to be humanized in the various distinct goddesses. For instance, Artemis bathing in the waters as a water deity is the human form separated from the natural form. In the early periods the human form coalesces with the natural form. Marija Gimbutas calls the frog goddess "the birth patron." The fact that the frog is a batrachian, at home in the water and on land, shows the relationship between the two realms, the realm of the womb and the realm of the outer world.

The twin goddess is the mother of the two worlds and of our two lives, the world of our life in time and space, and the world of our death, our life in the mystery zone beyond. The labyrinth motif connects the Goddess as the personification of those powers that exist beyond the labyrinth of our life.

The pig is associated with the Goddess in Romania, Bulgaria, Macedonia, Northern Greece, and Mycenae.[17] If you look at the figurine (Fig. 22), you'll notice that not only is she wearing a porcine mask, but her body is marked with a geometric pattern: the labyrinth, the mystic way. It is through the Goddess that you enter the world of the spirit. She is the maze, and she is also your guide.

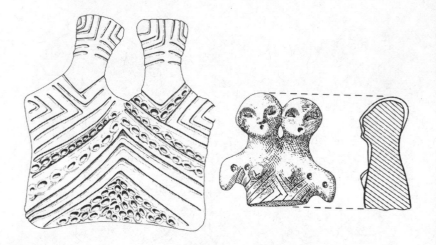

FIGURE 21. Double-headed goddess (terra-cotta, Chalcolithic, Romania, late sixth millennium B.C.)

FIGURE 22. Vegetation goddess wearing a pig mask (terra-cotta, Chalcolithic, Romania, mid-fifth millennium B.C.)

In *The Golden Bough*, Sir James Frazer suggested as early as 1890 that the great goddesses of Eleusis—Demeter and Persephone—were pig goddesses.[18] When Persephone was abducted by Hades a whole herd of pigs went down in the underworld with her, and when her mother went to find her, she couldn't follow the footsteps because they were covered by those of the pigs. Demeter's and Persephone's association with the underworld, death and rebirth, the labyrinth, and the pig echoes all the way back to the Neolithic.

The labyrinth is a gate through which only those who know can go safely. It is associated from very early times, and particularly in Southeast Asia, with the journey of the dead. The passage through the labyrinth is a decisive adventure, one in which you are deciding whether or not you are going to experience eternal life.

This legend, from West Ceram in Indonesia, is archetypal for planting cultures: At the beginning of the world the men would dance the labyrinth dance, while the women would stand in the center. The labyrinth dance consisted of a spiral of nine circles. (Nine is associated with the moon.) In the very center, a little girl, Hainuwele, was handing out what in India is called betel for the dancers to refresh themselves. One night, instead of handing out betel she began handing out beautiful presents. Night after night, the beauty of the gifts increased until the people became very jealous and frightened. It just seemed too frightening that this little thing should be the source of that which is inexhaustible—so they trampled her to death in the labyrinth. Then they buried her and from her body grows all the food plants that the people eat.[19]

We tend to think of death as the end of life, but death and life are counterparts. So this is the prime agricultural myth of a body that is a deity's body, so that in eating the plants we're eating God. This is carried over, then, to the idea of Jesus's sacrament: "This is my body, this is my blood." It is the labyrinth that knocks Hainuwele down and the Goddess becomes angry at the people for this act of murder, so that she fashions a gate that is a spiral labyrinth, and those who can come through the gate she strikes with the arms of this girl, and that strikes them dead. Those who can't come through become either animals or spirits, so that the one who dies is the human one. Animals die, but the animals are a negative power, spirits are negative powers, and the human beings are those who have come through and been touched with the sight of death. So one way or another going through the labyrinth

FIGURE 23. Labyrinthine goddess holding a child (terra-cotta, late Neolithic, Greece, 5900–5700 B.C.)

takes you through a psychological or spiritual crisis, transforming you into a full human being; in the stories that I've been telling, it brings you to death and immortality. Either way, it is a dangerous, difficult passage that only those who know can accomplish.

The serpent is a tremendously important figure in all the planting cultures of the world. It is associated with the power of life to throw off death because the serpent can shed its skin and be born again; it sloughs its skin, just as the moon sloughs its shadow. The moon is the energy of life engaged in the field of time, the energy of life absolute, and the moon symbolized in the bull is the celestial spirit that dies.

It's a peculiar twist of our biblical tradition that the serpent is condemned, as are women and nature. For other cultures the serpent, while dangerous, is one of the three great symbols of the power of life in the field of time. Serpent, bull, moon: the sun pounces on the moon and the moon dies into the sun; the lion pounces on the bull; the eagle, the sun bird, pounces on the serpent—this is a basic triad of paired symbols. What the moon, the bull, and the serpent represent is the power to throw off death and be born again. So the bull becomes the principal sacrificial animal in Europe, just as the pig was in Melanesia.

COPPER TO BRONZE: CRETE

Old Europe changed dramatically after 3500 B.C. when the Indo-Europeans began pouring into the area, changing the whole system. They swept down through the Balkans into Greece. They didn't cross from the Greek mainland over into Crete until about 1500 B.C., however, so you find in the Aegean a continuation of the old Mother Goddess system.

After the Second World War, a young man named Michael Ventris, who had been a flier and a translator during the war, turned himself to decoding Linear B, a script found in the Minoan palaces from about the thirteenth century B.C. Linear B had baffled scientists since Arthur Evans had first discovered it while excavating Knossos in the early twentieth century. Ventris found that Linear B was a very early form of Greek, an Indo-European language, indicating an Indo-European influence in the islands, though they hadn't yet dominated in the same way that they had on the mainland.

In Crete, the principle divinity was the Goddess. She stands with the double-ax in each hand. The ax of sacrifice is called the *labrys*, after which the labyrinth itself is named. The *labrys* is the prime symbol of Crete, a double-headed ax with a lunar curve—you can't have

FIGURE 24. Goddess with double ax (fresco, Minoan, Crete, second millennium B.C.)

something new unless something old is going to die. So she's the goddess of death in the end as well as of birth in the beginning. Death and birth belong together. With the *labrys* in her hand, the Mother Goddess stands clearly dominant, and the blood spilled in sacrifice is the mother's, whether it's animal sacrifice or human sacrifice. The principal sacrificial animal was the bull—always male. One did not sacrifice female animals, as the female is not that which dies and is resurrected; she is that which carries death to resurrection—she is the transformer.

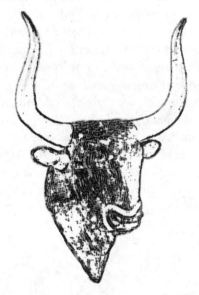

FIGURE 25. Bull's-head rhyton with lunar horns (carved soapstone with mother-of-pearl and gold, Minoan, Greece, c. 1500 B.C.)

Let me say a word here about the female sun and the male moon.

Later on we will be coming to the male-oriented mythologies in which the sun is masculine and the moon feminine, but this earlier Neolithic and high Bronze Age system shows the female sun and the male moon. In German, one says *der Mond*, ("moon"—masculine), and *die Sonne*, ("sun"—feminine). In France, one says *la lune* ("moon"—feminine), and *le soleil* ("sun"—masculine). If you know and appreciate with equal pleasure the two systems, you will recognize the source of this deep, dark quality in the German sense of the tragic. It is a mystical culture with a mystical language, whereas French is characterized by *la clarté du français*, the light and the shine of Gallic reason.

A little myth occurs among primitive people in the Northern circumpolar area about the sun sister and the moon brother. A young woman was approached every night by a lover whom she did not know and could not see in the dark. Finally determined to find out who this was, she blackened her hands on the coals of the fire and one night embracing him, left her handprints on his back. In the morning she discovered it was her brother and in shock, ran away. In zeal, he pursued. Every now and then he catches up with her and there's an eclipse of the Sun. This is an old story and it is another mythology of a deep tragic quality, not at all in the way of the solar mythologies that we will be coming to presently.

The famous Minoan bull games represented on the murals like this tiny one from the Palace of Knossos (Fig. 26)—could this have happened, or is it a fantasy?

When I was a student in France I went to Bordeaux to see a bull ring exhibition where the bull was not to be killed. The idea of the game is to have a bull—with horns like needles—come rushing at the matador, who must step aside moving only one foot. Well, I can tell you it was hair-raising! If the bull's horns had a bit more extension

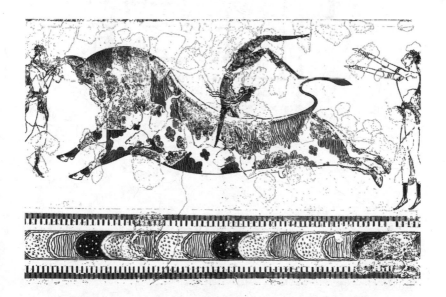

FIGURE 26. Bull-dancers (fresco, Minoan, Crete, seventh–fifth centuries B.C.)

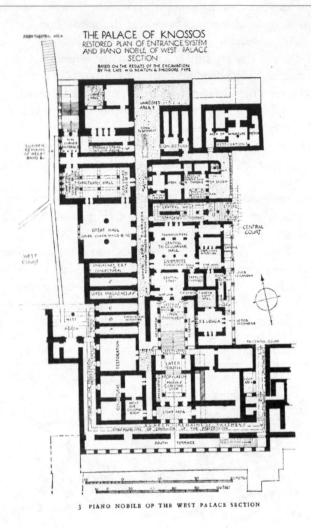

THE PALACE OF KNOSSOS
RESTORED PLAN OF ENTRANCE SYSTEM
AND PIANO NOBILE OF WEST PALACE
SECTION
BASED ON THE RESULTS OF THE EXCAVATION
BY THE LATE W G NEWTON & THEODORE FYFE

3   PIANO NOBILE OF THE WEST PALACE SECTION

Map 2. Palace of Minos

"The Palace of Knossos is not an artistic unity. As a Greek temple reveals the spirit of a people caught at a particular moment, so the Palace, like a Gothic cathedral or the temples of Karnak and Luxor, reveals the history and progress of its builders. Older structures are adapted to a new plan; old foundations, once built over, lie in what at first seems a confusing labyrinth where the spade has uncovered them."—J. D. S. Pendlebury[20]

Archaeologists use the term *Minoan*, derived from the famous King Minos, to describe a variety of cultural epochs covering the whole of the Copper and Bronze Ages in Crete.

than the matador had anticipated, the matador's shirt was torn off and perhaps a bit of the matador was taken with it.

But what was so exciting was when one chap, with the bull rushing wildly at him, started running at the bull himself! And when the bull approached him closely, he somersaulted right over the animal. Now, you sometimes wonder years later, "Did I really see that or was it a dream?" And then a few years ago I ran into a book that had actual pictures of this kind of bull game in southern France. It can be done.

What is the sense of a game like that? It is interesting that today the matador, when the bull is killed as part of the event, has to go right over the horns for the coup de grâce to take place. In this very dramatic confrontation, he is the sun god. The sun kills the moon once a month and as the moon—that which dies and is resurrected, that which begets itself—is masculine in these Neolithic and early Bronze Age traditions, so the sun is feminine.

Frazer, in *The Golden Bough*, made the point that the prime sacrifice in the old, early kingships was the king himself. There is a cycle of about eight years associated with the appearance of the planet Venus at the same point in the sky, at the end of which the king was to be killed. (Venus, as we shall see, was associated with the Goddess, whether she was called Aphrodite, Isis, Ishtar, or Inanna.)

The attitude of antiquity toward sacrifice is something I don't think we can appreciate fully. The animal or the young person sacrificed was to be *perfect*. Anyone with a flaw was unworthy to be sacrificed, and so the king himself was the primary sacrifice. One never finds a picture of him old. His throne (Fig. 27) shows the lunar form underneath the seat, and it is flanked on either side by a griffin that comes right down into the late Middle Ages, as Dante interpreted the half-eagle, half-lion griffin as representing the dual nature of Christ—both true man and true God. So the king straddles the threshold between this world and the next.

Sir Arthur Evans dubbed this gold disk (Fig. 28), found near the Peloponessian city of Pylos, "the Ring of Nestor" after Pylos's legendary king. At the center is a tree: "The seal is structured by the gnarled and knotted Tree of Life, which grows out of a mound covered in fresh shoots in the centre, with its two lateral branches dividing the scene into the underworld below and the after-life above."[21]

The group of dancing female figures with griffin heads is associated with the Goddess, possibly the one who distinguishes or judges

FIGURE 27. Throne Room, Palace of Knossos (fresco, Minoan, Crete, c. 1500 B.C.)

FIGURE 28. Ring of Nestor (gold seal, Minoan, Greece, c. 1500 B.C.)

the mortal from the immortal part. Wherever female figures are dominant in the cult there is an accent on the experiential side of religion, the rapture of religion that naturally moves into rhythmical movement and dance: the dance rather than the dogma, for the theoretical side comes up with the masculine mythologies. The women ask for the experience and they call it forth through the dance and this comes back with the Bacchae and the re-bursting-forth of this Dionysian dance after years of suppression.

FIGURE 29. Goddess with a *labrys* beside the Tree of Life (engraved gold, Minoan, Crete, 1500 B.C.)

In this system the experiential is often associated with the vegetable world, a motif that later returns in the Greek mysteries. In the vegetable world an important motif is that of rot, decay, that out of the disintegrating vegetation comes fresh life. So you see that the motif of life out of death is there with respect to vegetation, the moon, and the serpent shedding its skin.

The two serpents symbolize that whenever you have time, you have duality, birth and death. The serpents represent the dying and

FIGURE 30. Goddess with snakes (faience, Minoan, Crete, c. 1600 B.C.)

"The goddess is holding a snake high in each hand with all the ritualized gesture of divine statement. The net pattern on her skirt, which gathers significance from its Paleolithic and Neolithic ancestry, suggests she is the weaver of the web of life, which is perpetually woven from her womb. Her skirt has seven layers, the number of the days of the moon's four quarters, which divide into the two waxing and waning halves of the cycle, like the Neolithic cross inside the circle. Although seven was also the number of the visible 'planets,' this is probably a lunar notation of series and measure, so that sitting in the lap of the goddess, as the overlapping panel of her gown invites, would be to experience time supported by eternity, and eternity clothed in time."

—Anne Baring and Jules Cashford[22]

resurrecting, and the lion on her head represents the other principle into which the moon dies and out of which it is born. The moon represents the power of consciousness and life in the field of time and space, where it puts on bodies and puts them off. As it is said in the Bhagavad Gītā, "The soul accepts a new body / As a man puts on and puts off clothing."[23] This bull/serpent/moon principle is that of life engaged in the field of time and space, in the field of phenomenal apparitions and dis-apparitions of forms. The sun, on the other hand, is never shadowed except in eclipse, and so does not carry its death within it; thus it represents consciousness disengaged from the field of time and space.

Now, this is a basic motif in Bronze Age symbology, a motif that comes right down through all the high symbolism of the Indian tradition, right into yoga, with the two nerves *iḍā* and *piṅgālā*—the one representing the lunar principle, the other the solar. The great mystic realization is that these two aspects of consciousness are in fact one consciousness, so that your consciousness here in the field of life is at the same time consciousness disengaged from this field. The paradox of relating oneself to these two aspects of one's own true being and entity is the great mystical balancing act. It is a dangerous path—the sharp edge of a razor—the path between the knowledge of yourself as consciousness in the field and knowledge of yourself as consciousness in disengagement from the field. You can tip either way—and then there comes an inappropriate attitude, inflation or deflation of one kind or another.

The goal of all meditation and mystery journeys is to go between the pair of opposites. In the early thirteenth century, when Wolfram von Eschenbach wrote his *Parzival*, he described the Grail as a stone vessel brought down from heaven by the neutral angels. There had been a war in heaven, with God and Lucifer in battle, both with their tribes on the different sides, but apparently there were neutral angels who didn't participate. One problem when you have God and Devil is that you have a pair of opposites, but the transcendent transcends the pair of opposites, so the Grail was brought down. And indeed, the hero of von Eschenbach's poem, Parzival, takes his name from the French *Perce le val* ("pierce the valley")—the middle way.

So there we have the Goddess, holding the serpents. She has the

FIGURE 31. Goddess on the World Mountain (engraved gold, Minoan, Crete, 1400 B.C.)

whole thing in her hands: they are all part of her Mother conscious-ness, and her being incorporates both aspects—the solar and the lunar.

Images of the Goddess frequently show her atop a mountain. The whole mountain is the Goddess. This goes back to the old Sumerian times, when the cosmic mountain is represented in the ziggurats. In India, Parvatī is the goddess of the mountain, even as she is the moun-tain—that's what her name means: "mountain."

Here (Fig. 31), the Goddess has two lions as her attendants, and there is a male standing in reverence before her. So here is a whole concentration: the pair of opposites; the sign of the trident between the pair of opposites that goes past birth and death, careless of the phenomenality of the realm of time; the horns as symbol of the moon; and the lions as symbol of the sun. The trident becomes the symbol of both the god and the middle way that brings you to the place of the sacrifice, which is the altar of the Goddess.

The Goddess is the connotation of the energies both of solar absolute time and of the reflection of solar continuity and energy in the field of time. Now, if you think that the world's center is the center of your particular cult symbol, you are relating yourself not to the spiritual mystery, but only to your own social tradition. As I've said, this is an important point about symbols: they do not refer to historical events; they refer through historical events to spiritual or psychological principles and powers that are of yesterday, today, and tomorrow, and that are everywhere.

"And I saw that the sacred hoop of my people was one of many hoops that made one circle, wide as daylight and as starlight."[24] Black Elk's saying matches perfectly the Hermetic text that was translated from Greek into Latin in the twelfth century called *The Book of the Twenty-Four Philosophers*: "God is an intelligible sphere known to the mind whose center is everywhere and circumference nowhere."[25] This little sentence has been quoted by Ravalli, Nicholas of Cusa, Voltaire, Pascale, and by a great many others.

But the cult gives you a center and that is of historical moment. All studies of mythology have these two aspects: one is the provincial, the social, which links you through your social group to transpersonal powers and principles; the other is the transsocial, the nonlocatable, that of the spiritual principle to which the society is introducing. So symbols function in two ways, and since they come from the psyche, the psyche recognizes them with fascination. Shakespeare says that art "holds as 'twere a mirror up to nature";[26] the nature that's holding the mirror up is the inward nature too, like an X-ray mirror, and you see the symbol with fascination. When the symbol is working, you are fascinated. You don't have to be told what it means, you know what it means—and yet you don't. And that fascination, when it is rendered through the symbols of the group, link the individual to his group, and through the group to principles that are beyond those of his personal interest.

Then there comes a time when the group dismisses you and says, "We had you, but we've got another generation now." Furthermore, you've probably had it with the group, and so there comes the time when you say, "Tell me what's new. I've seen this before and that before, and I'm a little fed up." Because of the disengagement that takes place, you begin to turn inward and you find the real source-land of the messages that were rendered through the social forms.

Now, in India, the social aspect of the legend and myth is called the *deśī*, which means *that which has provincial location*, and the general or universal aspect is called *mārga*, a word from the root *mrg*, which refers to the path or track left by a game animal. So the symbols of the *mārga* are the path, the track left by the animal of the soul, and by following that track you find it: the transcendent meaning of the symbol.

The two relationships working simultaneously has one linking you to the social duty and world of history, and the other linking you to that which is beyond duty, beyond the pairs of opposites, beyond good and evil. It links you through that door of the clashing rocks, which those two leopards represented, into the realm that is both of the sun lion and the moon serpent; and there the Goddess, the mother of us all, shows Herself in both aspects. That's the important point of this whole subject. Once you get it, the whole thing begins to talk, and when you haven't got it, it links you into historical exercises that sometimes drive you crazy.

About 1480 B.C., a volcanic eruption exploded the whole interior of the island of Thera (now known as Santorini). Thera was known along with Crete as the capital of the Aegean culture of the Goddess.

The magnitude of the eruption has not been surpassed since; the closest thing to it was the eruption of Krakatau in Indonesia on August 26, 1883. Scientists estimate that tsunami from the Krakatau eruption could have been as high as nine hundred feet. Afterward, the atmosphere of the entire planet was filled with debris for several years, causing strange effects at sunrise and sunset. The force of the larger eruption on Thera wiped out much of the island. A huge tidal wave would have slashed into Crete, as well as into Palestine and Egypt, and the reports we hear of cataclysms of that time may be echoes of the event.

Up to that time the dominant powers in the Hellenic sphere were the Cretans, with the Mycenaeans receiving their cultured influences from Crete. This eruption really marked the end of the old pre-Bronze Age tradition, and in the Aegean, it ended the dominance of the Minoans—that is to say, the early Mediterranean Cretans. This was followed by the rise of the Mycenaeans and the mainland Greeks, the Indo-Europeans who had come down from the North, having entered Europe around 3500 B.C. After the destruction of Thera, the

Mycenaeans became dominant in the Greek sphere, so you have a shift in accent from Mother Goddess to male god. Both the goddess and god were present, but the goddess was no longer in the dominant role. From this date, just a little after 1500 B.C., the Minoan power declined and the male-oriented, bronze-weapon–oriented culture took over.

FIGURE 32. Goddess in seven-tiered dress (hematite seal, Sumerian, Iraq, c. 2150–2000 B.C.)

CHAPTER 3

──────●──────

Indo-European Influx[1]

MARIJA GIMBUTAS's extensive archaeological excavations and studies have established the influx of the Indo-Europeans from the north into the Neolithic agricultural societies of what she dubbed Old Europe.

At the same time, Akkadians and other Semitic tribes began pushing up into Mesopotamia from the south. Around 3500 B.C. those planting people were between two striking forces—the Semites from out of the desert, and the Indo-Europeans out of the north. The Semites were herders of sheep and goats principally, and they came with increasing force in the course of the years. Sargon and Hammurabi brought an increasingly powerful male accent into the Semitic sphere, with the Hebrews representing the extreme whereby the Goddess was utterly rejected.

The Indo-European people were herders, not of sheep and goat, but of cattle. Earlier in the Neolithic period of Old Europe, animal husbandry focused on pigs. The mythology of the pig is of a lunar character and now it becomes that of cattle, the bull. As Jane Harrison points out in her book *Prolegomena to the Study of Greek Religion*, the horns of the bull point upward and the sacrifices to the deities of Olympus were skyward, or ouranic. The tusks of the boar point downward and so the sacrifices to the powers of the earlier swine herders are to the earth, or chthonic.

In this chapter, we will look at the historical evidence of the impact of the Indo-European male-oriented warrior culture on Macedonia and Greece and show how the impact comes most strongly around 1200 B.C., at the time of the Trojan wars. In later chapters, we will see how, by about 700 B.C., the female powers come back again

MAP 3. Indo-Europeans' movement into Old Europe

in a new mode—not in the mode of fertility and of the Earth but as the Goddess of the Mysteries: She as the one who initiates us into a spiritual transformation. Formerly the initiation was more material, but in the Classical age we will be seeing a spiritual approach, and it's going to come as a consequence of this duality of the two systems, the Indo-European and Old European, coming together.

SPEARS AND LANGUAGES

There are two main alloys of bronze being used from about 4000 B.C. In the Caspian Mountains where copper is mined, it is alloyed with arsenic, and you get a bronze that is a sturdier metal than copper. The later, great, classic bronze first appears in Mesopotamia, alloying copper with tin. It's here that we have the dawn in Southwest Asia of what we've come to call the Bronze Age.

The first copper instruments were not weapons; they were tools for shaping objects and tilling the soil. The Indo-European peoples north of the Black Sea were warrior cattle-herding people and the first conquerors of the horse. When they learned about bronze they turned the new metal into weapons. The spear points show bolts and holes by which the metal blades were riveted to a staff, creating a lance or spear. This is the key implement, and wherever it is found it indicates that the Indo-Europeans were there, starting approximately between 4000 and 3500 B.C.

Around 4000 B.C., the Indo-Europeans began striking into the Old European world—what we would call Central and Eastern Europe and the Balkans. They then moved down into the Near East and to the east, into India and Persia. The Indo-Europeans who struck into India would compose the Vedas, and in Persia these peoples became the Zoroastrians. There are hymns of Zoroaster in a language that is so close to Sanskrit that we know that a division between the Persians and the Hindus took place after the Aryan invasion.

When the British conquered India in the eighteenth century, they intended to govern as far as possible within the Indian tradition—that is to say, to find out what the laws were of India, to take them over, and to adapt them to a contemporary world. It was found, however, that nobody could read Sanskrit and translate it into English. A group of *pundits*, Brahmin scholars, was brought together and they published a work called *Vivādārṇavasetu* (*Bridge Across the Ocean of Dispute*). So you can imagine what those meetings were like. And nobody could translate it; it had to be translated into Persian and then out of Persian into English. It was finally published as *A Code of Gentoo Laws* in 1776.

Clearly, somebody English had to learn Sanskrit, and so a man named Charles Wilkins went to Benares and put himself in school with the Brahmins there. Then he published a translation of the Bhagavad Gīta in English (*Bhagvat-geeta, or Dialogues of Kreeshna and Arjoon*) in 1785. This was the first bit of news out of India into Europe. The Bhagavad Gīta struck like lightning in certain places: Goethe and the Germans were simply enraptured, as was Carlyle in England, and Emerson and Thoreau in America. This is the beginning of the movement toward the mystical point of view in the Christian tradition— Emerson, Thoreau, Carlyle, Goethe. Then the translation appeared of *Śakuntalā*, a beautiful play by Kālidāsa, the Shakespeare of India, from the fifth century A.D. And again Goethe is enraptured. He said,

"If you want the springtime and the fall, the blossom and the fruit, read the *Śakuntalā*."[2] And there are certain features from *Śakuntalā* that he incorporated in *Faust*. So this Indian thing was becoming a smash. And what was it? It was the religion of putting yourself back in accord with nature in all of its aspects.

In 1783 an English lawyer named Sir William Jones was sent to Calcutta to serve as a judge. He was the first competent linguist to come to India from the European sphere, knowing Latin and Greek as well as the basic languages of Europe and something of their histories. It was Jones who recognized that Sanskrit is related to the languages of Europe. The term *Indo-European* derives from a paper he delivered in 1786 discussing the context of this widespread family of languages.[3]

He also recognized that the Indian pantheon of the Vedas matched that of the Olympians in Greece. As these Indo-European tribes struck at different places across the Eurasian continent, they carried with them their mythologies, so there is a related mythology in these areas. What we suddenly find intruding into the earlier Goddess cults in these areas is the mythology of a warrior people whose main deity, whether named Zeus or Indra, is a thunderbolt-hurler. This is not very different from Yahweh, whose people are striking up from the desert into Mesopotamia at about the same time.

There were two main divisions of the Indo-Europeans, the eastern and the western branch. The dividing line can be imagined to be where the Iron Curtain once fell.[4] Eastward, we have the Satem people —that is the Sanskrit word for "one hundred." Westward, we have the Centum people—that is the Latin name for "one hundred." (There are laws for linguistic modification between these languages: *C* becomes *S*; *E* becomes *A*, and so forth—and so we have the same word.)

On the eastern, Satem side, the main languages are the Slavic tongues (Russian, Czech, Polish, and so forth), Persian, and the languages of India (Sanskrit—the word *Sanskrit* means *syncretic*; Pali— the language of early Buddhism; and all the languages of northern India—Hindi, Marathi, Rajasthani, Urdu, and Bengali). The Centum languages to the west are Greek, the Italic or Latin languages (from which come French, Spanish, Italian, Rhenish, Provençal, and Portuguese), the Celtic languages (which survive in the British Isles—Scottish, Welsh, Manx on the Isle of Man, and Irish), and the Germanic languages (including English, the Scandinavian languages, German, Dutch, and the old Gothic languages). And Jones recognized that all these are the linguistic traces of related peoples that had come out of this same world, the Northern European plains, and their mythology was one mythology in different languages. Everywhere they had expanded, this mythology had spread in on top of the Mother Goddess cults of the people.

After the discovery of the Indo-European languages, we then had the same method of comparative linguistics applied to the Semitic group. Now, that is a more circumscribed area and the Semitic languages are more like one another than the Indo-European languages. The range of races speaking Indo-European languages is considerable, but the Semitic language family is a much more unified group. The early Semitic languages are Akkadian, Babylonian, Aramaic, Hebrew, and Arabic—the languages of those tribes that had swept into the different areas of Southwest Asia.

Another family of languages is found eastward of the Ural Mountains: the Uralo-Altaic people, or the Mongols in the east, the Finns in Scandanavia, the Hungarians in Eastern Europe, and the Turks.

Separate from these language groups of Europe and Western Asia, we have still another language family associated with the Chinese complex, and another one with the Australasian languages that go out then into Polynesian, and so forth. So when you are studying comparative mythology, you have to be aware of these unifying, integrating systems that always then come into touch with the locally land-based systems.

In these different zones that we have been discussing, the Indo-European peoples appeared on the scene as men in control of the war chariot, and when early anthropologists realized during the nineteenth century that all the high civilizations of the later periods seemed to have shared this origin, the idea of Aryan or Indo-European supremacy sprung up. *Ārya* is a Sanskrit word meaning "noble." The recognition that one after another of these later civilizations seemed to have been an outgrowth of the arrival of the so-called Aryans appeared to bear out this idea of their superiority.

However, further archaeological research proved that the Indo-Europeans' arrival was a comparatively late development; the modern dating of ancient Sumer and of Egypt, along with what we now know of Old Europe before these people came in—all this has changed the picture considerably.

We now see that the Indo-Europeans came in as warrior-ravagers and that in each region they knocked down the civilization that was already there. Then they absorbed the influence of the earlier civilization and out of that synthesis came the high golden period of Greece. The earlier civilizations belonged to the Goddess; the later to the gods. There is a perfect parallel in Southwest Asia, with the Semites arriving in Mesopotamia, Egypt, and so forth, as they had as their principal interest a kind of rough nomadic warcraft.

Around 1800 B.C. the Indo-Europeans from the north mastered the horse and invented the war chariot. At that point, they were absolutely invincible, and the war chariot then appeared everywhere in Europe, Egypt, Persia, and India, and then in Chang-dynasty China at about 1523 B.C. The striking power of these people was enormous across the whole Eurasian world.

BURIAL MOUNDS AND SUTTEE

The characteristic monument of the Indo-Europeans is the barrow, or mound burial, and the Russian term for these is *kurgan*. Marija Gimbutas calls the different local areas into which this culture came Kurgan cultures. The Indo-Europeans came in wave after wave into the areas of Old Europe, the East Baltic, and the Mediterranean, which is where the Goddess cultures had already established themselves.

With the Kurgan influx, what had been farming and trading communities suddenly become warrior strongholds, and we have the emergence of what is called the *akropolis*—that is to say, a warrior stronghold. And the burial sites give evidence of a new social stratification. As Gimbutas says,

> Usually royal tombs are found separately from the cemetery of the other members of the society....The burial rites indicate not only social differences but also the man's dominant role in society: the first and central grave in a barrow usually belongs to a man, perhaps

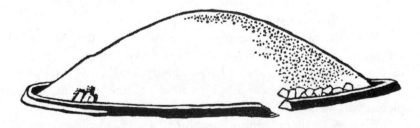

FIGURE 33. Alexandropol kurgan (burial mound, Chalcolithic, Russia, fourth century B.C.)

the father of the family or the village elder, and the women's and children's graves occupy secondary positions. The old Indo-European custom that the housemaster had unrestricted right of property over his wife and children and that the wife should die with her husband is indicated archaeologically by frequent double graves of man and woman and of an adult and one or two or more children buried at the same time. Parent-children relationship is shown by bone analyses."[5]

In these warrior mythologies the sun god dominated and the female was assigned to various planets and the moon. Suttee burial comes down from these periods right through to modern India. In the burial site known as the Grave of the Widow, located in Macedonia, the wife is buried along with the warrior. Together they go to the underworld and the hero deed of the wife is that of giving her life so that the two should become eternal together. The two are one: the husband and wife are the two aspects of one being. Usually the man dies first—he is out there getting beaten up in the battle, and so he dies and has gone to the underworld, and he calls the wife to come join him there for their mutual eternity. She becomes the savior of the dead hero. So when the goddess goes to the underworld as Ishtar and Brunhilda, this is the hero journey to bring the two—male and female—to eternal life.

It is important to note that *suttee* (the ritual live burial or immolation of a widow with her dead husband) comes from the Sanskrit word *satī*, and that this word is the feminine participle of the verb *to be*. In other words, to say that a woman is *satī* is to say that she *is*. This is a woman who has gone all the way with being a wife right through to following the husband in death. The woman who does not perform this duty is therefore *a-satī* ("nothing"). In such a traditional society one gains one's character by obeying the rules, by following the laws of the society exactly—all the way. There is a definite mythology associated with this attitude. In India, for example, you will see monuments to *satī* burial from the old days and there will be a woman's hand lifted in blessing, and that is the hand of Venus, goddess of love. By her act the woman has brought salvation simultaneously to both herself and her husband. The accent here is on the eternal character of their lives together, not the mere phenomenal.

Later on in Mesopotamia, in Egypt, and in China we find hundreds of people buried alive.[6] These burials just wiped out any accent on the personality, on individual experience, on pain and pleasure,

and on individual judgment. These people had the character of soldiers, and the good soldier obeys orders and is not responsible for
what he does but only for how well he does it. That was the way of
these societies and an important point to understand when we are
talking about these mythological periods.

So the problem today is to link ourselves—with our sense of individual value and responsibility—to these worlds without being swallowed up by them. When the Indian guru comes over to the United
States to teach today, he's teaching actually in terms of the devaluation of the individual mode of thinking that goes with the mythology
that he represents. However, *satī* burial is associated not only with the
god but also with the goddess, so this is an important matter.

MYCENAE

After the explosion of Thera's volcano, Indo-European Mycenae
became the dominant source of culture around the Aegean. The Aryan
influence is apparent in this Mycenaean stela showing a war chariot
(Fig. 34). Notice that in this wide, two-wheeled chariot you see the
mandala form of the wheel and axle. The axis becomes very important

FIGURE 34. War chariot (carved stone, Mycenaean, Greece, 1500 B.C.)

as the center around which all revolves. There movement and rest are at one, and the axle becomes symbolic of that point around which all movement takes place: the immovable point at the center of the psyche, the still point. It is this point that one must find if one is in performance, whether athletic or dramatic, or in the act of creative writing. There one is not entirely in motion—there is a balance between quietness in the center and movement around it. It is that spiritual point that this chariot wheel begins to symbolize, and the horse is symbolic of the violent dynamic energy of the body and the driver of the controlling mind.

At the great gate of Mycenae (Fig. 36), the goddess is now represented abstractly as the pillar with her guardian animals on either side—She is the axis. The missing heads from the flanking animals, and the space allotment for where the heads would have been, has led archaeologists to suggest that they may not be lions but rather griffins,[7] like those shown in Crete.

The warrior death mask (Fig. 35) found at Mycenae (which Heinrich Schliemann fancifully called "the Mask of Agamemnon") illustrates how the Indo-European people had heavy, sturdy bodies in contrast to the much more delicate bodies of the people of the

FIGURE 35. Warrior death mask (gold, Mycenaean, Greece, 1500 B.C.)

FIGURE 36. The lion gate at Mycenae (carved stone, Greece, 1500 B.C.)

Aegean. Two different races came together in this new culture of the Mycenaeans.

There is a sequence here that is quite characteristic of the period, and which works for both the Semitic and the Aryan invasions. First, these nomads come as warrior conquerors, and then they begin to pick up the much more elaborately developed culture system of the conquered peoples, and the invaders' mythology comes right along and gets grafted on top of the indigenous Goddess-oriented mythology, which becomes transformed into the later god-oriented mythologies of the Classical era. This sort of absorption of the older, higher culture and the transformation of its mythology to suit the purposes of the newer, less-developed culture is particularly conspicuous in the Bible, in the Books of Exodus and Joshua.

The same process happened in the Mycenaean world. Gradually, however, the Goddess began to reassert herself so that by the seventh century B.C. in Greece, around the date of the Homeric Hymns—that is to say about five hundred years after the final invasion—the Goddess is coming back again. The same thing happens in India almost simultaneously.

With the meeting of the Indo-Europeans and the Neolithic Old

Europe cultures, the matriarchal system was not replaced by a patriarchal world that arose from the same area, as some scholars have
tried to state in classifying European prehistory and its transformation. Rather, the Indo-European culture super-imposed itself upon
the Old European culture.

As Gimbutas writes:

> The study of mythical images provides one of the best proofs that
> the Old European world was not the proto-Indo-European world
> and that there was no direct and unobstructed line of development
> to the modern Europeans. The earliest European civilization was
> savagely destroyed by the patriarchal element and it never recov-
> ered, but its legacy lingered in the substratum which nourished fur-
> ther European cultural developments. The Old European creations
> were not lost; transformed, they enormously enriched the European
> psyche.[8]

In this ivory carving (Fig. 37), we have two goddesses with a little
male figure going from one to the other. It's the old double Goddess,
mother of life and mother of death. The female principle appears in
the two aspects, while the male represents the active power that moves
from one to the other, from night to day, from death to dark. That's
a power that lives in women as well as in men, just as the power of
the nature that these two female figures represents is in men—but it's

FIGURE 37. Goddesses and child (ivory, Mycenaean, Greece, 1300 B.C.)

a question of emphasis. The little male child is probably Poseidon, whose cult dates back to this period.

Poseidon is the lord of the waters with the trident, the central point between the pairs of opposites. The waters that Poseidon represents are not the salt waters of the sea but the fresh waters that come up from the deep under the Earth, the ones that fertilize the soil. In some representations Poseidon has a bull's foot: the animal of Poseidon is the bull. In the Christian tradition the inheritor of this symbolism is the devil, with his pitchfork and the cloven hoof. That is what happened to the Lord, who represented the dynamics of the zeal for life, when he was taken over by a system that considers every natural impulse sinful.

Śiva is the same god: his weapon is his trident, and his animal is the bull. He represents the *lingam*, the divine energy pouring world creative power into the womb of the Goddess. Śiva's principal symbol is the *lingam* joined with the *yonī*, the female organ penetrated by the male. Śiva and Poseidon represent that very old tradition when there was the diffusion of this mythology in the period of the Mother Goddess, the period of our earliest societies.

In Hindu iconography, Śiva is often shown with his Śakti, the goddess Parvatī. While Śiva has his trident and his bull, Nandi, Parvatī is frequently shown in a leopard's or lioness's skin, so here we are again: the god is associated with the lunar bull, while the goddess is associated with the solar lion. This is an old story, a continuity of tradition, not a suppression as we find in the biblical tradition. The Bible eliminates the Goddess, whereas in the Indian tradition the Goddess is celebrated as the Mother and in Greece the Goddess is powerful in her own right.

It is important to recognize the link here between these mythologies, so that when you are studying one you are also studying the implications of the other. The great mound burial, the *akropolis*, and suttee burial all belong to the same complex.

Another clue to this continuity to consider is the Linear B script that Michael Ventris deciphered as an early Greek language. When he opened up the late Cretan and pre-Mycenaean Helladic cultures, what did he find? He found the names of Dionysus, Athena, and Poseidon. These are not the deities of the Vedic pantheon but those of the earlier Cretan one, and this lets us know that before the Aryans came, these deities had already been there.

The Indo-Europeans invaded mainland Greece in different waves: first came the Ionians, then the Aeolians, and finally the Dorians were the last people that settled there. They came in not only down the Greek peninsula but also into Asia Minor, so that the people of Troy, who were being attacked by the people from Greece, were in fact the same race, Indo-European people who had established themselves in this very fortunate place that was at the entrance to the Bosporus (the "Cow's Strait," named after Europa, who was said to have crossed it in the shape of a cow), where Asia and Europe come together. Troy became a wealthy and very important city that had to be destroyed. The incursions began about 1200 B.C.; the period of the Trojan War is 1180–1190 B.C., and the civilization was practically wiped out. It begins coming back in the eighth century, and with that appears warcraft in the art. It is also the period of Homer, contemporary with the earliest texts of Genesis.

The Dorians brought with them two different styles of fighting and two different styles of weapons. One style was the bronze sword or spear with a heavy bull-hide shield that was slung over the body; the champion, who set the shield up, fought from behind it. The other, later kind of weaponry was a relatively light shield worn on the left arm with iron weapons. These two, totally different kinds of weaponry are both represented throughout *The Iliad*. The beginnings of *The Iliad* belong to Bronze Age, while it was finally completed in the late Iron Age, so you have both kinds of weapons.

There is one group of the Linear B tablets in old Nestor's palace at Pylos on the mainland that had to do with the distribution of troops; they show that an invasion was coming from the north during the period of the Trojan Wars and the same period as the Dorian invasions. So these Aryans came into the Aegean southern zone in waves. Remember that both the attackers and those defending Troy were of the same Aryan families. So in those clay tablets from Nestor's palace comes this last notice from the pre-Aryan Helladic period: some invaders are coming down, and the distribution of outposts is indicated as well as sanctuaries for the protection of the women and children. And the rest is silence.

FIGURE 38. Isis with infant Horus (bronze, Late Period, Egypt, c. 680–640 B.C.)

CHAPTER 4

Sumerian and Egyptian Goddesses[1]

THE ABSTRACT FIELD: RISE OF CIVILIZATION

In order to pick up the next part of our story, we need to move back to around 4000 B.C. and shift the focus to the river valleys of the Tigris, the Euphrates, and the Nile. Agriculture and animal domestication can be dated back to about 10,000 B.C. in Old Europe, but civilization in the areas that were formerly called the lands of the Fertile Crescent did not start until after 4000 B.C. People moved from those early Neolithic settlements in the Asia Minor and Southeast Europe to the great river valleys—and this is the beginning of the high cultures. Settling there, next to those enormous rivers, involved a lot of social organization in order to take care of the flooding and the channeling of the waters, but a big advantage was that the annual deluge renewed fertility in the land and quite large communities could develop.

It was in Mesopotamia about 3500 B.C. that the first cities arose, and there for the first time you have large societies with differentiated functions for the individual. In a simple nomadic community, all the adults are in complete control of the total culture heritage. Large communities develop when people can remain in one place with agriculture continually possible, and this development of a large, urban community finally encounters a large mythological problem, because the people in large communities begin to have differentiated tasks and specialized concerns—professional rulers, professional priests, professional traders, and so forth. People who are trading people, well, they never touch a plow. So you begin to have what in India has survived as the four castes: the priestly, the governing, and the money caste and then the servants. This means you now have a differentiated group of people to hold together, and it's at this time that the image of the mandala first emerges.

In each of these cities the central phenomenon was the emergence of a temple with a temple priesthood. A system of writing developed and a system of mathematical reckoning based on the decimal and on the sexagesimal systems, the unit of sixty by which we have measured all circles ever since. The observation of the heavens, coupled with writing, enabled the observers to record what they saw and lent to the recognition of an orderly procession of the planets through the fixed stars, the constellations, and the visible planets. The Earth was the first, and the sun, but then what the priest-astronomers noticed were the moon, Mercury, Venus, Mars, Jupiter, and Saturn—the seven bodies after which we name the days of the week. They recognized that there was a mathematical order to the movement of the planets and so a whole new concept emerged, namely, the idea of a cosmic order that was essentially mathematical in nature.[2]

Now, people from all times have been aware of the movements of the planets, in particular the sun and moon, but now they relate these movements to a mathematical system. I think this is probably the most important transformation of the notion of the universe in the history of human consciousness. The earlier plant- and animal-oriented people were interested in exceptional phenomena—this exceptional animal that comes and brings us a message, this marvelous tree here, or this pond—but now it's not the exceptional but the coordinated and predictable that becomes the essential concern. With that a whole new development of civilization takes place. We've jumped up from just Mother Earth and her children to Mother Cosmos and the order of the universe, and mathematics is somehow the key to the nature of the Mother Goddess whose world this is.

The concept of a mathematical cosmic order that encloses the whole world came to be held in the Goddess image that I discussed earlier: not Mother Earth, but the Cosmic Goddess, the enclosing sphere or womb of the sky within whose bounds we dwell. The Goddess became the dominant figure. The Fates—the Moirai and the Norns—were those goddesses that governed the passage of life, and this impersonal power is associated with the female principle. This is an idea symbolized in the early phallic imagery, which continues in India in the symbols of the *lingam* and *yoni*, where the male organ is represented penetrating the female organ from beneath. And when we are standing there regarding this symbol, which is that of the pouring of divine transcendent energy into the sphere of time and space within which we all dwell, we are, as it were, within the womb of the Goddess beholding and appreciating the mystery of the continuous creation, the continuous pouring forth of the transcendent principle into the temporal sphere. It is within the sphere of time and space that we all dwell, it is within the sphere of the pairs of opposites, the categories of thought that we all dwell. The goddess of logic as well as the goddess of time and space limits us in our thinking and in our action. And so even the names of god, even the forms of god, wherever god is worshipped, are those of Her children. She is the primary divinity, the Mother, and Her womb encloses us.

We first saw Her in the old cave art as those earliest figurines, and we have Her now, in the early mythologies out of which all our traditions derive, as the Mother of the world within whom even the gods dwell. Beyond Her boundary you are beyond concept, you are beyond all categories, you are beyond even the category of being and non-being. She is the first thing that is.

FIGURE 39. Abstract field (ceramic, Chalcolithic, Iraq, c. 5000 B.C.)

Around 4000 B.C., the concept of an organized, limited aesthetic field appears for the first time in the art of the Sumerian cities— abstractions of various kinds organized in an orderly, harmonious way. In the ceramic plate shown here (Fig. 39), from the Sumerian city of Halaf, you can see the idea of the blossom at the center, a little flower of the universe. In the center is the flower and in the center of the city was the temple. The emphasis on the four quarters is very important and it forms the unit. This is a composition of the whole city showing the four castes. When you go back to Paleolithic art you don't get this kind of bounded organization; there's another kind of organization of a cave and more-or-less naturalistic animals. This is essentially an aesthetic composition to please the eye and to coordinate the four quarters, the four castes. And what we have is the problem of the four points and the center—with an accent on the center.

FIGURE 40. Goddess with animals and swastikas (ceramic, Chalcolithic, Iraq, c. 4000 B.C.)

This cross pattern was often elaborated as the swastika motif, with the four points of the compass set in movement around an axis—an image of the axial center in motion, of the world in the field of time. Look at this piece, from Samarra (Fig. 40): See the aesthetic elegance, the simplicity of the forms. The cosmic tree in the center is the world axis and it is the goddess, and around her go the animals.

FIGURE 41. Female forms with scorpions (ceramic, Chalcolithic, Iraq, c. 4000 B.C.)

Another piece of Samarra ware (Fig. 41) organizes the whole in a pattern much more like that we saw in Figure 39.

The organization is in terms of fours, and four points with four points between them makes an eight. The women's hair blowing creates a swastika symbol, and once again, the female is the dynamic center.

Among the earliest temples excavated and reconstructed are that at Khafaje and the very similar one at Al-Ubaid, which dates from around 3500 B.C. and was dedicated to the goddess Ninhursag.[3] In all the old Sumerian cities, the temple is at the center of the community and is the largest structure, and the Goddess-dedicated temple compounds were in the form of a cow's vulva.[4] The sacred cow, which still exists in India, is the animal form of Mother Universe. The cow goddess is Goddess Mother of the world, and it is through her generation that all boons, all energy, all people proceed.

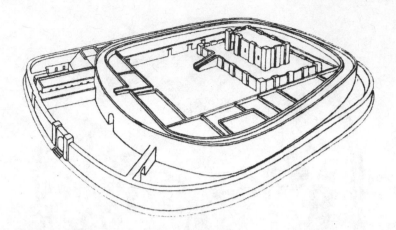

FIGURE 42. Temple Oval at Khafaje (artist's reconstruction, Sumerian, Iraq, c. 3500 B.C.)

In their study *The Myth of the Goddess: Evolution of an Image,* Anne Baring and Jules Cashford point out:

> Ki-Ninhursag was one of the principal Sumerian deities, "the mother of all living": mother of the gods and of humanity; mother of the earth itself, the soil and the rocky ground, and all the plants and crops it brought forth....
>
> [T]here is a suggestion that a lying-in place for women to give birth was associated with the temple, housing the sheepfold, cow-byre and granary within its precincts. All the produce and animal life belonged in the first instance to the goddess as the Great Mother and therefore to her temple, and from there was distributed by the priestesses and priests to her people and her animals.[5]

Note that in Sumerian, the word for *sheepfold, womb, vulva, loins,* and *lap* is the same.[6]

FIGURE 43. Frieze from the temple of Al-Ubaid (carved stone, Sumerian, Iraq, 3000 B.C.)

At the same time in Al-Ubaid we begin to see ziggurats emerging. In those temple compounds, the priests were cow herders of the very special herd and the milk of these cows was the milk of the Goddess, the sacred ambrosia, and this was drunk by the ruling family. It was meant as a symbolic matter and to brings one's mind through the symbolic associations so as to meditate on the mysterious source of one's being, and also the mystery of the function that one serves in the society.

As far as we know, the Sumerians were the first high civilized people in the world. For a long time it was thought the Semitic languages were the earliest, and then Sumerian is discovered and for a long time the scholars were saying, "Well, this was just the secret language of the Semitic priests." They had a hard time giving that one up, but finally they had to. Sumerian was related neither to the Semitic nor to the Indo-European languages.

FIGURE 44. Moon-bull and lion-bird (terra-cotta, Sumerian, Iraq, c. 2500 B.C.)

Now, I want to introduce you—or reintroduce you—to the Lion Goddess. In this Sumerian frieze from the Temple of the Bulls in Uruk (Fig. 44), you see a rehearsal of the old theme: the solar lion-eagle consumes the moon-bull. The lion and the eagle are equivalent symbols of the solar power. That is the Goddess. This bull is a mythological bull—from the joints of its legs there emanate energies, and the right forefront is down on a crescent that is on the top of a cosmic mountain. He is generating the energy of the Earth as though the bull were fecundating the Goddess Earth. And does he mind being consumed? No, he's smiling. This bull represents that mystery of the energy that pours into the world and is continually torn apart and revived, as may be seen with the death and resurrection of the moon each month.

FIGURE 45. God and Goddess, with snake behind her beside the Tree of Life (clay seal, Sumerian, Iraq, c. 2500 B.C.)

On this Babylonian seal (Fig. 45) we see the serpent goddess—much as we did in Crete. When this piece was discovered in the 1920s it was thought to be a prelude to the story from the Bible.

However, there is no Fall in this mythology. The tree we see here is the Tree of Eternal Life—the world axis of the Goddess—and the male lunar deity indicated by the horns seems to have come down to receive the fruit from the Goddess, behind whom is a serpent. This would be translated into biblical mythology as Eve and the serpent as the giver of the fruit to the male deity. However, in this Sumerian mythology it is not a fall. "Come in and be refreshed," she says.

The Book of Genesis is really a translation into patrilineal Hebrew mythology of the earlier Sumerian forms from a thousand years before Genesis was written.

In the famous Warka Vase, found in the ancient city of Uruk (Fig. 46), the priests are shown naked, carrying the vessels up to the top of the pyramid or mountain temple, and the break in the vase is where the king would have been standing, delivering the message or offering. And in front is another priest carrying the offering of the city for the king to the priestess, who might be called the incarnation of the Goddess—her name in Uruk was Inanna. The two uprights behind her are a standard or sign of the importance of the temple in this culture.[7]

FIGURE 46. The Warka Vase (carved alabaster, Sumerian, Iraq, c. 3000 B.C.)

The Goddess was the high divinity throughout Sumerian culture—whether she was called Inanna or Ishtar (as she appears in *The Epic of Gilgamesh*). In this carved head (Fig. 47), we see her in a tremendously important role as muse. This mask is the earliest representation of delicacy and charm of the female head and is unlike anything from this period. The eyes had been undoubtedly made of lapis lazuli, the eyebrows may have been of lapis lazuli or perhaps ebony, and on the head would have been a wig.

In the very early forms of the female from the old Paleolithic and Neolithic periods, we saw the accent on the breasts and the loins, on the woman as birth and fertility goddess. Here is another kind of fertility that the Goddess represents, and that's the fertility of the spirit. Just as the past is converted into the future by the Goddess, so is the material life translated into the spiritual. This is woman not as the generator of physical life, but as the muse, as the transformer of the spirit.

The virgin birth, the birth of our spiritual life—that is what is represented here. Other representations of the Goddess in this aspect lack the delicacy of this one, but they do tell us something of what is happening.

FIGURE 47. The Warka Head (carved marble, Sumerian, Iraq, c. 3200 B.C.)

FIGURE 48. Early Sumerian Eye goddess figurines (alabaster, Syria, 3500–3000 B.C.)

In the so-called Eye goddess figurines (Fig. 48), we see another representation of the shift in accent with regards to the Goddess from the source of physical generation to that of spiritual generation. The eyes of some of these figures seem to have been colored blue. The blue eye is the eye of the heavenly vault. This is an important point, for it moves us away from the Goddess as only the Earth goddess and associating the female just with fertility and the Earth. There is a whole range of goddess symbols that reference more than the physical Earth. The whole inspiration of life, whether physical or spiritual, comes from Her.

Now, you can trace the Eye goddess up to the British Isles and Scandinavia. This is the beginning of the age of bronze, which was, as I said, an alloy of copper and tin. Wherever tin was found—in Transylvania, in the Balkans, in Cornwall—there would be a mining community. So here we have the Bronze Age, with its beautiful works in bronze and gold.

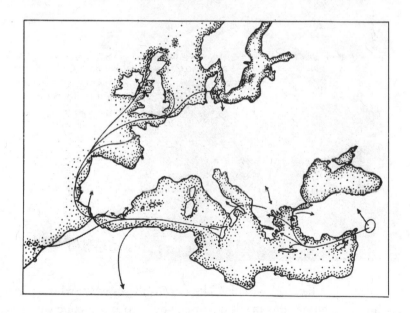

Map 4. Diffusion of Eye goddess monuments and tradition

During the 1920s the English archaeologist Sir Leonard Woolley excavated the ground in front of the ziggurat of Ur, and there discovered what are now known as the Royal Tombs of Ur.[8] Woolley found not only the king and the queen buried in these tombs, but their entire courts, the oxcarts, the drivers of the oxcarts, the nobility of the court, the dancing girls, and the musicians.[9] Based on the conditions of the skeletons, it has been surmised that the court had gone into the tombs alive; it is unknown if the king had been ritually slain or if he died naturally. The king was buried with his court and then the grave was filled in, and on top of that the queen (whose name, Puabi, is given on a lapis lazuli seal) was buried with her court. The woman was the cosmic order and also the awakener to future life, and when the man died the woman went down into the underworld to bring him to life. This is the motif of *satī*.

FIGURE 49. Headdress of the sacrificed Queen Puabi (gold, Sumerian, Iraq, 2500 B.C.)

What is a hero, essentially? The hero isn't someone who has hit six hundred home runs in his lifetime. The hero is someone who has given his life for a cause or for others. And this giving of life is here represented in the female role as the wife who goes into the underworld for her husband because she is one with him, and brings him back to eternal life. We find this in the great story of the underworld journey of Ishtar to bring the god, her spouse Tammuz, back to life. This is the great myth of the Goddess, how She descends to the underworld to bring immortal life to her spouse and herself. This image of the woman's role not only as creator of the cosmos but as rescuer within the cosmos is the basis of the old traditions.

FIGURE 50. Inanna (terra-cotta, Sumerian, Iraq, c. 2300–2000 B.C.)

One of the oldest recorded hero journey tales—possibly predating *Gilgamesh*—is the Sumerian myth of the sky goddess Inanna's descent to the netherworld.[10] *The Descent of Inanna* was inscribed as an epic poem on tablets dating from around 1750 B.C.; they lay buried for close to 4,000 years in the ruins of Nippur, Sumer's cultural and spiritual center.[11]

> *From the "great above" she set her mind toward the "great below,"*
> *The goddess, from the "great above" she set her mind toward the "great below,"*
> *Inanna, from the "great above" she set her mind toward the "great below."*
> *My lady abandoned heaven, abandoned earth, To the nether world she descended,*
> *Inanna abandoned heaven, abandoned earth, To the nether world she descended,*
> *Abandoned lordship, abandoned ladyship, To the nether world she descended.*

At each of the seven thresholds that Inanna crosses into the under-world she must remove an item of clothing or jewelry so that ulti-mately she arrives at her sister's kingdom naked, divested of all worldly items. When she finally reaches the very depths, her sister Ereshkigal, who rules the underworld, kills her with "the eye of death," and hangs Inanna on a hook for three days.

When Inanna does not return from the underworld, her compan-ion, Ninshubur, seeks the help of Enki, god of crafts, and he sends helpers into the underworld to seek the goddess's release. When Enki's minons arrive, Ereshkigal is suffering birth pains and they empathize with her, thereby winning Inanna's release; Inanna ascends to the upper world, where all had been mourning her disappearance—all except her husband, Dumuzi. Since Inanna must find a replacement for herself in the underworld, she chooses Dumuzi.

THE SEMITIC INFLUX: SARGON AND HAMMURABI

The arrival of the Bronze Age, of course, heralded the coming of the invaders, with their weapons and their male-oriented mythologies. In Mesopotamia, this was signaled by the arrival of the Semitic Akkadians.

FIGURE 51. Sargon of Akkad (bronze, Sumerian, Iraq, c. 2300 B.C.)

The first great Semitic monarch was Sargon I, who ruled around 2300 B.C. His story will sound familiar: His mother was a simple woman who lived on the river, and when her son was born, she prepared a little basket of rushes, which she sealed from the water with bitumen. Then she put her baby into the little basket, and it floated down the stream to the king's gardens.

He was pulled out of the river by the gardener in the estate of the emperor, and the goddess Ishtar loved him. The emperor regarded him with respect and he grew up to be Sargon I.

FIGURE 52. Hammurabi receiving the law code from the god Shamash (carved granite, Babylonian, Iraq, 1780 B.C.)

Hammurabi ruled as the lord of the new city-state of Babylon until his death in 1750 B.C. In one of the stelae that recorded his famous code of laws (Fig. 52), you can see Hammurabi receiving the law from the god Shamash, the god of the sun, from whose shoulders rays of light are rising. In the mythologies of the warrior people, for the first time, we find that the sun is male and the moon female.

Sargon (c. 2300 B.C.) and Hammurabi (d. 1750 B.C.) mark the incursion of the masculine traditions into the Mesopotamian city-states—the Semites came raiding out of the Syro-Arabian desert.

They were ruthless fighting people. They were not going to ask the stars, "Is it time for me to go into the grave?" They were going to let somebody else do it for them and offer substitute offerings and assume a commanding role themselves.

Now, the appearance of the Semites in this old world of the Goddess is expressed in a new kind of mythology: the great story of Marduk, the masculine solar and sky god who goes against the goddess of the abyss, Tiamat, who is the grandmother of all the gods.[12] The male pantheon has assumed control, and now they are the ones who are going to create the world. And what happens? Tiamat comes out of the abyss, Marduk goes against her, and she is called a demon. She is actually the Mother of the Gods. He kills her, cuts her up, makes the heavens out of the upper part of her body and the underworld out of the abyss. He creates men from her blood, and so forth and so on.

Well, that's a nice thing to do to Grandma. This is the beginning of the masculine assumption of the creator role.

When I first read that, I thought, "Well, if he waited a couple of minutes, she was going to do it anyhow." She does become the world; she gives her body willingly, but makes it look as though he were doing it. But the next interesting thing about this—and this is something else we learned from psychology—is that where the male come in, you have division, while where the female comes in you have union. For instance, it's the wife of the buffalo who unites what appear to be opposites—the human and the animal worlds. The mother brings together all her children. It's with the realization that the father is different from the mother that separation and differentiation come in.

And so, with these masculine Semitic mythologies, we have for the first time a separation of the individual from the divine, and this is one of the most important and decisive motifs in the history of mythology: that the eternal life and oneness with the universe are no longer ours. We are separated from God, God is separated from his world, man is turned against nature, nature is turned against man.

You do not have this separation in the mythologies of the Great Mother.

Now, there's another interesting thing about the Semitic mythologies: All other mythologies that I know have as their primary divinities those representing nature—the gods of the heavens and of the Earth, and the powers of nature, which are within us as well as out there. And in those mythologies the tribal ancestor is always a secondary god.

In the Semitic mythologies, this situation is reversed. The prime divinity in all the Semitic traditions is the local, ancestral divinity. As I pointed out, when you have the same divinities as everybody else, you can say, "He whom you call Zeus we call Indra." But when your principal divinity is your local tribal divinity, you cannot say this.

And so we have a pattern of exclusivism here; we have a pattern of social emphasis or social laws, and we have an antinature accent. The whole history of the Old Testament is Yahweh against the nature cults. The Goddess is called the Abomination, and she and her divinities are called demons and they are not given the credit of being divine. And along with that comes the feeling that the divine life is not *within* us; divinity is out there. The attitude of prayer now is outward, whereas in the old days it was turning inward to the immanent divine. After this change, how do you get to the divine? By means of this particularly endowed social group: the tribe, the caste, the church.

Now this is the masculine emphasis against the Goddess emphasis; when this occurs in individual psychology you're overemphasizing the father role: you repudiate nature, you repudiate women. This is what Nietzsche calls the Hamlet experience, bowing to the father and saying, "Ophelia, you can go drown yourself."

"Oh, that this too sullied flesh would melt"[13]—one hates one's body, one hates nature, one wants to get away from it. This is completely opposite to the attitude of the Goddess cults. In the biblical tradition, which is the last great tradition of this Semitic line, there is not even a goddess in the tradition. Here's a Father God with no Mother Goddess—a very strange thing.

What happens to the Mother Goddess? She is reduced to the elemental level. She is the cosmic water; that's there where God's spirit hovers, above the water. He is given the human personification, and she is not. The Chaos is exactly Tiamat, the goddess of the abyss, who now has been deprived even of her personality. This places a terrific stress on our culture.

Then you realize also that within the Jewish tradition, the covenant is symbolized by the circumcision. You can see that woman is out altogether.

And so we have the most radical split here in the history of civilizations and mythologies anywhere between the masculine principle, which is given all power, and the female principle, which is deprived of it, and her world of nature and its beauty is impugned. Even beauty is rejected in this tradition as a distraction, as something seductive.

EGYPT

The power and effect on world history that has come from Egypt is
absolutely astounding. Around 4000 B.C. the Nile Valley begins to be
settled, and little villages are scattered—along with the goddess. Egyptian history begins in the north, its middle period is in the middle,
and its late period is in the south. The Nile is the whole thing, and
on either side beyond is desert; Egypt was well-protected. There is
only one way that any people of any power could get in, and that was
through the delta.

FIGURE 53. Goddess figurine (terra-cotta, Predynastic, Egypt, c. 4000 B.C.)

In a little tomb at Hierakonpolis that dates back over five thousand years to before the first pharaohs, there are wall decorations de-
picting animals (Fig. 54). The likeness of these motifs to the images
from Iraq, the animals in circular movement, suggests that Egypt received its high culture during the very early period from Mesopotamia. Indeed, it has been determined that Mesopotamia is the earlier
culture. We see then that around 3200 B.C. the Egyptian style had not
yet been achieved.

FIGURE 54. Wall decorations from the Hierakonpolis tomb (paint and plaster, Predynastic, Egypt, c. 3500 B.C.)

In northern Egypt there is the prehistoric Neolithic culture to about 3200 B.C., and then you have these very early dynasties, 3200–2685 B.C., then comes the Old Kingdom, which is the time of the building of the pyramids, the Third to Sixth Dynasties, then there comes what's called an intermediary period around 2280 to 2060 B.C. —and every scholar has his own dates for Egypt—a period of two hundred years when Egypt was in chaos.

Following the intermediary period comes the second key period, the Middle Kingdom, from 2200 to 1650 B.C. The capital is now Thebes from the Eleventh to the Thirteenth Dynasty. This is the period when the pharaohs were buried in mountainsides because the pyramids were being plundered by grave robbers.

Then comes the second intermediary period, and this is something very special: 1650 to 1580 B.C., a hundred years after Hammurabi, there was an invasion into the delta by West Asian people. It is thought that this may have been the time when the Hebrews came into Egypt.

However, those West Asians were thrown out around 1580 B.C. Having been invaded, the Egyptians decided they were going to defend themselves, and they start up the coast and they go as far as Turkey. This period is called the Egyptian Empire—it is also the Egypt that appears in all the biblical stories.

The Persians conquered Egypt around 525 B.C., and Alexander the Great conquered Egypt around 332 B.C. Then the Romans conquered

Egypt around A.D. 30—that's the time of Cleopatra. That's quite a history for that thin little sliver of river valley.

FIGURE 55. Narmer Palette (carved siltstone, Old Kingdom, Egypt, c. 3200 B.C.)

In any case, around 3200 B.C. we suddenly have Egypt as we recognize; it's amazing the way the style suddenly appears. The Narmer Palette (Fig. 55) shows the king of Upper Egypt conquering the king of the delta and uniting the two lands. On the upper corners of either side are cows' heads—this is the goddess Hathor who guards the horizon and is called the House of Horus. The pharaoh wears her on his belt—before, behind, and on each side, and so he is said to fill the horizon. This pharaoh is the earliest pharaoh known and was the highest god. He incarnates as the highest power of the divinity, but Hathor is the horizon within which he lives, the binding power. The pharaoh is wearing a bull's tail and so he is the incarnation of the god Osiris, who is the moon bull god who dies and is resurrected, dies again and is resurrected, the model of the death and resurrection of any deities. The hawk is Horus, represented as the totem of the Upper Egyptian king, while the plant under the totem represents the papyrus swamp of the Delta, which he has just subjugated. The head represents the king of the papyrus swamp held by Horus. That's the mystical sign of the physical facts of the king with the crown holding the king of the Delta by the hair and killing him. The conquering pharaoh is wearing the crown of the Lower Kingdom, and before him go the signs of the four points of the compass and his power. From now on the pharaoh experiences two coronations, one as lord of the south and next as lord of the north, and then the crowns are united so that the later Egyptian crown is a combination of these two.

FIGURE 56. The pyramids at Giza (Old Kingdom, Egypt, c. 2560–2540 B.C.)

During the Fourth Dynasty (2613–2494 B.C.), the four great pyramids of Giza are built. The symbolism of the pyramid is connected with the annual flooding of the Nile. This flooding is associated with the death of the god Osiris: the moisture from his decaying body fertilizes the soil. When the land is wiped out by the annual flood, it is as though the world had been returned to its first condition simply as water—all is water. As the flood subsides, there appears the primal hillock symbolic of the seed of the universe, and that's the pyramid. This primal hillock is the Goddess and contains all the generative power of the universe, and within the pyramid is the king, buried as the generating energy within the world mountain—he is the counterpart of the dead Osiris. This architecture has a symbolic meaning: the pharaoh is the dead Osiris within the primordial hillock, which is the first sign of life returning to the world that was flooded at the time of his death, and his death is the fertilizing principle.

FIGURE 57. The Great Sphinx (carved limestone, Old Kingdom, Egypt, c. 2500 B.C.)

The sphinx symbolizes the continuity of pharaonic power; pharaohs come and go, but they are all carriers, or vehicles of the pharaonic power. The sphinx is the child of that wonderful lion goddess Sekhmet and a strange deity called Ptah, who is always represented in the form of a mummy and is actually a moon god. The moon rays fertilize the lion goddess, and this is the source of the sphinx.

In Egypt, the sky is the goddess Nut, and the Earth is the god Geb, her husband. The sun is born from her womb in the east, passes over her on its daily passage by barge, and enters her mouth in the west. The next morning, it is born again from her womb in the east.

In Mesopotamian and Greek mythology, the god is the sky and the goddess is the Earth, as rain came from the sky and fertilized the Earth. Originally Earth and sky were one being and were then separated, and this is sometimes thought to be a result of a sin, or simply an accident. In the great Greek story, the sky (Ouranos) was lying so closely on Gaia, Earth, that their children couldn't get out of her womb, so she handed a sickle to her son Kronos, who castrated Ouranos and pushed him up. Here in the Egyptian myth it is just the opposite: it is the goddess who is being pushed up (Fig. 58).

FIGURE 58. The separation of Nut and Geb (papyrus manuscript, Egypt, date unknown)

MYTH OF ISIS AND OSIRIS

The goddess Nut gave birth to two sets of twins. The oldest were Osiris and Isis, and the second were Nephthys and her consort Set. Osiris is the lord and generator of the culture of the society. The goddess Isis, his sister/bride, has on her head a throne. She symbolizes the throne on which the pharaoh sits, so the throne of Egypt is the Goddess, and the incarnate god sits on it as her agent. This continuity of the Goddess is very strong in Egypt.

Now, Osiris one night slept with Nephthys thinking she was Isis. This is an inattention to detail that never ends well in stories of this kind, and the result was that his brother Set, Nephthys's husband, decided to take revenge. Set planned his revenge by having a beautiful, rich sarcophagus made exactly to Osiris's measure. On one evening at a fine party Set comes in with this sarcophagus and says, "Anyone whom this perfectly fits can have it."

Well, all tried it, like Cinderella's glass slipper, and when Osiris lay in the coffin, seventy-two accomplices came in, clamped the lid down on the coffin, bound it up, and threw it into the Nile. So that's the end of Osiris.

FIGURE 59. Osiris standing between Isis and Nephthys (bas-relief, Ptolemaic, Egypt, second century B.C.)

Just as the goddess had to go down to rescue her husband, in the Mesopotamian tradition, so Isis goes to find her husband Osiris. He floats down the Nile and is washed up on the beach in Syria (what we would think of as Lebanon), and a beautiful tree grows up around the coffin and encloses it.

FIGURE 60. Osiris in the Erica Tree (bas-relief, Ptolemaic, Egypt, first century B.C.)

The king of the Syrian town nearby wanted to build a palace, and when he went down to the shore, the aroma from this tree was so beautiful, so ravishing, he decided to cut it down and put it in the palace as the principal pillar in the living room (Fig. 61). Meanwhile, his wife had just given birth to a little boy.

Isis came a long way, and these gods, they have a certain way of intuiting things—she comes to the area where Osiris had been washed to shore. So she takes service as the nursemaid of the child who had just been born in the palace, where her husband is in the main pillar of the living room. Then in the evenings she had a little ritual: she put the little boy in the fireplace to give him immortal life and to burn away his mortal character, and she turned herself into a swallow and went flying around the column that enclosed her husband, twittering mournfully.

One evening the mother of the little boy came in and saw her little boy in the fireplace with this silly swallow twittering around the column, and no nurse present. She let out a scream that nearly broke the spell, and the child had to be rescued from incineration.

Then the swallow turned back into Isis, saying that her husband was in the column and that she wanted to take him home.

So Isis got the pillar with her husband in it and put it on a barge heading home. She then uncovered the sarcophagus and lay on her husband and conceived from Osiris her son Horus. This is a very important moment in the whole mythology. Horus, the son of Osiris, is begotten of Osiris while he is dead. Isis is terribly afraid of Set, who has taken the throne, so she stays in the delta and gives birth to Horus there in great pain.[14]

Isis landed in the papyrus swamp and gave birth to Horus in sorrow and pain. The sun god Amon-Re and the moon god Thoth, guide of the dead, were her only support in the birth pains. Isis is one of the principal models for the Madonna in the Christian tradition; this is the motif of the mother giving birth to the child without the father present, and this standard motif comes right down in later folklore and in epics.

Meanwhile, Nephthys had also brought forth from her union with Osiris a son, with the head of a jackal, whose name was Anubis.

One day Set was out hunting a boar—our chthonic friend the boar with the down-turned tusks who represents death and resurrection. Set followed the boar into the papyrus swamp and found Isis

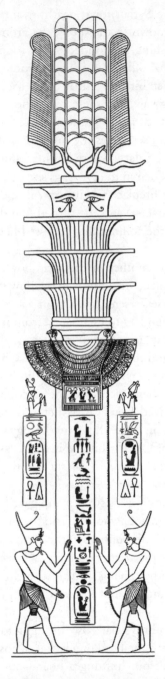

FIGURE 61. The Djed pillar (bas-relief, Ptolemaic, Egypt, first century B.C.)

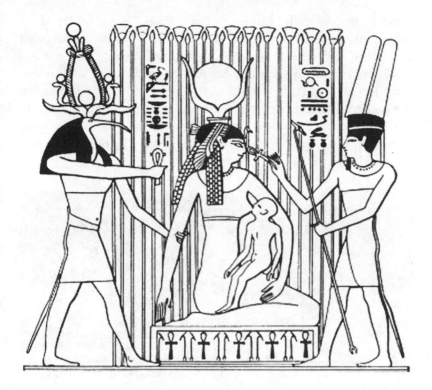

FIGURE 62. Isis and Horus in the Papyrus swamp (bas-relief, Ptolemaic, Egypt, first century B.C.)

with little Horus and the body of Osiris. He tore Osiris into fifteen pieces and flung him all over the place.

So Isis had to go on a hunt for him again. This time, fortunately, she was joined by Nephthys and little Anubis, the jackal-headed boy, who sniffed around after pieces of Osiris. Of the fifteen pieces they recovered fourteen—the fifteenth piece, which happened to be his genital organs, had been swallowed by a fish. And so the dead Osiris becomes associated with the fertilization of the Egyptian soil that occurs every year with the rise and flooding of the Nile. When his body has been reassembled by Isis, Anubis took the role of the Egyptian priest and embalmed the body.

This was a rite of resurrection, the restoration of life. When the priests of Egypt embalmed bodies they assumed the mask of Anubis and reenacted the whole myth.[15] In the scrolls and rituals, the person who had died was called Osiris N ("Osiris Jones," if you will), and the goal of the ritual was that Osiris Jones should go to the prime Osiris and recognize the divine power as identical to himself.

Now, Horus gave battle to Set to avenge his father, and in that battle lost an eye. That eye is called the Eye of Horus and is regarded as the sacrifice that resurrected Osiris and gave him immortal life, and so Osiris became the judge of the dead. The dead pharaoh was identified with Osiris in the underworld whereas the living pharaoh was identified with Horus.

FIGURE 63. The heart being weighed (papyrus, New Kingdom, Egypt, 1317–1301 B.C.)

When people died they were embalmed as Osiris was, and guided then by Anubis to the scale that weighed their heart against a feather (Fig. 63). The feather is the symbol of the spiritual, and the heart is the symbol of the physical. But if the heart is no heavier than a feather, then the person is worthy of spiritual immortality. Otherwise a demonic alligator monster there will consume the person. A feather on the top of the upright beam of the scale is the feather of the goddess Ma'at, who represents the whole that might be called the cosmic order, the order and law of the universe.

FIGURE 64. Ma'at (painted bas-relief, Ptolemaic, Egypt, first century B.C.)

FIGURE 65. Artemis (bronze sculpture, Classical, Greece, c. 330–320 B.C.)

CHAPTER 5

•

Goddesses and Gods
of the Greek Pantheon[1]

THE NUMBER OF THE GODDESS

Gods are metaphors transparent to transcendence. And my understanding of the mythological mode is that deities and even people are to be understood in this sense, as metaphors. It's a poetic understanding. It is to be understood in the same sense as Goethe's words at the end of *Faust*: *"Alles Vergängliche ist nur ein Gleichnis"* ("Everything transitory is but a reference").[2] The reference is to that which transcends all speech, all vocabularies, and all images. I think of the more prosaic style of thinking about these references as theological rather than mythological. In theology, the god is taken as a final term, a kind of supernatural fact. When the deity is not transparent, when he doesn't open up like that to the transcendent, he doesn't open up to the mystery that is the mystery of our own lives.

In the poetic mythological systems, the power that one is addressing out there is a magnifying image of the power that's operating in oneself. One's deity is a function of one's own ability to experience and conceive of the divine. It is the reflex of one's own position in the spiritual hierarchy. As the Chāndogya Upaniṣad puts it about 900 B.C. in India, *"Tat tvam asi"* ("Thou art that"). The mystery of your being is that mystery which you cannot conceive of, which lies beyond the touch of the tongue, and which is metaphorically referred to by the images of your pantheon. There is also a saying in the Bṛhadāraṇyaka Upaniṣad: "People say, 'Worship this god! Worship that god!'—one god after another, this whole universe itself is God's creation!"[3] Those who seek their worship out *there* do not understand at all. Turn inward, and *there* you will find the footprints of the mystery of being.

And this is an idea that we've seen already in the Egyptian Book of the Dead, where the person who dies is called Osiris N—"Osiris Jones." He is on his way, in the underworld and afterlife journey, to the throne of Osiris, the god who died and was resurrected and sits as judge of the dead, precisely the model for Christ. The individual on his way to Osiris is himself Osiris: you're it. On the way Osiris Jones becomes aware of the fact that all the deities that he has worshipped are simply functions of his own mystery; he goes through a gray area in the underworld and says, "My hair is the hair of Nu, my face is the face of Re, my eyes are the eyes of Hathor"—every part of my body is part of some god.[4] Then he says, "I am yesterday, today, and tomorrow and have the power to be born a second time. I am that mystery that has given rise to the gods."[5] That you yourself are what you see reflected outside there in your pantheon and must come to acknowledge as being within yourself is the realization of the initiation of mythology.

In prosaic mythology, however, which I call *theology*, the god is taken in the final term: he's not *in here*, he's *out there*, and you are not to *identify* with him, you are to *relate* to him. So I'm making a distinction between that system and the one that points to identity with those powers or to the operation of those mystery powers within your own life, through your own organs, and coming out in your dreaming vision. When the great yogis in India who worship Śiva as their god come to this realization, they dress as Śiva and say, *"Śivo'ham* ("I am Śiva"). Now, in life you can live as though you were the manifestation of Śiva, and by living that way long enough, consistently with that faith and belief, you would come finally to the realization that you are. This is called in Shintō Buddhism the "awakening phase," and then you know nobody can take away from you that internal life of consciousness and energy that you see supporting the stars, and the galaxies, and the birds in the forest and the trees, because it is also supporting you. You are a participant in this eternal mystery.

In the theological perspective, then, where the deity who has created you is an external fact, it is the height of blasphemy to say, "I am divine." Christ got crucified for saying it, and so it's a lie. The biblical religions—Judaism, Christianity, and Islam—are religions of relationship rather than identity, and they are institutionalized. How do you relate to God? You relate to God by being a member of a certain community, and there are two kinds of communities. One is the biological community; these are tribal religions in which you are born into that god's community. The other I like to call world religion, in which you are baptized into the community, and that's the only community that relates you to God.

The three great world religions are Buddhism (which is really a mythological rather than a relational religion), Christianity, and Islam. Now, Buddhism is related to Hinduism as Christianity and Islam are related to Judaism. Hinduism and Judaism are tribal religions: One is born a Hindu—not only born a Hindu but born a Hindu in this, that, or another caste—and one is born a Jew. This can make it difficult for modern Jews who become disillusioned with respect to the theological aspects of the religion. Since they can lose their religion and still be Jews, there's a double bind.

Judaism, Christianity, and Islam are quite different from the Indian religions, in that they are prosaic rather than poetic, whereas Hinduism and Buddhism are fundamentally metaphoric.

What we're dealing with in the Goddess mythologies of Old and Classical Europe is a body of material that dates back to the origins of agriculture and animal domestication. The earlier small nomadic hunting and gathering groups have a totally different psychological problem from that of the later settlement communities in which you begin to have differentiated societies. In the early nomadic forms, every adult within any given community was in control of the whole cultural heritage. There were still distinctions in these societies. The first significant difference was between the roles of male and female. The second difference was among the age groups—children, youth, mature people, and the aged—and the third differentiation was between the general community on the one hand and, on the other, the shaman, who had had a deep psychological crisis in which she or he had experienced from within the dynamic energies that are symbolized in the myths of the society.

However, when cities started to spring up in the Near East around 3500 B.C., a truly differentiated, specialized society developed. Now you had professional governing families, professional priests, professional trading people, professional tillers of the soil, and then professional craftspeople—potters, woodworkers, and so forth. At that time a very strong sociological mythology developed, signifying that in spite of the differences we are all one. This view is very clearly stated in the Hindu caste system: we are all of one body, and each individual is a cell in one of the great organs of the body. The Brahmins, or priests, are the heads of the social body, the *kṣatriya*, or governing caste are the arms and the hands of the society who enforce the law given by the Brahmins, the *vaiśya*, or merchants, are the body, the torso of the society. These three constitute what are known as the twice-born castes and are educated and intellectually informed. Then there is the fourth caste, which is quite separate: the *śūdra*, who constitute the legs and feet and support the body.

Around 3500 B.C. in the Near East (a period known as Sumerian Uruk B), priests began systematic observations of the heavens, writing was developed, and the reckoning of time and space was developed in terms of both the decimal system and the sexagesimal (based on the number 60) that we still use for regular schedules, whether they're segments of time or segments of space.

With these writing and recording systems it was possible to precisely track the movements of the planets through the fixed constellations. The visible planets are the moon, Mercury, Venus, the sun, Mars, Jupiter and Saturn, and the priests soon recognized that they moved at a mathematically determinable rate through the fixed stars. The mythology of a mathematically determined cycle of time, a cosmic order, comes out of this. The earlier primitive mythologies were interested in the exceptional, this particular tree, this interesting stone, strange little shapes, an animal that behaves in a peculiar way. In this new cosmic mythology now the interest is only in the great orders, and so mystical mathematics begins at this time. Since the great cosmic order is the enclosing womb within which all lives exist, it is identified with the female power, the Goddess, the Mother Universe.

This universe has an innate mathematics, and the number 9 becomes the great number of the Goddess. Nine, the number of the Muses, is three times three, the triads of the Graces. The three Graces are (as we'll see) the three aspects of Aphrodite, and the rhythm of her energy going forth into the world, coming back, and then herself enclosing the two movements.

Four hundred thirty-two is another interesting number: add those numerals up, and you get nine. In India the Purāṇas tell us that 43,200 is number of years in the *Kālī Yuga*, the current, last, and shortest of the cycles that make up the still larger cycle, or *mahāyuga* of 4,320,000 years. One day I was reading the *Poetic Edda* of Iceland—one of the great Norse sagas—and it tells us that in the warrior hall Valhalla, to which all the great war dead go, there are 580 dogs and at the end of the cycle of time, when the world's going to end and start all over again, 800 warriors go through each of those doors to give battle to the antigods in the mutual destruction of the universe. Well, I noticed: 800 x 540 = 432,000.

In the second century B.C., a Babylonian priest named Berosus described, in Greek, the Chaldean mythology of Babylon, and he pointed out that the period from when the first city (in that tradition the city of Kish) arose until the coming of the mythological flood that is the model for the flood of Noah, 432,000 years had elapsed. There's that number there again, in the second century B.C. in Mesopotamia. During that period of 432,000 years just ten kings reigned.

Where else do you think of finding long lives like that? Turning to the Bible, how many patriarchs do we count from Adam to Noah, including Adam? Ten. How many years elapsed between Adam and Noah's Flood? One thousand six hundred fifty-six years in these great long-lived patriarchs. I spent about three frantic days trying to factor 1656 into 43,200—I'm no mathematician, and it wasn't working, but then I said to myself, *Well, someone has worked this out.*

It was actually a Jewish Assyriologist named Julius Oppert in 1872. I went to his paper titled "The Dates of Genesis," and there it was. Both totals of the years of reign of the antediluvian kings of Berosus and the antediluvian patriarchs of Genesis contain 72 as a factor, 72 being the number of years required in the precession of the equinoxes for an advance of one degree along the zodiac: 432,000 divided by 72 = 6,000, while 1,656 divided by 72 = 23, so that the relationship is of 6,000 to 23.

In the Jewish calendar, one year is reckoned to have 365 days; after twenty-three years (plus the five leap-year days of that period), that amounts to 8,400 days, or 1,200 seven-day weeks. Multiplying 1200 by 72 to find the number of seven-day weeks in 1,656 years (23 x 72) yields 1,200 x 72 = 86,4000, which is twice 43,200.

That was all very astounding. There it is hidden in the Bible and there it is exposed in Berosus.

Here we've got the same number popping up in Iceland, in India, in Babylon, and in the Bible. Where is it coming from?

I started to ask myself another question: Due to the precession of the equinoxes, we're going into the Aquarian Age. We're now in the Age of Pisces, and formerly we were in the Age of Aries, and before that we were in Taurus, and so forth. How many years does it take for a complete cycle of the equinoctial zodiac? 25,920 years. Divide that by the sexigesimal 60, and you get 432.

A friend once sent me a book titled *Aerobics* to help me learn how much exercise I had to get in order to stay healthy. I'm reading along, and a footnote states that a man in perfect physical shape at rest has a heartbeat of approximately one beat per second, sixty seconds. In twelve hours it is 43,200. So this number of the rhythm of the universe is the number of the rhythm of our own heart, the microcosm and the macrocosm for one cosmic order. So when you are in health your rhythm is in tune with that of the universe. When you get off, your rhythm gets off. The whole basis of this mythology is rhythm; the ritual year is the rhythmic year, and so you are kept in rhythm with the universe and you are pulled back in. Disease is getting off rhythm and the myth rhythm is what pulls you back, and so we have these mythologies of cures. These days among the Navaho the myth and rituals that used to be for hunters are used for curing so as to bring people back into accord—to help them become transparent to the transcendent.

The great rhythmic number is 9. Add the numerals: 4 + 3 +2 = 9, and that is the number of the goddess. In India the Goddess has 108 names and in the great temples of the goddesses the priest pours into the *yōni*, which is the altar, a red powder that women put on their foreheads, and he counts out and recites the 108 names of the Goddess. Multiply 108 by 4, and you have 432. In Buddhist thought, there are 108 earthly desires that bind us to this sorrowful world of illusion—of *māyā*. One hundred eight is the Goddess number at this moment, at that moment, at the equinox season, at the solstice season and at dawn, at day-rise, at noon, at midnight, and so forth. She's the one who encompasses and binds you in your life.

Of course, add 1 + 0 + 8 and you get 9. Three times every day in the European countries you'll hear the strain of the Angelus bell, ringing one, two, three; one, two, three; one, two, three, four, five, six, seven, eight, nine. The Angelus prayer addresses itself to the Annunciation, the angel of the Lord declaring to Mary that she has conceived a child by the Holy Ghost, and so it indicates the pouring of divine energy into the world.[6]

This is the mythology of which the Greek goddesses are the local manifestations.

We have seen the deep archaeological roots of the Goddess in Old Europe, where from the very earliest times of the agricultural community she's the dominant figure as both the cosmic center and the surrounding protector. The Indo-European warrior people invaded in the fourth, third, and second millennia B.C., bringing a collision of two totally contrary mythologies—one in which the matrilineal or mother line is dominant and one is related primarily to the mother, and the other, the patrilineal line, in which one marks one's identity through one's father.

In the Greek tradition, this collision comes to a climax in the Oresteia story, in *The Eumenides*, when Apollo and Athena, representing the male line, cleanse Orestes of the guilt of his matricide.

In *The Odyssey*, we will see the female power coming back, increasing in power and glory. Looking into the Classical Greek pantheon and its evolution, we will see how divinities changed character and were recombined in new guises as the society itself changed. A mythological pantheon is fluid and as the needs and the realizations of the society change, so do the relationships and the gods. Deities are really time- and space-conditioned; they are shaped from inherited ideas, inherited traditional imageries, but they are put together in terms of a local context of time and space.

One of the great disadvantages of a literary or scriptural tradition like the biblical one is that a deity or context of deities becomes crystallized, petrified at a certain time and place. The deity doesn't continue to grow, expand, or take into account new cultural forces and new realizations in the sciences, and the result is this make-believe conflict we have in our culture between science and religion. One of the functions of mythology is to present an image of the cosmos in such a way that it becomes the carrier of this mystical realization, so that wherever you look it's as though you are looking at an icon, a holy picture, and the walls of space and time open out into the deep dimension of mystery, which is a dimension within ourselves, as well as out there.

This dimension can open through the science of today even more wonderfully than it opened through the science of the second millennium B.C. There is absolutely no conflict between science and the religious mood or the mythological realization—but there *is* a conflict between the science of the twentieth century A.D. and the twentieth century B.C. This is what we are getting in our religion, because the whole thing became petrified in the fourth century at the time of Theodosius when the authority of Byzantium came down with St. Augustine to establish the beliefs that had to be accepted. From this came the petrifaction in our tradition and the split between the scientific and the religious view.

This is not the case in the Greek world. One of the great things about Greece is that there never was a scripture. Rather, the Greeks had the playful world of Homer and the Homeric Hymns, Hesiod's tales, and so forth. There are versions of the stories in which Eros is the youngest of the gods, and versions (such as Plato's *Symposium*) in which he is the first and eldest. The Greeks had the rituals but there was no authority with the power to say, "This is it."

In a way that is true in India as well, as there never was a single orthodox cult, an authority that was in such a position as to say, "This is the way it all must be believed." So you have a proliferation of cults, and the individual can find his or her way to deity through this variety of manifestations. There was a terrific explosion of ways to interpret the mystery that was presented in these symbols both in the Greek world and in the first centuries of Christianity.

And so you have the Great Goddess appearing in the Greek myths in a variety of guises.

ARTEMIS

Take a glorious deity like Artemis, for example. What is wonderful about the Greek world is that she is manifested in no end of different ways in the different cults. Martin Nilsson, the great authority on classical Greek religion, says that she was *the* prime goddess. In the

FIGURE 66. Leto, Artemis, and Apollo (red-figure krater, Classical, Greece, c. 450 B.C.)

familiar Classical tradition, Artemis was known as the virgin goddess, but that is only one definition of her character and role.[7] She is, as every goddess, a total goddess. With her I want to introduce us to this set of problems.

Here she is in the Homeric Hymns:

> *This is about*
> *brilliant Artemis*
> *her golden arrow,*
> *her hunting of deer,*
> *her pride in arrows,*
> *the sacred virgin,*
> *the sister of Apollo*
> *in his gold sword,*
> *Artemis*
> *She loves to hunt,*
> *in the shadow of mountains*
> *and in the wind*
> *on mountain-tops*
> *she loves to take her bow,*
> *her solid gold bow,*
> *stretch it*
> *and shoot off*
> *groaning arrows*
> *The peaks*
> *of great mountains*
> *tremble*
> *The forest*
> *in its darkness*
> *screams*
> *with the clamor of animals,*
> *and it's frightening*
> *The whole earth*
> *starts shaking*
> *even the sea,*
> *the sea-life*
> *She has a strong heart,*
> *she darts in and out*
> *everywhere*
> *in and out*
> *killing*
> *all kinds of animals*
> *And when she is satisfied,*
> *when she is through*

watching for animals,
when her mind has had its fun,
she unstrings her bow.
She goes to the great house
of Apollo,
the brother she loves,
in the grass country,
Delphi
she goes there
and arranges
a chorus
of Graces
and Muses
And when she has hung up
this unstrung bow,
when she has put away her arrows,
she puts on
over her flesh
a beautiful dress
Then she begins the dances
and their sound
is heavenly
Their song
is of Leto,
whose ankles are so lovely,
Leto
whose children stand out
the best of gods,
the best in their counsel
the best in their acts
Farwell
children of Zeus,
and of Leto,
of Leto whose hair is beautiful
I will think of you
in my other poems[8]

Artemis was originally a goddess associated with the bear. The bear was probably the first worshipped animal in the world, and this goddess goes way back. At Brauron, a very important sanctuary east of Athens, there was a festival where little girls danced in honor of

Artemis, and they were called the "little bears." The name Artemis is related in Europe to Arthur: both these names are related to Arcturus and the bear.

Artemis and Apollo are deities with two totally different origins, yet they have been combined in the Classical Greek tradition as brother and sister, born of Leto in the island of Delos. Leto was the daughter of the Titans Coeus and Phoebe, and Hesiod claims that she was Zeus's wife before Hera. When Leto was pregnant with Artemis and Apollo, she was relentlessly pursued by Hera until she finally came to the island of Delos. Artemis was born first and helped her mother birth Apollo, hence Artemis's title Eileithyia (believed to have been one of the names of the goddess in the Minoan culture): "Artemis Eileithyia, venerable power, who bringest relief in labor's dreadful hour."[9]

A late pulling together of old ideas, the twins represent two powers: Apollo the power of the protector and the rational mind, and Artemis the power of nature. Personified in Artemis are the nature powers that inform the whole natural world.

FIGURE 67. Artemis with deer (marble relief, Classical, Greece, fifth century B.C.)

Artemis is associated with the bow and consequently with the hunt, and in this role the death that she deals is a sweet and swift one. The Muslims have a wonderful saying about the Angel of Death: in his approach the Angel of Death seems terrible, yet when he has arrived he's sweet.

Originally Artemis herself was a deer, and she is the goddess who kills deer; the two are dual aspects of the same being. Life is killing life all the time, and so the goddess kills herself in the sacrifice of her own animal. Each life is its own death, and he who kills you is somehow a messenger of the destiny that was yours from the start. So it is with the animal and the deity. If the animal kills the deity as the boar killed Adonis, or if the deity kills the animal as Artemis hunts deer, these are two aspects of the same life mystery.

Actaeon was out hunting stags with his dogs and followed a stream up to its source, and in the pool at the source of the stream was the goddess Artemis bathing naked with her nymphs. Actaeon, the

FIGURE 68. Artemis and Actaeon (red-figure krater, Classical, Greece, 470 B.C.)

poor chap, saw this glorious naked body and he looked at her with eyes not of worship but of lust.

This is an improper relationship to a deity. Seeing that look in his eye, Artemis simply splashed him with some water and he was turned into a stag, and his own dogs then consumed him. The dogs themselves, like the sailors on Odysseus's ships, are representations of the lower appetites, while the stag represents his lower, merely animal nature; that is really what consumed him when he was in the presence of the Goddess herself.

Here is the problem in encountering a deity: if you're not ready, you're going to make a mistake and get blown to pieces. The deity represents a certain concentration and focus of power, a power center. In myths, the individual human character represents a less powerful focus of spiritual power than the deity, and so the mortal must prepare for this incongruity of power fields through meditation in order to put the mind in the proper mode for regarding the deity-as-deity—naked, in a word.

Like an electric circuit with a fuse that isn't able to carry the charge, if the power is too great for the individual's capacity, he blows. So before approaching a goddess or god, there are manners of preparing oneself, of insulating oneself, as it were, to meet, receive, and subdue the power of the deity.

The varied powers that have been brought together in Artemis are indicated by her various images and associations. We've seen her as a deer and we've seen her bathing in the water as the water nymph, which brings us back to the Old European fish goddess from 6000 B.C. (Fig. 19).

In Sumer, we saw the Goddess in her role as Lady of the Wild Things (Fig. 40). In this guise, she is the World Mother—that is to say, the whole world is of her, and all are her children. And in Greek myths too, the Mistress of Beasts appears in the avatar of Artemis. As Baring and Cashford point out, "Artemis became the Goddess of Wild Animals, a title she was given in the *Iliad—Potnia Theron—*inheriting her role from the Paleolithic Goddess of the Wild Animals of the Hunt."[10]

All the animals of the forest are under Artemis's protection, and so in the later, somewhat more sentimental literary tradition, she is represented as the huntress. This is her more cosmic representation; the wolves and cranes are associated with the goddess-as-initiator, and

FIGURE 69. Artemis as the mistress of beasts (black-figure vase, Archaic, Greece, c. 570 B.C.)

the swastika represents the cycle of time. That's the image implicit in my number 432,000, the cycle of the revolving spheres.

All this has come together in that one great goddess; this is all Artemis.

The doves on this figurine's headdress (Fig. 70) signify that the goddess whom the priestess serves is Potnia Theron, Lady of the Wild Animals. The bull's horns in the center suggest the sacrificial rites of the bull that were a part of the goddess cult and worship, as seen in the symbolic imagery at Çatal Hüyük and Knossos. The doves and the bull's horns symbolize the Goddess's power in the realms of both life and death.

FIGURE 70. Priestess of the Goddess (terra-cotta, Minoan, Crete, 1500–1300 B.C.)

The center of Artemis's cult was in the city of Ephesus, on the Aegean coast of Asia Minor. On this statue from her temple (Fig. 71), Artemis Ephesia's crown is surrounded by a nimbus of horned animal figures with upraised arms. Her heavy necklace carries the signs of the zodiac. On her arms appear to be lions, and the column of her body is covered with animals, including lions, bulls, and rams. On the base of the statue are the remains of the hoofs of stags that originally flanked her.

In his book *The Eternal Present: The Beginnings of Art*, Siegfried Giedion said of this statue, "The most revealing of all her traits are perhaps the stag hoofs upon her pedestal, all that remains of a pair of life size stags that stood on each side of her. It is just these footprints which give the clue to the origins of this deity, who has undergone so many transformations.... The origins of this cult idol are rooted in

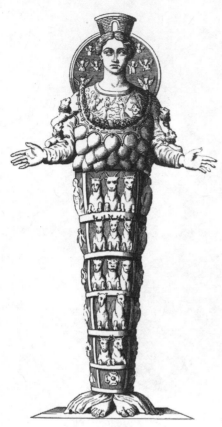

FIGURE 71. Artemis Ephesia (carved marble, Hellenistic, Turkey, first century B.C.)

FIGURE 72. Hekateion (carved stone, Classical, Greece, c. third century B.C.)

prehistory.... Artemis Ephesia is the result of a long process of anthropomorphism which began when the dominion and veneration of the animal came to be replaced by the power of deities in human form."[11]

Artemis, along with Selene and Hekate, was one of the Greek triads representing the Old European three-bodied or triune aspect of the Goddess. We can see this represented in this figurine (Fig. 72) of Artemis as part of three-fold Hekate. First you have the pillar—the goddess mother is the axis of the universe herself. Round about are three representations of the Goddess, including Artemis, and Hekate, who represents the chthonic underworld—the magic aspect of the Goddess—and then dancing in a relaxed, fluent manner around about we see the three Graces.

Artemis is the giver of abundance: Our Lady of the Wild Things, and the All-Mother of the many breasts, who bears the totality of the entities of the natural world. This is something very, very different from the image of the virgin goddess and the mere huntress that we have normally associated with her.

APOLLO

Apollo,
it is for you
that the swan sings
so loudly
self-accompanied
on its own wings
beating
beating its way
to the shore of the river,
the Peneus
stirring
It is for you
that a poet shapes
language,
holding in his hand
a lyre that is loud too.
First and last and always
it is for you.
Here is my prayer.
Here, god, is my song.[12]

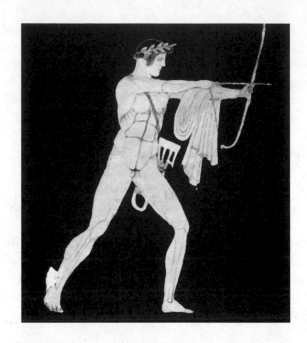

FIGURE 73. Apollo (red-figure krater, Classical, Greece, 475–425 B.C.)

FIGURE 74. Hittite King Tudhaliya IV in the embrace of the god Sharruma (bas-relief, Hittite, Turkey, thirteenth century B.C.)

Nilsson finds Apollo to have been associated originally with the Hittites.[13] The Hittites were Indo-European people who came into Asia Minor when the Homeric Greeks were going down to the Greek peninsula, so there is an actual ancestral relationship. The Hittites came into the Aegean area and entered into a different context of relationships from the Greeks. Apollo was on the Trojan side in the war of Troy, and it is now since believed that he stems ultimately from Yazilikaya, Porsuk Çayi, and Alaca Höyük—areas within the great Hittite domain.

At the entrance to a great mountain sanctuary of Yazilikaya in Turkey stands the image (Fig. 74) of the Hittite god Sharruma protecting the king. Now, regarding such sanctuaries, we have seen the

FIGURE 75. Apollo Belvedere (Roman marble copy of Greek bronze statue, 350–325 B.C.)

motif before of the guardians—lions or leopards—representing the threshold from the world of secular experience into the transcendent realm. The Hittite word *upulon* means "gate" or "wall-guardian," and Nilsson suggests this is the antecedent of Apollo. Likewise, Nilsson argues that the Babylonian word *ubulu*, which also means "gate," is a linguistic support to this matter of Apollo's background as representing a threshold guardian, a protecting figure at the entrance to shrines.

When the Greeks incorporated him into their pantheon, Apollo came to be identified as Artemis's twin brother—the god of human culture to balance the nature goddess.

Note the serpent winding its way up the column in the famous Apollo Belvedere (Fig. 75).

Over time, Apollo became associated with healing and with the serpent, which we still see in the caduceus, medical staff, representing the power of life in the field of time, the casting off of its past and the moving into the future: throwing off death. That's a powerful role that later is assigned to the god Asclepius.

The great female figure associated with Asclepius was his daughter Hygieia, the goddess of health, after whom we have the word *hygienic*, and she too is associated with the serpent power. This is the serpent power that in the Book of Genesis is cursed, but in these, as in most nonbiblical cultures, it represents the vitality of the energy and consciousness of life in the body in the field of time, the vitality of spiritual consciousness in the life in the world. In the carving, Hygieia stands with the serpent. The Goddess herself feeds the symbolic animal that represents the vitality of the living. This is allegorical of a situation of hygiene, or the austerities and disciplines of good health: we must give life and food and sustenance to the serpent power of our own bodies, which keeps us in health, and throw off the shadow of disease.

Here (Fig. 76) we see Asclepius with his *śakti*, Hygieia. Asclepius leans on a club that may have belonged to Heracles,[14] but it is entwined with a snake, symbolic of his cult. Hygieia's arm rests on a tripod that is connected to Apollo's temple at Delphi. When I discussed this piece in my book *The Mythic Image*, I pointed out that above her "are ritual utensils suggesting the symbolism of the mystery cults: to the right a wine pitcher with an emerging snake, to the left a basket (*cista mystica*) containing along with a second snake a divine child. Below, near the goddess, stands another appearance of the child."[15]

Asclepius, the god of medicine, was simply taking over a role that had been Apollo's earlier, and that Apollo had taken over from an

FIGURE 76. Asclepius and Hygieia (ivory relief, Roman, Italy, late fourth century A.D.)

earlier deity—whom we don't know. As Nilsson points out, whenever you find an Apollonian shrine, the god has come in late and taken the shrine over from an earlier god who was in the role, one way or another, of a protector.

Asclepius's great temple at Epidaurus was a sanatorium to which people went for health cures. Now, how was healing handled at Epidaurus? It was a great and gloriously beautiful sanctuary of harmony and beauty that included dormitories, temples, and parks. The individual would come to the sanctuary and meditate and pray under the instruction of the priest but would then go to sleep and dream in the sanctuary of the god, and in the dream the healing power would appear.

Carl Kerényi, in his handsome although rather difficult volume *Asklepios*, brings to our attention with great emphasis the aspect of the various levels of dream expression and language in Classical medicine. In the Asclepian sanctuaries of healing, Kerényi writes:

> The patient himself was offered an opportunity to bring about the cure whose elements he bore within himself. To this end an environment was created which, as in modern spas and health resorts,

FIGURE 77. The Serpent god Amphiaraus (relief, Classical, Greece, fourth century B.C.)

FIGURE 78. Omphalos of Delphi (carved marble, Classical, Greece, fourth century B.C.)

was as far as possible removed from the disturbing and unhealthful elements of the outside world. The religious atmosphere also helped men's innermost depths to accomplish their curative potentialities. In principle the physician was excluded from the individual mystery of recovery.[16]

One very illuminating votive offering (Fig. 77) shows a young man in the dormitory dreaming, and he dreams of himself as being healed by the god who touches his shoulder, but at the same time he dreams of a serpent power emerging from his body touching his shoulder. This is the same act in two aspects. Did they not know something? The whole function of the Epidaurian experience was to awaken that healing power in ourselves and bring about a psychosomatic cure. This picture shows this: the youth dreams of the serpent power coming from his body while at the same time he dreams of the god curing him. Dreams are saying two or three things at a time and here he has two ways of understanding.

At Delphi the whole sense of a classical world as distinct from any other comes to you. The omphalos is the world's navel, the *axis mundi*, and was guarded by Apollo. The accent in the early goddesses of the Earth was on the navel motif, and the omphalos is the navel of the Goddess at Delphi.

Here (Fig. 79) is one of those sixth-millennium B.C. goddess figures, and there is the navel, the center of the cosmic quadrangle. She is the world's center; she is the world's encompassor.

Delphi was the site of the oracle, the priestess who would enter a trance and answer questions, whether on matters of state or of personal problems. The simplest person or the highest could come to her, and she would provide answers.

When Athens was threatened by the invasion of the Persians, the Athenians went to the oracle at Delphi to ask, "What do we do?"

And the oracle gave them the advice, "Take your wooden walls." This was interpreted as, "Go to your ships. Leave your city. Let the Persians take your city. Get into your ships."[17] And they did and wrecked this whole terrific navy of Xerxes in just that way.

An individual could come and ask his questions, and the answers were always given in a kind of enigmatic way by a woman seated on a tripod inhaling some kind of smoke or steam, and she was certainly in a trance state. She was called the "pythoness" because she was the consort of the cosmic serpent—the earlier deity of this area had been the python. This snake Apollo slew (thereby gaining him the name

FIGURE 79. Goddess of the World Navel (terra-cotta, late Neolithic,
Hungary, c. 5500–5000 B.C.)

Pythian Apollo), and then the god took over the shrine. So here again
we have that motif of Apollo coming in and taking over; he becomes
the protector now of the oracle. This is the way when a new mythology comes in: the older deities are slain and their energy is incorporated by the new god.

Sitting in the theater at Delphi, one sees the backdrop of Mount
Parnassus, where the Muses lived. This is where Greek spiritual life
took root and flowered, and you can just see how close to the natural
world it is.

In Martin Buber's book *I and Thou*, he says, "The *I* that is related
to *thou* is different from the *I* that is related to an *it*."[18] Think about it.
Think of yourself: do you have a *thou* relationship to an animal or an
it relationship? There is a real difference.

In Delphi, you're living in an environment that is a *thou*. It is alive—the trees, the birds, the animals, all are looked at as *thou*. If you live, as I do, in a city like New York, your environment is buildings that have been made out of dead bricks and so forth; we relate to our environment as an *it*. This is one reason why it is so challenging for valid, authentic poetry to come out of the city. You get complex metric problems and various ways of handling the language and all that kind of stuff, and it gets very interesting for the literary critics, but who reads it? It's only the rare poet who can make a real breakthrough and turn the city into a *thou*. In the Greek world, they never got in the *it* psychology, only the *I* and *thou* psychology, the mystic mode that is entered by relating to your environment as a living being.

FIGURE 80. Phoebus Apollo (red-figure krater, Classical, Italy, fifth century B.C.)

Another role of Apollo is as the sun god Phoebus Apollo. Here he is driving the chariot of the sun across the sky (Fig. 80), sunrays encircling his head, while *ephebes* (the little star-boys) fall into the sea. This is an example of how a number of different deities have been brought together into one, and then the whole mythology becomes something that wasn't there before.

DIONYSUS

One of the great religious sanctuaries was the theater. It was a field devoted primarily to Dionysus for the display of mythic themes in a kind of enacted ritual. A ritual is the enactment of a myth, and by participating in the ritual you are participating in the myth. Symbolically the myth is the manifestation of spiritual powers, and by participating in the myth you are activating the related spiritual powers within yourself. Now, instead of simply having individual participation in a ritual action we have the community participating in the enactment of the myth in the form of a tragedy or comedy.

FIGURE 81. The Theater at Delphi (limestone, Classical, Greece, fourth century B.C.)

One of the greatest things about the Classical tradition is that you have these two deities who are polar opposites to each other brought together: Apollo representing the rational principle, the light principle, the consciousness principle; and Dionysus representing the dynamic of what we would call the unconscious. Dionysus, who in a Near Eastern tradition would be associated with the diabolical powers and was a nongod, an antigod, was recognized as copowerful with Apollo, so we have this idea of balance and interplay between the two. It was quite a period in the late seventh, sixth, and fifth centuries B.C. when the Apollonian tradition began to yield to the Dionysians with those terrific, orgiastic rites that were the scandal of the period. But Dionysus was finally united into the tradition, with his rapturous song with satyrs and obscenities serving in quite a vivid contrast to the Apollonian principle.

The best study of Apollo and Dionysus is still Friedrich Nietzsche's *The Birth of Tragedy*. There he wrote that where the mind has broken through to the transcendent, it is filled with awe and terror and fascination, and it is from this breakthrough that the arts derive.[19] The two aspects of attention, then, are to the wonder and marvel of the world as it is and of everybody in it.

Within the field of differentiation, within the field of time, we have these forms that are manifestations of the transcendent power, and the artist in rendering the form is giving us a sense of the immanence of the transcendent in this body. The body becomes dreamlike in its wonder. This is called the Apollonian aspect.

On the other hand, we can be interested in the terrific energy that shatters everything and brings forth new things—that is to say, the projecting aspect rather than the in-form aspect, and that is the Dionysian.

The Apollonian represents the fascination with that which is in this poignant, passing moment, while the Dionysian represents identification with the energy that is shattering and bringing forth new forms. These two must function together in art.

Neitzsche sees sculpture as the principal art-representing form, and he sees music as the principal art-representing the dynamic through time and process, and so we have to have both in a work of art. If the dynamic is not formed, all you have is the scream, the cry, and if the form does not take into account the dynamic, you have simply a petrifact, a piece of dead, dry sculpture.

When you combine the two, you break through to this mystery, the *mysterium tremendum et fascinans*; the experience of the sublime when you break through, is of the *tremendum*. This is why religion is called *the fear of god*; the other name for it is the *love of god*. You haven't caught the sense of the mystery, how shattering it is to your whole system and your ideas and everything else, unless you get both senses.

Goethe says that *"der Menschheit bestes Tell"* ("the best part of man") is this experience, the *Schaudern* ("shudder")[20]—it's a kind of noumenal ripple, a realization of how momentary you are in this vast explosion that is the universe, and that's what you get through Dionysus.

ZEUS

Now, finally, in this context, I want to speak of the Aryan gods. Zeus, who comes in with the Indo-Europeans, has no connection to the Goddess cult of this area. Zeus's name is related to the word θεός (*theos,* "god"), which is related to the Sanskrit देव (*deva,* "god"); the gods of the Sanskrit world are related, then, to the Aryan gods of the Classical world. Zeus is definitely an Indo-European god who came into Greece with the invading people in the fourth, third, and second millennia B.C.

> *Zeus*
> *who is the best*
> *god*
> *and the greatest*
> *is who*
> *I will sing*
> *he sees*
> *far he rules*
> *he*
> *finishes things*
> *he converses*
> *wisely*
> *with Themis*
> *at his side*
> *be kind*
> *son of*
> *Cronus*
> *who sees far*
> *you're the most*
> *famous*
> *of all*
> *you're the greatest* [21]

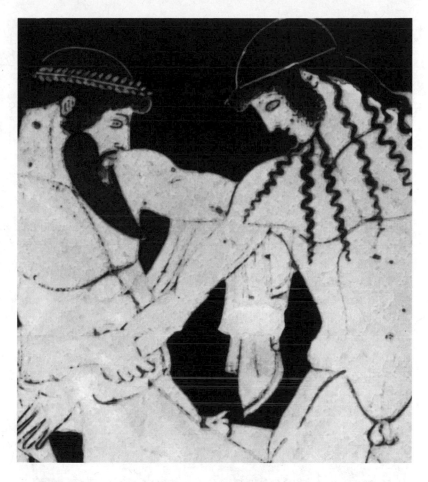

FIGURE 82. Zeus abducting Ganymede (red-figure kylix, Classical, Greece, c. 475–425 B.C.)

The Homeric Hymn to Aphrodite tells how Ganymede came to Olympus:

> Verily wise Zeus carried off golden-haired Ganymede because of his beauty, to be amongst the Deathless Ones and pour drink for the gods in the house of Zeus, a wonder to see, honored by all the immortals as he draws the red nectar from the golden bowl... deathless and un-ageing, even as the gods.[22]

The kylix above shows Zeus carrying off Ganymede to become his water boy, to serve at his table on Olympus. This is the role of the men's rites that I spoke of earlier: to separate the little boy from the mother world. Zeus, however, manages to get himself linked up with the older mythologies.

Zeus becomes absorbed by the older, longer-standing mother-right tradition.

Below (Fig. 83) you can see him with Hermes and Leto, the mother of Apollo and Artemis in the classical tradition.

Artemis, as we remember, came from the Minoan culture. Apollo originated with the Hittites. Leto was the Old European Mother Goddess. And Zeus was the thunder-hurling chief of the Indo-European pantheon.

In other words, we have four totally different divinities of four totally different provenances brought together here in a syncretic myth, a myth that has put together conflicting and contrary mythologies. The problem was to unite these two societies, the society of the Mother Goddess and the society of the male god.

Now, ordinarily the deities of these warrior peoples are not subject to the Goddess. Indo-European deities are not born; their deities are eternal powers representing the powers of nature and of the spirit within us, the nature within us, but here she takes over and we have the birth of little Zeus. Kronos, the father of Zeus, had castrated his

FIGURE 83. Zeus, Leto, Apollo, and Artemis (carved marble, Classical, Greece, fourth century B.C.)

own father, Ouranos, and was therefore afraid that his sons might castrate him, and so he began to eat his children as they were born. Rhea, his wife, substituted a stone in swaddling clothes for little Zeus when he was born and she spirited Zeus away to Mount Ida on Crete, where he was taken care of by the nymphs and by *kouretes*—young warriors. The *kouretes* performed a great dance, clashing their shields with their swords in order to make more noise than the baby's cry, and so to hide the infant Zeus from Kronos.

Here we see the wedding of Zeus and Hera (Fig. 85), where she is about to unclothe herself and he, in love, regards her.

While Classical Olympian mythology claims Hera as Zeus's wife, she is a much older goddess, predating the Indo-European Bronze Age syncretism. She was therefore independent of, and more powerful than, Zeus at the time of that mythology's appearance. As Harrison points out, "In Olympia, where Zeus in historical days ruled if anywhere supreme, the ancient Heraion where Hera was worshipped alone long predates the temple of Zeus.... Homer himself was dimly haunted by the memory of days when Hera was no wife, but Mistress in her own right."[23]

FIGURE 84. *Kouretes* dancing around the infant Zeus (terra-cotta relief, location unknown, date unknown)

FIGURE 85. Wedding of Hera and Zeus (carved marble, Classical, Sicily, c. 450–425 B.C.)

Baring and Cashford continue:

> In one story even [Hera's] marriage comes by subterfuge: during a thunderstorm in which Hera was separated from the other goddesses and gods, sitting alone on the mountain where her temple was later to be built, Zeus transforms himself into a cuckoo, wet and bedraggled from the rain, and settles in Hera's lap. Taking pity on the poor bird, she covers him with her robe, and Zeus reveals himself. Here, Zeus is drawn as the intruder who steals marriage, not the great god who claims it.

Kerényi comments, "by this unique mythological creation Zeus is *precisely fitted into the history of the Hera religion of Argos.*"[24]

ARES

Ares, superior force,
Ares, chariot rider,

Ares wears gold helmet,
Ares has mighty heart,
Ares, shield-bearer,
Ares, guardian of city,
Ares has armor of bronze,
Ares has powerful arms,
Ares never gets tired,
Ares, hard with spear,
Ares, rampart of Olympos,
Ares, father of Victory
who herself delights in war,
Ares, helper of Justice,
Ares overcomes other side,
Ares leader of most just men,
Ares carries staff of manhood,
Ares turns his fiery bright cycle
among the Seven-signed tracks
of the aether, where flaming chargers
bear him forever
over the third orbit!
Hear me,
helper of mankind,
dispenser of youth's sweet courage,
beam down from up there
your gentle light
on our lives,
and your martial power,
so that I can shake off
cruel cowardice
form my head,
and diminish that deceptive rush
of my spirit, and restrain
that shrill voice in my heart
that provokes me
to enter the chilling din of battle.
You, happy god,
give me courage,
let me linger
in the safe laws of peace,
and thus escape
from battles with enemies
and the fate of a violent death.[25]

FIGURE 86. Ares and Aphrodite (fresco, Roman, Italy, date unknown)

Another deity who comes from the Indo-European context is Ares, the god of war. We have seen him linked up to Aphrodite, the goddess of the morning star, like Inanna and Ishtar; like them she is the Great Goddess, the personification of the feminine divine. Ares gets into relationship with the Goddess in this way.

The principal deities of the patriarchal traditions were male deities. The most extreme example of this masculine accent is in our own Old Testament, where there are no goddesses. In the biblical tradition, the old goddesses were simply eliminated, whereas what the Greeks did, as we've already seen, was to marry the god to the Goddess, or to make the god the protector of the Goddess, or to make the Goddess the protector of the god. They established a relationship that tied themselves and their own deities to the land and the local cult in an interactive way.

This is quite in contrast to the pattern we get in the story of Judah and Israel and the Yahwist attempt to superimpose the cult of Yahweh on the other Semitic people, who had gone over to the land. This history of the Old Testament is really the history of kings who abandoned Yahweh to sacrifice on the hilltops to the gods and the goddesses of the nature world and of the attempt of the Yahwists to establish their deity against this.

You don't have that kind of thing with the Greeks. Rather, what you have is the development of a relationship between the masculine and feminine aspects of the divine.

ATHENA

I'll start this singing with
that grand goddess,
Pallas Athena,
bright-eyes,
so shrewd,
her heart inexorable,
as virgin, redoubtable,
protectress of cities,
powerful,
Tritogene,
whom shrewd Zeus himself
produced
out of his sacred head—
bedecked in that
spangly gold war armor
she wears—
what awe enthralled
all those immortals
who saw her

jump suddenly
out of his sacred head
shaking
her sharp spear,
right out of Zeus
who holds the aegis!
Great Olympos itself
shook terribly
under the might
of bright-eyes,
the earth groaned
awfully and the ocean
was moved to foam up
with dark waves,
then as sudden
the salt sea stopped.
The glorious son of Hyperion,
the sun, stood
his fast-footed horses still
for a long time,
until the girl
took that god-like armor
from her immortal shoulders.
Shrewd Zeus
laughed
And so, greetings to you,
daughter of Zeus,
who holds the aegis.
I will remember you
in another song.[26]

The birth of Athena from the head of Zeus is another example of this patriarchal culture assimilating the Goddess. Metis, an Oceanid titan and—by one reckoning—Zeus's first wife, is pregnant, and an oracle tells him that Metis will have two children: one will be wise and powerful, but the second will kill him. Zeus doesn't like that idea, so he turns his pregnant wife into a fly and swallows her. In the course of things, Metis gives birth. Then one day Zeus has a terrible headache and calls in Hephaestus with his ax, who splits open Zeus's head—and out pops Athena, fully armed.

FIGURE 87. Athena of Piraeus (bronze, Classical, Greece, c. 360–340 B.C.)

FIGURE 88. The birth of Athena (black-figure kylix, Archaic, Greece, c. 560 B.C.)

FIGURE 89. Athena with Jason, disgorged by dragon (red-figure vase, Classical, Greece, c. 490–480 B.C.)

FIGURE 90. Athena with Gorgoneion and snakes (red-figure amphora, Classical, Greece, c. 530–520 B.C.)

This remarkable piece (Fig. 89) was first made generally public by Jane Harrison. It shows Athena wearing the breast plate of the head of Medusa—the same goddess in her apotropaic or dangerous, repellent aspect, with the tongue out—and in her hand is the owl of Athens, which is her totem bird. There is Athena in her character as

an inspirer and protector, or *śakti*, of heroes. You can see Pegasus on
her helmet—Pegasus having been born when Medusa was beheaded.
You were not to look at the head of Medusa, as she would turn you
to stone, and so Athena offered the shield to Perseus, and looking at
the shield by reflection he slew her. Then when Perseus took Medusa's
head and put it into a bag, Pegasus, the winged horse, was born from

FIGURE 91. Goddess with snakes (faience, Minoan, Crete, c. 1600 B.C.)

her severed neck, and Medusa's head then became the *Gorgoneian* on Athena's breastplate.

In these two pieces (Figs. 90 and 91) we see the goddess behind the whole thing, the Great Goddess of Crete. *Athena* actually means "protectress of the port"—thus you can have Athena of Athens, Athena of Pireaus, Athena of Ephesus. She goes back to this Mycenaean and Minoan protector figure with the serpents (Fig. 91). This is a perfect example of the way deities were assimilated and transformed into Classical shapes.

FIGURE 92. Paris abducting Helen (carved marble relief, Roman, Italy, date unknown)

CHAPTER 6

Iliad and Odyssey

RETURN TO THE GODDESS[1]

The Iliad represents the male-oriented Indo-European world and Zeus, Apollo, and the Olympians in general figure in it the most prominently. Following *The Iliad*, we come to *The Odyssey*, where we have the return of the Goddess.

It was Samuel Butler who said that *The Odyssey* was probably written by a woman.[2] The change in mode and mood from *The Iliad* and its the male war- and achievement-oriented psychology to that of *The Odyssey*, where learning about life from the goddess, is very important. I want to tell the story of *The Iliad* and *The Odyssey* with a certain little inflection that's all my own.

The Odyssey is the tale of Odysseus's wanderings from the time of his fleet being blown about by the gods to his final return home, cast ashore asleep on Ithaca. In the first part of the story, he is dealing with human beings on the surface of the Earth. Once he lands in the Land of the Lotus Eaters, he's in the world of myth and monsters, and the characters he meets are all mythological: the Cyclops, Scylla and Charybdis, Laestrygonians, monsters; Circe, Calypso, and Nausicaa, all nymphs. When finally he wakes up at home again and goes to his palace, he finds that during his absence his wife's suitors have been usurping him, and then comes the conclusion—the routing of the suitors and the reunion with Penelope. This is obviously a mythological journey, and the principle transformative experiences are with these nymphs—that is to say, the female principle.

Consider Circe, Calypso, and little Nausicaa. When we study these figures, we see that Circe is the temptress, Calypso the wife, and Nausicaa the virgin. Now, think back on the cause of the Trojan

War: three goddesses, Aphrodite, Hera, and Athena, are competing, with Paris as the judge, for the beauty prize. These are the dominant goddess principles, and they represent aspects of the manifestation of female power.

THE JUDGMENT OF PARIS

Aphrodite is the erotic impulse absolute, and her counterpart in *The Odyssey* is Circe. Hera, the spouse of Zeus, is the matron, the household mother of the universe, and her counterpart is Calypso with whom Odysseus lived for seven years. Athena is the virgin goddess, born from Zeus's brain, the daughter of the Father, she who is the inspirer and patron of heroes, and her counterpart is little Nausicaa. Each represents these aspects of the female power, aspects of the energy of life: *śakti*.

FIGURE 93. The Judgment of Paris (red-figured stamnos, Classical, Greece, c. fifth century B.C.)

When Paris is asked to judge the three goddesses, says Jane Harrison in her wonderful book *Prolegomena to the Study of Greek Religion*, it amounts to a male put-down of the Goddess. For here were the three major classical goddesses, the three aspects of the one Goddess who is manifested in these three modes, and here is Paris, a languid young man, judging them as though in an Atlantic City beauty contest! And they are vying for his vote by giving him bribes and promises.

Aphrodite says, "Choose me and I'll get you Helen of Troy. Helen, the most beautiful woman in the world—only inconveniently married to Menelaus, but so what, I'll get her for you."

Hera says, "Choose me and I will give you majesty, dignity, and power among men."

And Athena says, "Choose me and I will give you heroic fame."

Now, what is actually happening here, as Jane Harrison points out, is that this young man is choosing a life's career: deciding which of these patron goddesses he is to follow as the dominant one. He is choosing his spiritual mistress as guardian and guide, and the reinterpretation of this is nothing but a patriarchal put-down of the Great Goddess herself.

So there you have the supposed cause of the Trojan War, ten years of he-man stuff—woman and booty. When Achilles, the great Greek hero, goes off and sulks in his tent, what is the big quarrel between him and Agamemnon about? The argument that caused Achilles to neglect the war—is it strategy or tactics? No, it is "who gets the blonde?"

Now, this is an attitude toward the female that is totally different from that which is proper in a dialogue between the sexes.

After Odysseus has had ten years of this war, he starts for home with his fleet of twelve ships—and as soon as you hear the number twelve you know that it is a mythological situation. The twelve ships represent aspects of Odysseus's own essence. He and his men go ashore on the way home, and there they rape the women and ravage the town just for fun. But when they return to their ships the gods say, "This is no way for a man to return to his wife!" He needs to be reintroduced, or as they would say today, debriefed.

So for ten days the gods blow the ships about until they come ashore at the Land of the Lotus Eaters. From then on they are in the realm of dreams and visions, the world of myth. Odysseus will encounter three nymphs, and not one of them can be pushed around, because he must meet the female principle on her own terms. Of course, he gets help from Hermes, and it is interesting to note that in *The Odyssey* the warrior hero's guiding god is not Ares, the god of war, nor Apollo, nor Zeus, but Hermes: the messenger-god who guides souls to rebirth in eternal life. And through the initiation by the three goddesses who were slighted in the beginning by the Judgment of Paris, he is made ready to return home to his wife, Penelope, and rescue her from the suitors.

With Penelope there appears another interesting motif: that of weaving. During Odysseus's absence, she has been weaving daily a tapestry and at night unraveling it. This is a ruse to keep her suitors at bay, for she has promised she will choose one when she finishes her weaving. Now, all the female figures to whom Odysseus is introduced pick up this theme: Circe of the braided locks, weaving a tapestry; Calypso also of braided locks weaving a tapestry; and little Nausicaa, doing the laundry. This is the female as Māyā, weaver of the world of illusion, creator of the tapestry of the world.

Odysseus kept a herd of swine with three hundred sixty boars (the cycle of the conventional year of the old traditions), and he had been gored in the thigh by the tusk of one of these boars. Adonis was slain by a boar; the Irish hero Diarmuid was killed by a boar; Osiris the dying and resurrected god of Egypt was killed by his brother Set while hunting boar—this relationship to the chthonic boar, to the dead and resurrected god, is a theme throughout mythology, and throughout *The Odyssey.*

If the moon and the sun are in the same sign of the Zodiac at the spring equinox, it will be twenty years before they are in the same position. How long was Odysseus gone from Penelope? Twenty years. The problem of coordinating lunar and solar mythologies was a major one in this period, and the story is steeped in that context.

Now, I have pointed out that the sun, which has no shadow within it and which represents life eternal, is the symbol of consciousness disengaged from the field of time and space. The moon, however, which dies and is resurrected monthly, is exactly consciousness *within* the field of time and space. The realization is that the two are one, that our eternal and temporal life are one; we are not to ask, "Shall I be alive after my death?" but to experience the eternal principle here and now. This is the main point. What is the relationship of that solar to this lunar life we are living? This is the problem represented in *The Iliad* and *The Odyssey* by the effort to coordinate the two mythologies, and the answer comes in terms of the powers of the goddess.

As I have said, every one of these goddesses is the whole Goddess, and the others are inflections of her powers. Aphrodite is the divine goddess whose powers are inflected throughout the world as the power of love, of the dynamics of the energy represented by Eros, who is Aphrodite's child and a major deity of the classical pantheon— in Plato's *Symposium* he is the original god of the world. In her one aspect of lust she plays a role in the triad in which Hera also takes a role and Athena another, but she actually could play all the roles herself. As total Goddess, she is the energy that supports the *śakti* of the whole universe. In later systems, the three Graces come to represent three aspects of her power to send energy into the world, draw energy back to the source, and unite the two powers.

In the old mythology, the Goddess had been seen as the dominant creative energy of the universe. When the male mythology came in with the Indo-Europeans, we find a change of accent. As I mentioned earlier, the story as told by Hesiod is that the heaven god Ouranos was lying so closely upon the body of his mother Gaia, who had become his consort, that the children in the Goddess's womb could not be born. By the magic of her ancient power, Gaia gave to Kronos, the eldest and most courageous of the sons in her womb, a sickle with which to castrate his father. So Kronos castrates Ouranos and separates heaven from Earth.

Now this theme of the separation of heaven and Earth is one that occurs in most mythologies in one way or another. We see it in the Egyptian myth of Nut, the sky goddess, being pressed up from the Earth god Geb. There's an amusing version from Nigeria in which a woman is pounding grain in a great big tub with a great big pole, and the top of the pole keeps hitting the sky, so the sky king moves up, and up, and up.

One way or another, we have this separation of heaven and Earth, which in the beginning were one, and the original cosmic androgyne becomes male and female. After Kronos castrated his father, he simply

FIGURE 94. The birth of Aphrodite (carved marble, Classical, Greece, or possibly Italy in a Greek style, c. 470–460 B.C.)

flung the genitalia over his shoulder into the sea, where they kicked up great foam—and out of the foam was born Aphrodite.

With this story you see another put-down of the Great Goddess, since she was already there, but now the story has been turned upside-down so that she becomes only a manifestation of Ouranos's sexual powers. And in art she is often represented on a seashell, as in the famous Botticelli work, and she was known as "the foam-born" or "ocean-born." In later Hellenistic and Roman representations, during a period of prudery, she was shown covering her genitals, but in the earlier mode of the Goddess it was precisely these that represented the power of her being.

FIGURE 95. Ares, Aphrodite, and Eros in the war against the Giants (red-figure amphora, Classical, Greece, c. 400–390 B.C.)

As love and war are irrevocably connected, Ares is represented as Aphrodite's lover. Aphrodite's first relationship is to Ares (Fig. 95), and the words "All is fair in love and war" belong to him. Venus and

Mars are the two planets that are represented on either side of the sun in the classical astrological system.

Aphrodite's other male association is with Hermes (Fig. 96), the lord who guides us through to immortal life. This is the *śakti* energy inspiring both war and mystic illumination. Hermes represents the way to mystical illumination. The little chariot is drawn by two horses named Eros and Psyche.

FIGURE 96. Aphrodite and Hermes (terra-cotta, Classical, Greece, 470 B.C.)

Ares and Hermes are the two prime relationships from the female point of view. One is to the young male, the defender, the warrior, the dragon slayer, while the other is to the wise, older Hermes who guides the souls to immortal wisdom and immortal life. The staff of Hermes, called the caduceus, has two interlocking serpents representing solar and lunar energy. He is often portrayed with his totem animal, the dog. The dog can follow an invisible path, and the path to a longer life is the path that Hermes gives us. Hermes was normally represented as the one in relationship to Hera, Aphrodite, and Athena in the Judgment of Paris.

FIGURE 97. The Judgment of Paris (red-figured krater, Classical, Greece, fifth century B.C.)

Jane Harrison shows us yet another picture of the Judgment of Paris (Fig. 97), describing the scene fittingly as a beauty contest.

Hermes comes to Paris to invite him to make his choice among the three goddesses. Aphrodite is being fixed up by Eros to make her very attractive—he puts a bracelet on her. You see Hermes's dog and the deer, which is associated with Artemis but can also belong to any of these goddesses. Hera is in a very decent way arranging herself nicely as befits a proper matron, and Athena, in the words of Jane Harrison, "is just having a good wash."[3]

Then comes the judgment whereby Paris, by his choice of Aphrodite, brings about the abduction of Helen, wife of Menelaus of Sparta, which launches the world war of the twelfth century B.C., undertaken to recover Helen.

FIGURE 98. The Judgment of Paris (red-figured krater, Classical, Greece, fifth century B.C.)

Harrison then goes on to propose a very different interpretation of these events of Paris's Judgment. In this red-figured vase from the fifth century B.C. (Fig. 98), you see the three goddesses, no beauties in any man's view, standing each with the sign of the world cycle, the wheel of destiny, in her hands, and Hermes is telling Paris, "You've just got to face it, boy." Paris, however, is trying to run away from the responsibility of choosing the course of his life, his destiny, as represented by the goddesses. As Harrison puts it,

> Hermes actually seizes Paris by the wrist to compel his attendance. There is here clearly no question of voluptuous delight at the beauty of the goddesses. The three maiden figures are scrupulously alike; each carries a wreath. Discrimination would be a hard task.[4]

These are the three *śakti*, representing three life paths: What is the youth going to have as his career? Are you going to follow the way of Athena to the heroic life, are you going to follow the way of Aphrodite to the erotic, or are you going to follow the way of Hera to the way of royal rule, majesty, and dignity?

The powers symbolized in the personifications of the deities are the entities that inform ourselves as natural objects, as well as the natural world in which we live, so they are both out there and in here, within us. The way to approach them may be either through outward address, and this is the attitude that's represented by the address of prayer, or in the Hindu way, which is that of meditation.

Now, we have enough statements by shamans, as well as material from the traditional scriptures of the world, to know that this is the way deities are understood. The energies that inform the world may be thought of as one variant of a single energy, or as differentiated entities, pairing this, that, or another aspect of nature with our own lives. So the deities may be thought of either as total or as specified.

Max Müller coined a term when he began to realize that the Hindu deities could be addressed either as specifically informing the fire or the winds or the solar light, or on the other hand, as total deities: *henotheism*. That is to say, an individual god can be understood as representing to the mind a totality of the entities of the universe. In this case, he would be the divine creator figure, though not really a creator, but rather one through whom the entities of creation come.

On the other hand, a god may be addressed as representing this, that, or another specific inflection of the totality. So it goes with these goddesses of the Greeks. The Greeks participate in this mutual manner of experiencing deities.

I have said that a deity or a myth is a metaphor transparent to transcendence. After seventy years of thinking about these things, I finally discovered this term in the work of the Jungian psychiatrist Karlfried von Dürkheim. A deity or myth is a metaphor—you have to remember it's a metaphor—transparent to transcendence, and then it can lead you beyond your powers of knowledge.

That's the same idea that comes to us through the German Romantics, as well as out of India. To Goethe's *"Alles Vergängliche ist nur ein Gleichnis"* ("Everything transitory is but a reference"),[5] Nietzsche adds another point: *"Alles Unvergängliche—das ist nur ein Gleichnis"* ("All things eternal are only references as well").[6] That's the point of deities: they are personifications, metaphorical representations of the powers that are operating in our lives right now. There's a truth in them—it is the truth of our own lives and attitudes. The god that one chooses to revere as one's primary deity represents a choice of the powers that are going to be prime in one's life. One chooses one or another aspect of one's living as the possibility that one is going to represent among the real.

Now, in our open society we can make our own choices. In a traditional society, individuals can minimize risks through this, that, or another career, each of which might be seen as being under the aegis of this, that, or another, actual deity. This is the problem of the judgment of powers and the whole Classical idea of Paris as choosing the most *beautiful* of the goddesses: he was being required to choose the deity who was going to be his *śakti*, the energy that defines the meaning of his life. Because this is what the female powers represent in these myths—the energies of which the male is simply the agent— and as a muse, or as a mother goddess, or as the inspirer of a heroic life, these goddesses are reflections of the main force that the female represents, as one who is herself open to nature. Her life is one that is moved by nature in a way that the male is not.

These three goddesses are Paris's three possible fates, and his choice has to do with the relationship of the male and female powers. All the goddesses are to be talked about in the way of relationship, and as far as I know there are no representations of goddesses or gods out of relationship with the polarities of the world.

Paris chooses Aphrodite, and she rewards him with Helen.

THE ILIAD

Helen was Menelaus's wife—apparently they were both originally deities of Sparta. There are two aspects of Classical mythology: one is that which got put together by the literary people after the seventh and sixth centuries B.C., and the other is that of the local cults. When you go to Sparta or Boeotia you find locally grounded cults that are associated with local rituals. In what might be called the Athenian literary redaction, the characters are deracinated—lifted out of their roots—and played into an epic narrative.

So Helen is abducted and Menelaus goes to his brother Agamemnon and says, "This Trojan guy, he's run off with my wife!"

Agamemnon says, "Hmm, that won't do, we've got to go get her back!" This is wife-as-property. So they got together an army of heroes and had ships carry them to Troy.

Now, none of these heroes want to go on this expedition. Odysseus makes believe he is insane to avoid conscription. He has just married and his wife has had a little boy and so he wants to stay home.

But Agamemnon has a fine idea: "Mad, are you?" he says, and puts the little boy Telemachus into the furrow before the plow that Odysseus was driving. Odysseus stops and the game is up and off he goes to war.

Agamemnon and Odysseus then recruit the warrior Achilles, as he's the one without whom they can't win.

Now comes a very unfortunate event: the ships are all assembled, ready to sail to Troy, but there isn't any wind: Agamemnon's troops have offended Artemis by killing a pregnant hare. Calchas, the fleet priest, advises Agamemnon that a sacrifice is needed to get up a wind—a human sacrifice. So Agamemnon sends home to his wife, Clytemnestra, for his youngest daughter, Iphigenia, and she is sacrificed to make the winds come up. And of course when Agamemnon finally comes home after the war, his wife kills him. And who could blame her?

In this Roman representation (Fig. 99), Iphigenia's father, Agamemnon, is on the left and he can't look. At the right is the priest, who is saying, "Should we *really*...?"

Up at the top is Artemis. Martin Nilsson, one of the great authorities on Greek religious antiquity, writes that Artemis was the total Great Goddess and represented all the powers of nature. With the

FIGURE 99. The sacrifice of Iphigenia (fresco, Roman, Italy, c. A.D. 79)

differentiation of the goddesses and the departmentalizing of powers, Artemis came to be associated with the nature world and the forest; she became the Mother of the Wild Things. In Euripides's version, just as Iphigenia is to be sacrificed, Artemis substitutes an illusionary Iphigenia and goes off with the real Iphigenia, who becomes Artemis's priestess in Tauris.

In *The Iliad*, however, Iphigenia is sacrificed and this brings the wind and the army heads to Troy.

Achilles is the hero of *The Iliad*, but he's not described as the noble man—that title belongs to Hector the Trojan. The Greeks are just as much interested in the enemy as in their own troops, and they describe them with dignity and compassion and appreciation.

A very interesting illustration of this occurs when Odysseus and Diomedes capture a Trojan named Dolon. There is a sense of respect for the other side: champions are matched as equals, and this is particularly Greek. This is characteristic of these epics and tragedies. Aeschylus wrote his tragedy *The Persians* only a few years after he himself had been in battle against the Persians, and the humanity with which he treats his former enemy is something typically Greek.

The Homeric epics date to almost exactly the same period as the Book of Judges. Read the Book of Judges and see the way in which the Semitic Israelites regard their enemy. It's a very different story.

Homer begins *The Iliad* with the words, "I sing the wrath of Achilles." Now, why was Achilles angry? There are two reasons, and they come in two stages.

FIGURE 100. Briseis and Achilles (fresco, Roman, Italy, c. A.D. 20–50)

The first concerned Briseis, a beautiful captive woman. Achilles had her, but Agamemnon wanted her and he pulled rank to get her. So what is Achilles's response? He broods in his tent and won't come out and fight. And since Achilles is a hero and a powerful fighter, the battle can't go on without him. Eventually, Odysseus is sent to Achilles's tent to persuade him. Here we have the guru or instructor being played by Odysseus. Still Achilles doesn't come out—until his buddy Patroclos is killed while wearing Achilles' armor.

Now, in his wrath, Achilles is going to avenge the death of his friend.

FIGURE 101. Andromache and Astyanax bidding farewell to Hector
(red-figure krater, Classical, Italy, c. 370–360 B.C.)

Now comes Hector's crucial moment. He is the only one capable
of meeting Achilles as he is the hero of the Trojans. In this krater
(Fig. 101), Hector's wife, Andromache, is carrying their little boy
Astyanax, "the little star." The child is frightened by his father's war
helmet and Hector puts it on the ground and fondles his son. Andromache begs him not to go, telling him he will be killed. Hector says,
"No man has avoided his death by cowardice."

Now, this reply is the Greek counterpart to Kṛṣṇa's exploration
in the Bhagavad Gītā (itself a chapter in the great Hindu epic, the
Mahābhārata) of the same problem: the warrior and the virtue of war.
The Mahābhārata comes from the same kind of people fighting in the
same period as *The Iliad*, and in the Bhagavad Gītā you have what
might be called the mysticism of war. Arjuna, the chief warrior of the
Pandavas (who are trying to get back their territory), asks Kṛṣṇa to
be his charioteer. As the battle is about to start, Arjuna asks Kṛṣṇa to
drive him between the two battle lines before he blows the trumpet
to signal the beginning of battle. When Arjuna is there between the
lines, he sees men on both sides whom he admires, whom he holds as
his masters in philosophy. Arjuna drops his bow and says, "Better I
should die here than precipitate this battle."

Kṛṣṇa asks him, "Whence comes this ignoble cowardice? This is
not befitting a warrior."[7] Kṛṣṇa then recites that wonderful phrase

of the transcendent, which is the battle cry of Gītā: "That which no sword can touch, rain does not wet"[8]—the eternal is not touched by your sword, but processes of history are underway, and it is your duty to participate. Kṛṣṇa gives Arjuna this wonderful clue to the performance of action as yoga. It is the yoga of war—the yoga to perform your duty without fear or desire of the results.

What is the basic principle of action? If you get interested in the results you're going to get thrown off-center, and your performance is going to suffer. Just go right in there without fear or desire, either for yourself or for others, and do what has to be done; take the big step. That is the counterpart in the Indian way of speaking to the stoic words of Hector.

Hector then mounts the chariot and goes to his death. This is the moment of acting, of doing, without fear or desire. Hector is of course killed in battle by Achilles, who does what to us is a really horrible thing: he tied the corpse to his chariot and dragged it around and around Troy. Some say that Hector was captured alive and killed in this way.

Now, was this simply a brutal act of revenge against the once powerful enemy? It isn't made clear what Achilles's motive was, but another interpretation is that the walls of Troy were not only physical walls of stone and mortar but also magical walls, and that this was a magical act to unwind the protective magic of the Trojan walls.

Afterward Priam, the old king and father of Hector, comes humbly to Achilles to beg for the body of his son so he can perform a proper burial (Fig. 102). This was very important in these traditional cultures. The tragedy of *Antigone* springs from this custom.

Now we come to the fine adventure of the Trojan Horse, which Odysseus and Diomedes invent in response to a suggestion of Achilles. They prepare this enormous wooden horse and fill it with soldiers and then have the Greek ships withdraw, leaving this horse on the beach. The Trojans think the war is over and that this trophy has been left in their honor. They drag the Trojan Horse inside the city and then, that night, the soldiers break forth and open the gates, and the Greeks destroy Troy.

Now we come to the matter of the end of the war. Troy falls, the war has been won, and now we have what I call the *nostos*, or the warriors' return to their homes after ten years of battle.

It is on these homecomings that many of the tragic plays are based. The first, of course, is Helen's return to her husband, Menelaus.

FIGURE 102. Priam begging Achilles for the body of Hector (bronze, Archaic, Greece, c. 560 B.C.)

She's been captured in shame, and when she gets into the boat there must have been quite a memorable domestic scene! Again, however, Euripides, in his version of the scene, saves her reputation by saying that it was not Helen who was at Troy but only an image of Helen, an illusory presence, and that Helen was actually hiding in Egypt during the war.

The next big return is that of Agamemnon, and the cycle of killing that began with his sacrifice of Iphigenia continues with his own murder by his wife, Clytemnestra, and then her murder by her son Orestes. Now, in any culture murdering a mother is about as hideous a deed as can be performed, but in the Greek world of this time there's a question: Was Orestes the son of this mother or the son of this father? Are we reckoning relationships in the matrilineal line or the patrilineal line? If the inheritance is in the father line, and the father has been murdered, then it is the son's duty to kill the murderer of his father, in this case his own mother. If, on the other hand, the inheritance is in the female line, then killing his father's murderer is not his duty, as the father is inconsequential—it becomes a personal act and therefore a sin.

Here we see the conflict between the two systems: the earlier mother-right base that had survived in the countryside among the *pagani* (Latin, meaning "rustic people"—hence the word *pagans*), and the later, Indo-European, patriarchal father-right system, which was that adopted by the Achaean Greeks, and in particular by the city of Athens. As representatives of the patriarchal system, Apollo and Athena declare that Orestes was not guilty and they are going to allay or hold off the female power of the Furies by making a pig sacrifice over Orestes.[9]

In this image (Fig. 103), Orestes is being purified of his bloodguilt for killing Clytemnestra at Apollo's shrine at Delphi. (Notice that it is the omphalos he's sitting against.) Apollo is on the right bathing him in the blood of the pig—Orestes is cleansed in the blood of the lamb, as it were. The sacrifice of the pig is made to allay the wrath of the Furies, who represent the chthonic underworld powers and the mother line; the pig sacrifice is going to be very important in *The Odyssey*. Artemis stands behind Apollo carrying hunting spears. On the right are two sleeping Erinyes (Furies) whom Athena has put to sleep. The woman touching the sleeping Erinyes is the shade of Clytemnestra, bidding them to wake and avenge her. The Erinyes are ancient deities in the Greek tradition, "the avengers of offences against blood-relations on the mother's and father's side, of all offences against moral, and finally even natural law."[10] They represent "a human relation intensely felt…the outraged soul of the dead man crying for vengeance."[11]

Orestes is cleansed, and the male principle dominates.

The pig, as we saw in Çatal Hüyük, was the domestic animal representing the chthonic powers. The Achaeans come in with the cattle herds and their own gods, to whom a cow or bull would be sacrificed instead. The powers that have to be appeased in Orestes's case, however, are the powers of the Earth, the Furies, the Mother Goddess powers. Jane Harrison talks about the difference between the two sacrifices: the Achaean sacrifice is a meal shared with the gods, while the old pig sacrifice is what was known as a *holocaust* (literally, "a complete burning"): the killing of the animal, with the blood and ashes poured into the Earth, and so it is not a shared meal.[12]

FIGURE 103. The purification of Orestes (red-figure krater, Classical, Greece, c. 370 B.C.)

THE ODYSSEY

We now come to the great *nostos* story: the return of Odysseus.

As I see it, the quest of Odysseus is to return home, decently, to Penelope, his wife—not to *a blonde*, not to someone who is the victim and the booty of war, but to *his wife*. A wife is someone with whom one is in counterplay as the other side of the mystery of the androgyne, and so Odysseus has to be debriefed from his warrior attitude, where there is no idea of dialogue between the male and female powers.

I regard *The Odyssey* as a book of initiations, and the first initiation is that of Odysseus himself into a proper relationship to the female power, which was put down at the time of the Judgment of Paris when the male principle was dominant in an excessive way.

Now the female power must be recognized to make possible a proper relationship—what I call an androgynous relationship—in which the male and female meet as co-equals. They are equals, but not the same, because when you lose the tension of polarities you lose the tension of life.

There's a second initiation in *The Odyssey*, and that is of Odysseus's son Telemachus. When Odysseus was inducted into Agamemnon's army, he and Penelope had just married and had a little boy together. Odysseus has been away for twenty years—ten years fighting the war, and ten years lost in the Mediterranean—so Telemachus is twenty years old and he's been with his mother the whole time. Athena comes to him in the form of a young man and says, "Go find your father."

The first initiation, then, is Odysseus, the initiation of the mature man to the life of charity in marriage.

The second is the initiation of the male youth Telemachus to his manhood, leaving the mother and going to the father.

The third is the initiation of Penelope, the wife whose husband is away, and her endurance and faithfulness through the temptations of the suitors in loyalty to her spouse. So, this is a fantastic compendium of initiation as conceived in these countries: the initiation of youth, the initiation of full manhood, and the initiation of the woman.

With twelve ships Odysseus sets sail from Troy and goes north to the town of Ismarus. When the ships and warriors arrive, what do they do? They ravage the town and ravish the women. The priest of Ismarus actually thanks Odysseus for not raping his daughter. These men were that rapacious.

The gods say, "This is no way for a man to go home to his wife! This is not the proper relationship of a male to a female for a domestic existence."

So they blow those twelve ships astray for ten days. What Odysseus is going to have to do in order to get where he wants to go is to meet those three goddesses and appease them. Aphrodite, Hera, and Athena are going to appear in the forms of three nymphs Circe, Calypso, and Nausicaa.

I think it is utterly fascinating that the three powers that in the early Homeric period were disregarded in their majesty now have to be regarded in their full power. So we're going to see the story of the visionary journey of reintegration of the male and female into a reciprocal relationship, rather than an over-prominence of one or the other.

Blown by the wind, the ships find themselves in North Africa, and the Land of the Lotus Eaters. There they're all put to sleep, sent into dreamland—and from there until Odysseus wakes on the beach of Ithaca he meets not human beings but monsters and nymphs. That is to say, that from this point on his is a dream journey: Odysseus goes into the unconscious, down into that part of himself that has been disregarded and that he must assimilate.

When the troops on the twelve vessels eat the lotus, it sends them off to the dreamland, and Odysseus has to drag them back onboard one by one and tie them to the hull of the ship.

So now we know the problem: he is coming from a world that has rejected and denied the female principle, trying to dominate it or subsume it into the patriarchal system, and now he is going to have to face the sheer force of this and submit to it. We are passing from the world of latent consciousness to the world of dreams, from the world of rational objects to the world of mystic, metaphorical experiences. We're going to go through the mythological journey in a perfectly classic way. We're thrown out of the normal life, because something is missing—namely, a proper relationship of the male to the female.

We go into the mythic journey, crossing a threshold into dreamland, and the first meeting is with what is called a threshold guardian, the power that represents the transition from the realm of everyday to the realm of the mysteries. The threshold guardian is a threatening monster and is almost always a lower manifestation of the same power that you will encounter when you finally get to the end of the journey.

So the first power that Odysseus meets with is Polyphemus the Cyclops, that one-eyed figure. The one eye represents the bull's eye, the narrow gate through which one has to pass on the way to initiation. Polyphemus is a son of Poseidon, the lord of the abyssal waters who rules over this whole adventure—he is lord of the unconscious—and who is the Greek counterpart of Śiva. Odysseus and his twelve men go into the cave to see what land they've come to. They find there some jars and pots full of milk, cheese, and butter, and they know they have come to the dwelling of a shepherd of some kind.

Now, the shepherd comes in, and lo and behold, he's this enormous giant with one eye in the center of his forehead, and he's a man-eater. He says to Odysseus, "Well, who are you?"

Thinking quickly, Odysseus says, "I am no man." That's the first stage in self-divestiture as one goes into the magic realm. He doesn't boast; he doesn't say, for example, "I am Odysseus, haven't you heard of me?" No, "I am no man." We're going to see a succession of divestitures as he goes into the abyss.

The Cyclops says, "Well, there's a good meal here," and so he grabs two of the men and tears them apart, and things look bad.

FIGURE 104. Odysseus blinding Polyphemus (black-figure vase, Archaic, Greece, date unknown)

After Polyphemus has eaten his snack for a while, Odysseus says, "Would you like a little wine with your meal?"

Well, Polyphemus has never had wine, and so he accepts, and it makes him very sleepy and drunk.

Odysseus and one of his men then take a big beam, sharpen it, and harden it in the fire and then they drive it into the one eye of the sleeping Cyclops. The scene is described in beautiful detail—the beam goes in and you hear the moisture in the eye: *crickle, crackle, boil,* and *split.*

Polyphemus is still alive, so he shouts and makes a lot of noise and all the neighboring Cyclopes say, "What's the matter in there, who's hurting you?"

And of course Polyphemus screams back, "No man!"

"Well, then," the other Cyclopes grumble, "shut up."

So Odysseus has saved himself by divesting himself.

The Cyclops's eye is out, so he can't see, but he's there in the cave and Odysseus and his men have to get out—so Polyphemus sets himself at the gate. He's just going to wait for them.

Odysseus, man of many wiles, has an idea. He takes three of the sheep, ties them together, and puts one of his men under the central sheep and sends him out. Another, another, another, another—six times three, this is the eighteenth sheep. The Cyclops just feels all these that come by and says, "Oh, these are my sheep, they're going out to graze."

So all the men get out.

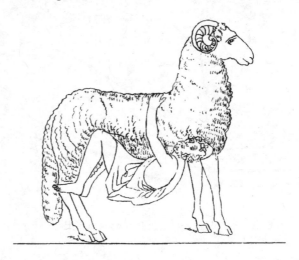

FIGURE 105. Odysseus under a ram (bronze, Archaic, Greece, c. 520–500 B.C.)

Odysseus gets under the great ram.

Now, in that period the ram was symbolic of the sun, the solar principle now as male power. In Egypt, the sun god Amon-Re was represented as a ram. Nobody would have read this account without

knowing that Odysseus here had identified himself with the sun journey. He has identified himself with the sun, and as we're going to find
out, he ends up on the Island of the Sun. This is important: he has cast
off his secular character and he has identified himself with the solar
energy, the solar consciousness, the solar life. He passes the Cyclops.

We have passed the threshold into the spiritual realm. Now, what
happens when you have passed into the spiritual sphere and left your
secular character outside? When you have cast off the material life,
you are in danger of what the psychologists call inflation: "I am so
spiritual."

Having crossed the threshold, Odysseus comes to the Island of
the Winds and the god Aeolus, the lord of wind, of *prāṇa* (Sanskrit:
"breath, spirit"). Now, this god has a curious custom: he has twelve
sons and twelve daughters, and he marries them to each other. He's
also a very generous host, so when this army of twelve ships arrives,
he takes them in and entertains them. When they're about to leave,
Aeolus gives Odysseus a gift, a wallet full of wind. "There's enough
wind in there," he tells Odysseus, "to get you back to Ithaca—only
don't open it all at once. Be patient."

They get aboard and as they're sailing back Odysseus gradually
falls asleep. The leader himself represents controlling consciousness,
but the crew represent the *id* power—the "I want" power. So when
Odysseus falls asleep, the men are curious and impatient, and they
open the windbag, and *poof,* that's the end of that: now they don't
have any wind. They are now becalmed.

This is known as *deflation*—and the whole cycle is manic-
depressive. This is a rather common psychological pattern: you think
you're divine and…oh, no, then you are not. We can't separate this
dynamic from being human. The temperament of the middle is the
virtue that is needed. So the crew have crossed the threshold, they
have passed through the narrow gate, they have experienced inflation,
and now nothing more.

So now they are back to rowing—could anything be more humil-
iating than a great battle fleet *rowing*? They row back to the island of
Aeolus, where they say, "Well, we blew it. Can you give us another?"

And the god says, "Nothing of the kind. Row."

So they go rowing, and the next adventure is that of total depres-
sion. We had inflation, now we come to deflation. They come to an
island that may be Sardinia, and they go ashore. This is the Island
of the Laestrygonians. As you read the epic you gradually become

aware of how horrible these people really are, and what great danger the Greeks are in. The Laestrygonians are cannibals, and when Odysseus sends three scouts ashore, they grab one and put him in the pot. The other two scouts flee but are pursued by the Laestrygonians, who hurl great boulders down and smash all the ships but Odysseus's own to splinters. So now Odysseus has only one ship left, and the men are madly rowing.

This is the abyss. This is divestiture in grand style: one ship, rowing. Across the threshold, past the narrow gate, inflation, deflation, and now we come to the Island of the Dawn, ruled by Circe of the braided locks, skilled in all enchantments but with no great fondness for humankind.

This is the great crisis of the story. We are in the abyss, we are down and out, and we come ashore here. We meet the first goddess, representing the temptress—and the temptress is the initiator. The temptress, the seductress: she is the one who leads the hero beyond bounds. She is the goddess Māyā in her initiating aspect.

There on her swampy island she weaves her tapestry, and all around her grunt beasts, those she transformed from human beings. This time Odysseus's scouts are offered a meal—which is drugged. No sooner do they begin to eat it than Circe turns them into swine.

Fortunately for Odysseus he didn't go with them. He's waiting for them to return when who comes but Hermes and says, "You are in trouble. I'm going to give you some help."

So Hermes gives to Odysseus a little plant called *moly* that is going to protect him against the bewitching power of Circe. And then Hermes says, "When you come in, she will be unable to enchant you. Threaten her with your sword, and she will submit—not only that, but she will invite you to her bed. When she does, go."

These are the two powers: the male physical power of action and the female power of magic—the magic power to attract, to repel, and to enchant. Circe and Odysseus face each other, and it's the first experience Odysseus has had of a woman who is his match. He can't push her around, but she can't overcome him because of the help of Hermes. Now comes the picture that I love: she has magic power, he has physical power. He forces her to return his men to their original form. Now we get this interesting statement: *When they were returned to their human form, they are handsomer and stronger and wiser than before.*[13]

FIGURE 106. Odysseus threatening Circe (red-figure lekythos, Classical, Greece, c. fourth century B.C.)

It has dawned on me that not only in this story but also in the Egyptian story of Osiris and in the Aztec story of Quetzalcoatl, the initiator is the temptress, the one who invites and leads the male into the realm outside the ropes, breaking the law.

Circe leads Odysseus through two major initiations: the first is to the underworld where the ancestors dwell. This initiation is into what might be called the biological ground, going down into the underworld to the realm of the ancestral spirits. Ancestors represent the biological generative powers of which we are all productions.

In the underworld Odysseus sacrifices an animal, and the blood attracts the spirits. Among the first spirits to come is the young man Elpenor, who was the helmsman on one of the ships that were sunk by the Laestrygonians. In this underworld the spirits are all just twittering shadows, with the exception of one, and that is Tiresias, who is a three-dimensional presence.

The story of Tiresias is always amusing: Tiresias was out strolling in the forest one day when he came upon two copulating serpents; he put his staff between the two and was transformed into a woman. Well, Tiresias then lived as a woman for eight years. She was out strolling in the forest one day and came upon two copulating serpents, and when she put her staff between them, she was transformed back into a man.

So one fine day on that sunny nudist mountaintop of Olympus, Hera and Zeus were debating who enjoyed sexual intercourse more, the man or the woman. "Well," they said, "you're on that side, I'm on this side. Who can tell? Aahh, let's ask Tiresias!"

So they sent for Tiresias, and Tiresias answered, "Why, the woman. Nine times more." Well, for some reason (which I at one time didn't understand), Hera took this badly and struck him blind. Zeus felt a certain responsibility here and so gave Tiresias the power of prophecy. Blind to the mere phenomenal surfaces, Tiresias could intuit the underlying morphological forms from which all things derive.

But why do you suppose Hera took it badly? Well, after one of my talks on this subject a lady came up to me and said, "I could tell you why Hera took it badly."

"I'm always willing to learn," I said.

And she said, "Because from then on she couldn't say to Zeus, 'I'm doing this for you, darling.'"

So Tiresias is the informer and the representative of this power that was the problem Odysseus had to face—the male not as dominant but as copartner and in counterplay with the other half of the androgyne, of which male and the female are the two parts.

The first initiation that Circe leads Odysseus through, then, is to the biological ground: traveling into the underworld, meeting the ancestors, and realizing that male and female are transcendently one. So Odysseus comes back and he tells Circe, "Well, I learned that lesson."

And she says, "Good. I've got another one for you." Having been initiated into the biological ground of our humanity, Odysseus now has to pass through the second initiation; he must be initiated into the light of consciousness. It turns out that Circe is the daughter of the sun god, Phoebus Apollo. So she says, "I will show you the way to the

FIGURE 107. Odysseus and the Sirens (red-figure krater, Classical, Greece, c. 475 B.C.)

isle of my father, the sun." She tells him the dangers of the way, and these are classic dangers.

First, there are the Sirens, whose song charms and allures sailors, wrecking their ships on the shore. What is the Sirens' song? It is the song of the mystery of the universe that makes it impossible to go on with mere phenomenal work. Later Hellenistic philosophers identified the Sirens with the spheres of the heavens, and their song is the music of the spheres, the music of the universe, which can so enrapture you that your earthly past is forgotten.

I heard the Apollo 9 astronaut Rusty Schweickart tell his experience of the Sirens' song on his flight around and to the moon. He had been given what they call an *extra vehicular activity*. He was to go out of the vehicle in the spacesuit, connected only by the umbilical to the module, and to do some work out there. This work was to be coordinated with something that was to go on inside the module. All those men were kept very busy, so their minds could not experience what he's about to experience. Something went wrong with the machine in the module, and Rusty had five minutes with nothing to do. He was out there, flying through space at the rate of 18,000 miles an hour.

There was no sound, there was no wind, and down below him was Earth, over there was the moon, and up above him was the sun. He said, "I asked myself what had I ever done to deserve this experience?" Now, it's this kind of transcending, mystical experience that can ravish you out of the task of your lifetime.

Another example of being "spaced out" is that of Saint Thomas Aquinas. He was at work on the *Summa Theologica*. He had written about eleven volumes of this thing and had a little bit still to go, when one morning while celebrating Mass he had a mystical experience. He put his pen and ink on the shelf and said, "Everything I have written is straw." Spaced out. After that experience, how are you going to go on with mere temporal work? Well, that's the song of the Sirens.

FIGURE 108. Scylla (silver coin, Classical, Italy, c. fifth century B.C.)

There is a revelation that transcends anything you can do or think, and that is the ultimate mystical experience. And this is what Odysseus wants to get and yet not be tossed on the rocks at the same time. So he stuffs his men's ears with wax and has himself lashed to the mast with no wax in his ears. He tells the helmsman, "No matter what I say, keep me lashed to the mast." For he knows that he is going to be ravished out of his skin.

After the Sirens, we have this strange and ugly business of Scylla and Charybdis. Scylla is a young woman marooned on a rock coast, a high sheer cliff, and the lower part of her body is a kennel of barking dogs. Over on the other side twists a whirlpool, and that is the other goddess, Charybdis. In the Hellenistic period, Scylla was identified with the rock of logic, while Charybdis was identified with the abyss of mysticism. One must sail between—as these are all instructions for moving down through the middle, between each pair of opposites.

After passing these two trials, Odysseus comes to the Isle of the Sun, home of Phoebus Apollo.

Now, there is a taboo on this island: you are not to kill and eat the oxen of the sun. That is to say, when you are in the presence of the ultimate deity you are not to concern yourself with economics. When it comes to this moment of the higher, ultimate experience of the consciousness and the energy of life's light, something happens. It's not, "Let's have a cup of coffee and a sandwich"—you don't have these concerns.

There's a story told of Ramakrishna, the great Indian saint of the nineteenth century in Calcutta. His major disciple was Narendra, who later became known as Swami Vivekananda. One day, as Ramakrishna was going into the temple of the goddess Kālī, whose priest Ramakrishna was, Vivekananda said to Ramakrishna, "You know, there's something I wish the goddess would do for me, to give me. Will you ask her to do this for me?"

Ramakrishna went in, and when he came out, Vivekananda asked, "Well, did you ask her?"

"Oh," Ramakrishna said, "I forgot." So next time he goes in, he's reminded. When he comes out he says, "I forgot."

The point is that when you're in the presence of God you don't have those secondary thoughts.

Odysseus goes to sleep, and his men misbehave and kill the sacred cows and roast and eat them. Apollo registers a complaint with

Zeus against this sacrilege, and when Odysseus and his men launch again, Zeus flings a thunderbolt at their ship, wrecking it and drowning all aboard except Odysseus, who saves himself by clinging to the mast, and he is once more swept back along the path he has just traveled.

He has come to that golden door through which consciousness could easily go into eternal life, never to be reborn, absolutely disengaged from the field of time. That is not his destiny; his destiny is to get back to Penelope and life. Odysseus gets brought back.

Now, there's a very interesting point here: when you have come to this point of high concentration and are about to have a breakthrough to the ultimate realization, all the mere earthly impulses have been held back, but if the concentration breaks, they sweep you back again.

There's a marvelous story from India that I ran into by chance one time when I was reading the Mahābhārata. A saint had been meditating in a pond for a hundred years or so, probably on one leg, and he was just at the point of a breakthrough when he heard a splash. Distraction. He looked. Now, if you let a little bit go, a lot's going to go. He looked—it was a *big* fish. It was a big fish swimming happily among a bunch of little fish. The yogi was overcome. "O, happy fish, with your progeny. Oh, dear, I wish I had progeny. I think I'll go get married."

So he got out of the pond and went to a nearby palace. And there, of course, is a king, and being a yogi this chap knew all about these things: the king has fifty daughters. Now, these yogis coming right from their meditation are a very unappetizing phenomenon. This stinking yogi walked into the palace and the king received him and the yogi said, "I'd like one of your daughters."

Well, the king looked and he thought, *Oh, my God!* Of course the yogi was reading his thoughts; knowing this the king said, "Well, we don't give our daughters away here; we ask them to choose their husband. I'll call a eunuch, and he will bring you to the seraglio and if any one of my daughters wants you, you can have her."

The eunuch came and brought the yogi to the seraglio, and just as the door was about to be opened, this yogi turned himself into a charming youth with eyelashes like a camel and beauty beyond thought.

When the door opened and the eunuch said, "Your father says that any one of you who would like to marry this man may go away with him," they all squealed; they wanted him, and he walked off with the fifty wives, according to the bargain.

Some little time later the king thought, "Well, I wonder how things are going." So he had his elephants prepared, and he got on them and went on a trek in the direction in which the yogi had gone with his fifty daughters. The king eventually came before fifty palaces. So he went into the first palace and saw one of his daughters among pillows, and he said, "How's it going, darling?"

"Oh," she said, "he's wonderful. Well, the only thing that makes me anxious is he's always with me."

So the king went to the next daughter. Same anxiety. "What about my other sisters?" Well, people will think it's worth practicing yoga to get to this point, but what happened actually in this situation was that the father went home thinking, *Well, they're all happy, you know. So what?*

Then babies began coming. Well, one baby is a delight, two babies are two delights, and three babies begin to be something else, and four? What about fifty? And the yogi thought, "Oh yeah, this is what I thought of in the first place. I think I'll go back to my puddle."

When he suggested this to his wives, they said, "Well, it looks kind of messy around here, I think we'll do that too." So they turned the children over to nurses and the yogi with his fifty wives went back to the pond, and there they all stood on one leg.

So this is what I mean by suddenly being brought back. Odysseus's boat has sunk, his crew is gone. He's all alone, hanging onto a spar, and he's traveled a long distance to the Island of the Sun, and *zing*—he's on the way back.

Now, you see, he's experienced the two initiations with Circe—one to the biological ground and the other to the solar life. But his journey isn't over yet; he has to return to the world of dual experience. Back he goes along the route he has just taken, and he is washed ashore, not on Circe's island, but on the Isle of Calypso, a sort of middle-aged nymph.

He lives with Calypso for seven years. This is *marriage*; this is actually coming into a real, practical relationship between two powers, the male and female.

There comes a time when he is sitting on the shore thinking about Penelope, and when he seems to have learned the lesson, Hermes comes again and says to Calypso, "You have got to let him go." Then he says to Odysseus, "It's time to get home to Penelope."

So Calypso, who must obey orders from on high—and Hermes, you will remember, is the messenger of the gods—has no choice but to prepare a raft and some provisions for Odysseus and let him go.

The tides carry him on, and now he's getting back to the place of the original threshold crossing. Turbulence, the other world coming in—this is a place of great difficulties for the mystic and for anyone else. The threshold crossing into the plunge is difficult enough, but coming back out and integrating with life is something else again.

Poseidon, however, is keeping a wary eye to avenge his son Polyphemus the Cyclops, and he wrecks the little boat, leaving Odysseus to be tossed about on the waves until he gets a little help from

FIGURE 109. Odysseus, Athena, and Nausicaa (red-figure amphora, Classical, Greece, fifth century B.C.)

Leucothea (the white goddess of the sea) and from Athena herself, and eventually is washed ashore on the Island of the Phaeacians.

The next morning, as he is sleeping on the beach, down comes little Nausicaa, daughter of the king, with her handmaidens. She's come to wash her linen in the stream that runs down to the sea. After the work is finished, the girls begin to play with a ball, tossing it to and fro, and the ball gets loose and bounces down onto Odysseus, waking him. And this great, big, naked man rises up out of the seaweed, covering his genitals with an olive branch. (Joyce said Odysseus was the first gentleman.[14]) All the girls are frightened to death, except Nausicaa. Now, she is the counterpart of Athena, the patroness of heroes. Here's this little girl who's been on this island where there haven't been any particularly distinguished young men around, and she thinks, *Ah!*

This is hero worship, and her hero has come.

Odysseus speaks to Nausicaa, who takes him under her protection and back to her father, King Alcinous. Alcinous invites Odysseus to a rich banquet and, once his guest has dined, asks, "Well, stranger, where are you from?"

Instead of saying something like, *No man*, he says, "I am Odysseus." He has returned to his name, the adventure is complete, and he's on the threshold of return.

The king says, "We've been waiting for twenty years to find out what happened to this chap, and now here he is!"

Of course, now Nausicaa realizes, *He is not for me.*

Odysseus then tells the story of his journey—and it's here that *The Odyssey* actually begins: the whole story is a flashback as he tells them what has brought him to this point.

Afterward, he asks for help to get home, and Alcinous gives him a fine boat. Odysseus is put aboard it asleep, exhausted from his travels and the revelry, and the boat sails to Ithaca, where he is put ashore on his home island at last, fast asleep. How beautiful: out of this dream he comes and now he's ready to go home to Penelope. And so ends his dream journey, during the course of which he has experienced the temptress Circe (Aphrodite's messenger), Calypso as wife (Hera's messenger), and the lovely little virgin girl Nausicaa (Athena's messenger).

Meanwhile, Penelope has been weaving and unweaving a web, like the moon. For twenty years her man has been away, the war is

FIGURE 110. Penelope and Telemachus (red-figure *skyphos*, Classical, Greece, fifth century B.C.)

over, the others have come back, but where is Odysseus? From the palaces all around have come young and middle-aged suitors saying, "A woman can't survive alone in this country, in a place like this. You must marry one or another of us."

Penelope has faith that her husband will return and she says, "When I finish this web, I'll make up my mind." So she weaves it all day and unweaves it all night. Odysseus is the sun, she is the moon— they are associated with a calendric mystery, symbolizing the relationship of solar and lunar consciousness, male and female consciousness.

Athena comes in the form of a young man and says to Telemachus, "Boy, go find your father." Now comes the initiation of a young man into his manly life through the quest for the father.

Nobody knows where his father is, and so Telemachus says, "Well, I think I'll go to Nestor." Nestor was one of the old advisors during the war, like an old football coach. He knows all the heroes, all the odds, the whole thing.

Once Telemachus leaves to see Nestor, the suitors set up an ambush to kill him when he returns. Telemachus is informed of this and so comes back by another route. He lands and enters the lodge of Eumaeus, Odysseus's swineherd.

Isn't it interesting that the father is going to find his son in the house of the swineherd? Odysseus was initiated by the woman who turns men into swine, Orestes was cleansed of his guilt by the blood of the swine—the swine is the high sacred animal of the deep mysteries of the underworld. When Odysseus arrives on Ithaca, the first creature that recognizes him is his old dog, but the second is the maidservant Eurycleia, who while washing his feet recognizes on his thigh a scar left by the tusk of a boar. Remember: just as Adonis was slain by a boar, and Osiris was slain by his brother Set when Set went into the papyrus swamp hunting for boar, so Odysseus was gored by a boar. This association of the boar with death and resurrection, with soul and rebirth, with the hero who has gone and come back—it is primary. When Eurycleia recognizes the scar and realizes who he is, she is about to speak and he covers her mouth and says, "Don't say a word," because if his name were announced, the suitors would have gotten him.

By synchronicity, Penelope finally gives up at this time and says, "Okay, I will marry the one who can string the bow of my husband Odysseus and send an arrow through twelve axes." Twelve again—going in the cycle of the zodiac.

They all try, and of course nobody can do it. Then the tramp who's just come in and whom nobody recognizes says, "Let me try." This scene is beautifully described. Odysseus takes the bow, he tests it to see whether during the years the worms have eaten it or anything. He strings the bow, takes an arrow, and sends it through the twelve axes. He reaches back, takes another arrow, and starts shooting the suitors. He is like the sun that has risen now, and the suitors, the stars that were there with the moon goddess, they are wiped out.

When Odysseus returns, that's the end of the suitors. So Penelope says, "Oh, darling, I guess you probably had some pretty interesting experiences."

FIGURE III. Odysseus slaying the suitors (red-figure *skyphos*, Etruscan, Italy, c. 440 B.C.)

Now, I don't know anyone who has read *The Odyssey* as an initiation in this way, but it seems to fit perfectly with what might be called the archetypal voyage into the night sea and the return to the time of being readjusted to the female principle, which had been downgraded ever since the Trojan War. The recovery of the Goddess and the reintegration of the female power represent a new dynamic, but while these myths speak of the anxieties and the problems of the moment, what are dealt with are always the same powers that now have to be integrated. The Kena Upaniṣad from India, written during the seventh century B.C.—around the same time as *The Odyssey*— tells of the goddess coming back as well. The Indo-European gods are standing around and they see coming down the road a strange, mysterious phenomenon. They say, "Now, I wonder what that is."

Agni, the god of fire, says, "I'll go find out who it is." He goes and confronts this strange power, and the power says, "Who are you?"

Agni says, "I'm Agni. I'm the god of fire. I can burn up everything."

The strange power throws a straw on the ground and says, "Let's see you burn that."

Agni can't burn the straw. He goes back to the others and says, "I don't know what this is. I can't do anything."

So Rudra, the lord of the wind, says, "I'll go. Let me talk." So Rudra goes and this strange power says, "Who are you?"

He says, "I'm Rudra. I'm the lord of the winds. I can blow anything down."

So the power puts the straw down again and says, "Let's see you move that."

Rudra can't move it. He returns to the others.

Then a female god appears, Māyā. This is her first appearance in the whole Vedic tradition, and she introduces the gods to *Brahman*, the supreme god. This is the female as the revelatory power—and that is just what we have seen in *The Odyssey*.

FIGURE 112. Goddess (carved relief, Classical, Italy, c. fifth century B.C.)

CHAPTER 7

Mysteries of Transformation[1]

The Once and Future Goddess

I've tried to give something of the historical background and the main lines of the counterplay of the dominant Mother Goddess tradition dating from 7000 to 3500 B.C., and the incoming Indo-European people of around 4000 B.C., who came in with their quite contrary mythological worldview. I didn't spend much time on what the Indo-European mythology itself was like; we have to reconstruct it by comparative methods, comparing the European with the Asian traditions —the Greek tradition versus the Vedic tradition of India, and so forth.

When you have agricultural people settled in a given area as was the case with the Mother Goddess traditions, the worship can be directed at specific objects: this tree, this pond, this stone, and this place. When, however, you have nomadic people, which is the situation both with the Semitic warrior people and the Aryans, the direction of the worship is to that which is extensive and everywhere: the all-covering sky, the all-spreading Earth, the wind, the moon, the sun. The altars are transportable and they are set up here, there, and elsewhere, and the altar itself then takes a symbolic form to suggest a cosmic orientation. The deities are not like the deities of the planting people and Mother Goddess culture world—deities who are born, mature, die, and are resurrected—rather, these deities are universal and eternal presences.

The background of the nomads is with the hunting people, and for hunting people the principal contact with the mythological world and the primary maintainer of the tradition is the shaman. The shaman is one who has undergone a psychological transformation of his or her own, an experience that we would call a schizophrenic crack-up. The shaman has gone down into the domain of the deep unconscious, found the deities, and come back, so there is a kind of authenticity about him or her.

Further, the deities that the shamans are devoted to are their own familiars: they are those who have come to them in dream and vision. In hunting culture areas, particularly in relation to the North American Indian hunters, the principle of the vision becomes democratized so that anyone can have a vision. We know when it comes time in many tribes for boys to have the initiatory experience, they are sent out into dangerous places in the wilderness to fast for four days or more, and during that fast visions come to them, and the visions tell the young men what their careers are to be. Are they to be great healers? Are they to be great chieftains? Are they to be warriors? In adulthood, if a man feels his power failing he can go out and fast again, and so there is a kind of personal experience that is essential in that hunting culture world.

In the planting world, meanwhile, the deities that are venerated are those normally of the village, and that is where you find the traditions of the priests and priestesses who are devoted to the culture deities.

When these two kinds of people come together, as they did during the Indo-European and Semitic invasions that I've discussed, these two principles get into action through their relationship to each other. The most inclusive intuitions about a mythological order of the history of humankind that I have found anywhere are in the writings of Leo Frobenius. Anyone who wants to know something about the real intuitions of mythological history should turn to Frobenius's *Paideuma* or his *Monumenta terrarum—The Monuments of the World*.

His great insight in relation to these two great culture fields was that the dominant pedagogical experience for the hunting people is the animals and the animal world. There the people struggle with the problem of killing animals all the time, and develop the terror and fear of the animals' revenge, of the evil eye. This brings about a system of rites in which the core idea is of a covenant between the human society and the animal society, and the principal center of this covenant is the principal food animal. This animal world gives itself willingly to the hunter, with the understanding that rituals will be performed to return the life to its source so that the animal can come back again. So you have this idea of an accord and covenant between the two worlds; it's a beautiful kind of mythology.

On the other hand, when you come to the people on the equatorial belt, the principal pedagogical experience is that of the plant world, and there you have the planting of the seed in the Earth, the rebirth, and the coming of the new plant. Here the dominant motif is death and resurrection, and it's in that sphere that human sacrifice predominates.

You don't get human sacrifice in a major way in the realm of the hunters, as they're doing enough killing and their experience of the guilt of killing involves them in rites of penance and of compensation to the animal world.

With the equatorial peoples you find the idea of death as the source of life, and this is where the tragic mood comes from. You regard the world of vegetation, and here are all these rotting leaves and rotting sticks in the jungle, and out of it come fresh shoots, and so the notion that out of death comes life leads to the next conclusion, that if you want to increase life, you need to increase death, and so there is an absolute frenzy of human sacrifice right across this glorious mother-right tradition. We always think of the Mother Goddess as so tender but just remember her with the axes in Crete, for example.

In its purest form, the matrilineal mother-right system existed in the European sphere from about 7000 to about 3500 B.C., and then the warrior people came in, beginning with the fourth millennium, and achieving real dominance on the mainland during the third millennium.

Just about this time the Semites were moving from their homeland in the Syro-Arabian desert into the Near East in two directions. They moved eastward into the Mesopotamian and westward into the Canaanite zones. Here you had this mashing together of two unlike cultures, and if you want to know what it might have been like to live in one of these little towns in those days, just read the story of Jacob and his twelve sons invading Sechem. There was a dust cloud on the horizon—was it a sandstorm or was it a bunch of Bedouins coming? It happened to be Bedouins...and the next morning everybody in the city was dead. These were terrific times when these two worlds were coming together.

The momentum of the old mother-right tradition survived in Crete and the Aegean, which can be seen in all those beautiful marble

Mother Goddess figures from the elegant world of Crete. That terminated with the Santorini volcanic explosion around 1500 B.C., and from that time on the male-oriented Mycenaean system dominated—though it had already absorbed the female contribution, so those beautiful Mother Goddess figures continued to be created there.

Then, around 1200 B.C., there came the final invasion of a northern Indo-European tribe, the Dorians, who came with iron and a smashing victory, and this was the time of the fall of Troy. This was also the time of the bardic celebrations of the great hero deeds, and these were all brought together finally in the Homeric tradition.

The Iliad and The Odyssey bring out the problem of the conflict between those two traditions—the mother-right and the male-oriented—in the Classical period, and we have to think of the Homeric epics in three main stages: first was that of bardic oral traditions; next came that of putting together the epics by whomever it was we think of as Homer in the eighth and seventh centuries B.C.; and finally we have Pisistratus in Athens in the sixth century consciously instituting a program for fashioning an Athenian mythology. That's the emergence of this literary, deracinated Classical mythology, which we have inherited through the plays and poems. The epics were refined then, and the more primitive crudities were wiped out. For instance, we don't have Achilles dragging Hector around Troy alive, we have him dead.

Here we find also the two kinds of shield in conflict, the two orders of battle: the Bronze and the Iron Ages, side by side. These epics became, you might say, the school texts, and the later, more refined urban ethic moved in.

Finally, The Odyssey shows signs of the reemergence of the female principle.

In the comparable periods on the mainland, in the Near East and in Egypt, we have the cults of death and resurrection, with burials of whole courts and the great story of Osiris.

Now we come to the mystery cults—the Eleusinian mysteries, the Dionysian mysteries, the Orphic mysteries—and the beginnings of the translation of all this into the new terminology of the Christian cult. Translated into Christian terminology, the main theme of the mystery religions is the death of the old and the birth of the new. In alchemical terms, this is the process of bringing gold out of base matter. This is the theme that came up into Christianity as the virgin birth: the birth of the spiritual life in the human animal. This theme shows how your whole concentration and focus can be shifted from the concerns primarily and exclusively of your animal existence to the awakening of a sense of a spiritual aim for your life, and the animal aspect of your life is to support and not simply frustrate this.

I believe that Saint Paul, who wrote his epistles and letters in Greek and was himself a Jew, caught between the two traditions of the hard monotheism of Judaism and the syncretic polytheism of the Greek tradition, suddenly saw the Crucifixion, the killing of this charismatic, young, prophetic rabbi, as symbolic of the killing and death of the mystery savior.

With that shift in focus, the Fall in the Garden became the fall into Māyā, into the realm of illusory pairs of opposites, and into the whips and scorns of normal, phenomenal life. The cross is now the second tree in the Garden of Eden, the Tree of Immortality, while Christ himself becomes the fruit of everlasting life. The Tree of Immortal Life is precisely the Bo Tree, the tree under which the Buddha sat, and so the image of the Buddha and the image of the Christ are equivalent. In the early centuries of Christianity there was considerable conflict concerning the nature of the Christian religion, conflict that still exists as implicit in the whole tradition. Was it simply a variant on the theme of the mystery cults, or was it something very special, a whole new thing?

What I want to show is that the mythologies of the mysteries served as a prelude to the basic mythology of Christianity. Further, a figure like Orpheus and the Orphic tradition played a big role in the shaping of the Christian mythology. Orphic imagery is the foreground to Christian imagery, and the mythology of Christianity is far more firmly rooted in this classical mystery religion than it is in the Old Testament.

That was another big conflict in the first four centuries of Christianity: was it a totally new religion that should therefore have broken free of the Old Testament, or was it a fulfillment of the promise of the Old Testament? When you look through a Christian Bible today, you see in the footnotes all kinds of cross-references showing Old Testament prophecies on the coming of Christ and so forth. However, one could say that not only the Old Testament but also Classical paganism and behind that even Asian mystery religions played a role in the development of Christianity. During the third century B.C., Aśoka, the great Buddhist emperor in northern India, had sent missionaries to Cyprus, Macedonia, and Alexandria, which would become one

of the centers of Christian theological argument. This is recorded in
what they call *The Edicts of Aśoka.*

People ask, "Did Jesus go to India?" He didn't have to—India
had already come to the Near East. One wonders how this idea of the
inward Christ came to this young Jewish prophet, because it's not in
the Jewish tradition at all. This I think is what knocked St. Paul off
his horse—when he realized that the actuality of Christ's death and
alleged resurrection was an actual historical enactment of the sense of
the mystery religions.

Now, I've lectured on these Asian and Classical European themes
for many years at Roman Catholic seminaries with Jesuit invitations,
so this is recognized by people in the Church. However, they feel
that there was something special about the Christian enactment of the
mystery religions: namely, that it was God himself who came among
us as the man Jesus.

That is a concretization of the idea of God, that God is a fact and
not a metaphor for a mystery. They say in one breath that the ultimate
mystery transcends all thinking, all imaging—just like the Hindus
do—but then they say, "But it's a little bit different because we know
and what we know is *it.*"

So you can read this thing any way you want. You've got good
authorities for seeing Christianity as a continuation of a mystery tradition, or as something really exceptional whereby God, if you know
what that is, came on into the world in a very special way.

The Gospel According to Thomas, discovered in 1945 in Egypt, is
a Gnostic gospel, and there's simply no problem in equating Buddhist
ideas with the Christian ones and with the Classical mystery religions.
When Jesus says there, "He who drinks from my mouth will become
as I am and I shall be he,"[2] he's saying just what Gautama would
say: *All things are Buddha things.* All beings are Christ beings and the
Christ within us is to be found, recognized, and transformed into the
source of our living. This is sheer Buddhism, using the term *Christ*
instead of *Buddha consciousness.* Then you can read *Buddha consciousness* back to the mystery religions. Part of that common universal tradition of death and resurrection—death to your animal nature and
resurrection of your spiritual nature—is inflected already from the
mystery traditions into the Christian tradition.

In the Old Testament biblical tradition you have the most ruthless patriarchal accent of any tradition I know. As I've shown, there is
no Goddess there at all. The Goddess herself (Inanna and Astarte and

Ishtar and the others) is actually called the Abomination.[3] Here is an absolutely masculine-oriented mythology in which you don't have the idea of an incarnation of the divine. The Hebrew idea of the Messiah is not as the Son of God but as a human being of such majesty and form that he is worthy to be *called* the son of God; you don't have this literal, Classical virgin-birth motif, which is actually repulsive to the whole Old Testament tradition. There, the Goddess is out.

What happens in the Christian tradition is that Paul turns it over to the world of the Greeks. Paul himself wrote Greek elegantly, and he bridged the two worlds of the synagogue and of Athens. The Goddess comes in with the Virgin as the Mother of God. The last two thousand years have seen a gradual ascent of the Virgin to being pretty nearly in the line of a goddess. She is now even called co-savior in her anguish and suffering, which was as great as the suffering of her son. She also brought him into the world, and her submission to the Annunciation amounts to an act of salvation, because she acquiesced to this saviorhood.

Even so, the Church very carefully distinguishes between the worship of God and the *veneration* of the Virgin. She is still human; yet in the fact that she is human and achieved such sublime realization, she actually represents a higher Bodhisattva symbol than the divine Christ himself. So she's getting there, my friends, and it's the old Goddess right back again—you can't keep her down.

I've talked about the deities of prehistoric times. Now, I have a word I want to say about the affair of their transformation into those glorious humane and human figures that we recognize. The problem with the Greek pantheon is that accenting the human may dilute the mythological import, but I don't think this happened in the actual Greek tradition itself—there was just too much recognition of the traditional mythological aspects of these deities. I think the problem only comes in our reading of it. In the Homeric epics we have the transition from the masculine emphasis that came in with the Aryan invasions toward a new, female-influenced outlook.

Now we move on to the post-Classical period, and we are no longer dealing with an agricultural society but with a society that is cosmopolitan. The people are not primarily concerned with the growth of crops, though that aspect remains, certainly; they are living in cities, and they are traders using the great trade routes of the world. They are, in fact, people like ourselves, who are disengaged from the soil and have psychological problems. So the death and rebirth theme is interpreted finally not in terms of the vegetable world, with decay preceding the little green shoots of spring, but in terms of death and rebirth in the psyche.

The interesting thing is that though thousands of people experienced initiation into the mystery cults, the secret of these cults was never revealed or betrayed. We have clues, but that is all.

What was the secret? Different scholars have different theories about what went on. I intend to show you a series of pictures illustrating the stages of the mystery cult in the belief that out of this you will get a sense of what happened, not, of course, of the details, but of how it happened generally.

FIGURE 113. Goddess of the Tree of Life (clay cylindrical seal, Sumerian, Iraq, c. 2500 B.C.)

Look again at this old Sumerian seal (Fig. 113). The Sumerian civilization was in the lower Tigris-Euphrates valley, a world of mud. But the mud was fertile and therefore big settlements could grow up there. The first cities of the world were there—Lagash, Erach, and the rest—and among what we've found there was this cylinder seal for stamping properties. As we have seen, there is a woman on the right with a serpent and a male figure, and the tree with the fruits of the knowledge of good and evil. It is easy to see how archaeologists might have interpreted an image like this as an early rendition of the Fall in the Garden.

However, from all we know of the Sumerian tradition—and there are other seals in which this tree is shown—there was no sense of *sin* involved in people's view of this tree. The deity that attended the tree was there to dispense its fruits, and the fruit of immortal life is *to be eaten.*

Now let us look at the question of the two trees in the Garden of Eden. God forbade the eating of the fruit of the two trees: one is the knowledge of good and evil and the other is the tree of immortal life. As we read in Genesis 3, when God finds that Adam and Eve have covered themselves with leaves, he knows that something is up. He asks, "What has happened?"

Well, they confess, and the man blames the woman, and the woman blames the snake, and God then curses them in certain degrees. The man gets the easiest out; all he has to do is sweat. The woman will deliver in pain, and the serpent has to crawl on his belly for the rest of his life. The text then says—and God is called in this text *Elohim* (אלוהים), a plural name, not the singular *Yahweh* (יהוה)—"The man has now become like *one of us*, knowing good and evil"—that is to say, the knowledge of the world, of phenomenality, life and death, right and wrong—"and now, lest he put forth his hand, and take also of the tree of life, and eat, and live forever: Therefore the Lord God sent them forth from the garden of Eden...and He placed at the east of the garden of Eden Cherubim, and a flaming sword which turned every way, to keep the way of the tree of life."[4] This is a religion of exclusion from immortal life.

All other religions that I know are religions of discovering immortal life—as I have said, the Tree of Immortal Life is the very tree under which the Buddha sits. When you approach a Buddhist shrine, you see two military-looking door guardians there. Those are the cherubim to keep you out. What do they signify in Buddhism? They signify your psychological fear and desire. The fear of death is the fear of death to your ego, and the desire that the ego should enjoy the goods that it is interested in—these are what keep you from realizing your immortality. Fear and desire are the clashing rocks that exclude us from the intuition of our own immortal character.

This is the big theme of the mystery religions of Buddhism and Christianity—Christ went through that door and becomes himself the fruit of immortal life by hanging on the tree. The tree of the cross is the second tree in the garden: this is St. Paul's illumination. This is the great Christian theme; it is the theme, as well, of the mystery religions that we're about to deal with.

Look at the motifs in the Sumerian cylinder seal: the horns on this

deity suggest the moon god coming as he is about to die to be resurrected in the area of the tree. The moon god with the horns of the
lunar power has come down into death for refreshment in the womb
of the Goddess, who is the tree, and then he is reborn. And later on
this is the tree by which the Goddess stood on the world mountain
(see Fig. 31). What one sees here is the male deity ready to receive the
Goddess, whose consort is the serpent, or has the serpent power to
give life. You shed your animal life in order to be born again in the
spirit: that's the whole sense of the mysteries.

Mystery Cults

The center of the Greek mysteries was Eleusis, which today is only
a short taxi ride out of Athens, during which you pass a big harbor
full of shipping and oil refineries; it is anything but the holy way you
expected.[5] The old legend is that it was at Eleusis that the art of agriculture was invented—or rather, was given by Demeter to the world.
Here wheat was supposed to have been first produced, and it was the
patron deity of this shrine who gave the wheat to the world.

FIGURE 114. Demeter and Plutus (stone relief, Classical, Greece, fifth
century B.C.)

At Eleusis, we find Demeter in a similar pose (Fig. 114). The
goddess sits, and in her right hand is the torch that represents the
chthonic, or underworld, journey, so she combines here the symbolism of herself, as the Earth Mother, and of Persephone, her daughter,
who descends into the underworld and is reborn every spring. The serpent has become here the serpent pair—it is an androgynous serpent.

It could be represented as one serpent or split into its two aspects, and these two aspects could show themselves either in purely serpent form or in the serpent/human form. Plutus, the lord of the wealth of the underworld, is receiving from Demeter the grain—wheat—to carry it to the world above.

There is a special historical legend associated with the Eleusinian center. Martin Nilsson pointed out that during the Classical period in Athens wheat was planted in the fall and harvested in the spring. In the Greek summer, fierce heat dries up the vegetation, so during the summer the grain that was harvested in the spring was stored in silos in the ground. Hence the wealth of the culture is in and under the ground, in the domain of Hades or Plutus, the lord of wealth and the underworld. From there it was taken out and sown and dispensed to humankind. So the lord of wealth allegorically represents the silo in which the grain is stored during the summer. In northern realms the reaping and planting seasons are reversed, and during the Hellenistic period these two notions of when one plants and when one reaps come into collision in the interpretation of the myth.

A deity like Plutus, who represents the primal energy of life, appears very often either as a boy or as an old man. The whole cycle of human life from childhood to old age has in its middle the period of participation in the historical society into which you have been born. The child is prehistoric in its character and has not been inducted into the way of its particular historical condition. The aged person, who has disengaged from the toils, concerns, and the prejudices of this particular society, again has gone back into the realm of the universal. So that figure of old age looking at childhood that we still use to symbolize the passing of one year into the next is one eternity looking at another, and in between is the time of historic action in the field of history. So the one who represents that eternal energy can be represented either as a boy, the *puer aeturnus*, who continues to be outside the historical context, or the old man. You can see this in the Arthurian romances, in which Merlin, the Druid sage of the Arthurian court, could appear either as a boy or as an old man.

One of the goals of initiation in the mystery religions is to introduce the individual, through a spiritual journey, to the grounds of existence, that source of consciousness and energy of which we are all manifestations. So the aim is to guide us to the knowledge of this power, and the cornucopia that is symbolic of the course of our life.

All the symbols of these mystery religions come from the agricultural period, and so their first level of reference is to agricultural experience and the wealth of the land, the production of flocks, the production of crops, the production of children. That is to say, the reference is biological. However, while the vegetation cults have periods of fasting and jubilation, later the accent is on spiritual regeneration. Many traditions of this time were translations into a spiritual exercise of the imagery that formerly and for many centuries had been associated with planting, with the fruitfulness of the Earth, and with the birth of the new seasons, and so forth.

These symbols, then, which in the period of agricultural accent specifically referred to the field, now, in what might be called an urban period, are seen as psychological metaphors. The people were going to Eleusis for refreshment, as we do today; most of us are not gardening and worrying about whether the plants are coming up; what we're worrying about is whether we're going to be bringing forth the potential of our own psyche that are in the underground of our unconscious. So the stowing of the wealth in the dark abyss becomes associated with the undiscovered gold of our own spiritual potential. The traditional agricultural symbols become specifically and emphatically psychological in their accent. The character of the mystery cults, in contrast to the character of the old agricultural cults, has the accent on the spiritual and psychological, and those who are using the symbols know it. This isn't something that had to be discovered by Freud and Jung; this is something that has been known, and artists and poets have always known it. So what we're doing now is translating all of this into psychological terms.

What the cornucopia represents is that vessel of our own psyche out of which the crop must come, out of which the flower must bloom, and the figure carrying it can be either the child, the *puer aeternus*, or the old man. The woman represents the fostering field itself, the very source. The male is simply the agent of the female in these systems: he is the one who represents the active arm, you might say, of the one whose body is really the body of giving, receiving, and nourishing.

We do not know what happened in the Eleusinian mystery cults; the rituals were kept secret and to betray the mystery was a mortal offense. Here is a mystery in every sense, a secret that was kept by hundreds of thousands. However, it is possible to reconstruct an idea of the sequence of action by reviewing a great number of pictures on vases and sarcophagi. What the specific act was that rendered it symbolically and made it a stunning statement—as Socrates himself said, "I cannot tell."

To get to Eleusis from Athens you walk along the seacoast road that was called the Sacred Way. It was along this way that the people of Athens would go in procession at certain seasons to partake of a barley broth, and then after that little ritual drink, attend a series of some dramatic representations of the mystery in the sanctuaries at Eleusis. There's a very interesting book by Gordon Wasson, Albert Hofmann, and Carl Ruck called *The Road to Eleusis*. In it they suggest that the barley used in the broth had been infected with a fungal parasite known as ergot, which contains a hallucinogenic compound that is a chemical precursor to LSD. The theory is that a very light dose of this ergot was in the broth. Therefore, the initiates had their own inner hallucinogenic powers activated in accord with the ritual demonstrations in the sanctuary. The family in charge of the rituals at Eleusis was there for many centuries. We don't know when worship at Eleusis actually began, but it probably went back to pre-Homeric times and sprang from the cult of the Mother Goddess. The ritual was a living-out of a hero journey to the underworld and back, such as the one on which Circe sent Odysseus.

FIGURE 115. A priest between Herakles and a young initiate (black-figure *skyphos*, Classical, Greece, fifth century B.C.)

So here we go: we're at the entrance. On this lovely black-figure vase (Fig. 115), we see the Dadouchos, the second priest of the mystery, standing between Herakles, the archetypal hero, on the left, and the initiate, the hero of this journey, on the right. The priest is handing the initiate the torch of underworld.

Having been admitted, the young man is led by the mystagogue, the psychopomp or soul guide Hermes, who guides one along the track into the vastness of the mystery sanctuary and to rebirth.

The Terra Nouva Sarcophagus (Fig. 116) gives a representation of the sequence of the mysteries, showing the whole course of the initiation, in three stages. Beginning on the left, first comes a standing figure whose name is Iacchos—*Iacchos* is the word that was shouted in greeting to the young Dionysus when he appeared in birth, and was

FIGURE 116. The purification of Herakles (carved stone relief, Roman, Italy, second century A.D.)

the cry that was shouted at the moment of revelation. Personified as the deity Iacchos, he would represent that moment of the illumination that comes at the high point of the mystery drama.

The tree behind him is a laurel, a tree that has the apotropaic power of warding off evil. Daphne was turned into a laurel tree, and there's a place called Daphne on the way from Athens to Eleusis. So this is a threshold where we leave the secular world to enter a protected, sacred space, and the first figure that meets us is an aspect of Dionysus.

Next on the way in we encounter the two goddesses: Demeter is holding her torch upward and purifying the upper air, while Persephone, her daughter, is holding her torch downward, purifying the lower, chthonic region.

You must make a distinction between the chthonic, or under-earth—the caves and darknesses—and the telluric, or upper-earth, on which we live, and of which we think when we think of Mother Earth. These are the two aspects of the Goddess, appearing as two goddesses. The role of Persephone in some of the Peloponnesian cults was played by Artemis, and the primary quality of the figure is that she is Kore, the virgin goddess. Kore, or Persephone, is abducted by Hades and taken to the underworld. She is the fruit of the fields in the underworld who is to come forth again. By going down into the underworld and coming up again she is reproducing the history of the grain, of the wheat, of the food of the people. She is a personification of this energy, but she's a personification of other things as well, namely the power of the underworld. From the point of view of the upper world, Persephone is the abducted daughter, but below the surface she is the queen of the underworld.

Demeter is seated on a sacred serpent-coiled basket, and from the mystic basket precedes the serpent, that which sheds its skin to be born again and which represents the engagement of life-giving consciousness in the field of time and space.

So the first stage of the initiation is the passage through the mystery of the two goddesses—the goddess of our life and the goddess of our death, who, as we have already seen from Mycenae, are a mother-daughter pair.

Between them walks the initiate; his head is covered and he is seated on a bench covered over by a ram's skin. The ram is the symbolic animal of the illumination of the sun. In other words, there is going to be a surprising revelation of some kind coming along. The mystagogue or guide is pouring a libation into the fire. Beside the guide is Dionysus and behind him is Hekate, who represents the powers of the night and the abyss.

The Lovatelli Urn (Fig. 117) depicts essentially the same situation but with a couple of additional elements. As Carl Kerényi points out, here the initiate-hero is represented as Herakles himself:

> A youthful Herakles, moving from right to left, enters upon the lustral rites that will prepare him for initiation. The hero-prototype of the man in need of purification can be recognized at once by his lion's skin.[6]

The door guardian on the left is a female guide, and in her right hand is a little bowl that comes from very early times, not only in Greek but in Assyrian reliefs as well. It is a bowl of the elixir of immortal life, ambrosia.

Seated on the basket is Demeter, and on her right is Persephone feeding the serpent. We see that the candidate, still veiled, is to have some kind of revelation from the basket, which is a *liknon*, used for winnowing wheat—separating the chaff from the seed, which is the

FIGURE 117. The purification of Herakles (carved stone relief, Roman, Italy, first century A.D.)

whole point of initiation. We separate the chaff of our lives from the seed, coming to the essential in our revelation.

The winnowing basket (Fig. 118) is filled with fruits and a phallic feature, so we know that it has to do with birth, fertilization, and new life. The candidate is about to have his head unveiled. Standing off to the right is a bacchante, a dancing girl with a tambourine on which is despicted a goat that represents not only solar energy but also the energy of sexual power.

FIGURE 118. Initiate about to see the contents of the basket (carved stone relief, location unknown, date unknown)

This picture (Fig. 119) shows something about one of the revelations in the mysteries. What is interesting in this newborn child is that it shows the motif of death and resurrection of the savior, and the revelation in the basket is now represented as the child, the reborn young Dionysus. The two aspects of the young boy and the old man both with torches are aspects of this Hades power representing the abyssal energies. And there was some kind of revelation here as though a curtain were withdrawn. In the hand of the boy on the left is a torch, so we know that it was dark; this must have been a fantastic experience.

Now, the people reaching this journey were being introduced in a dramatically moving way to the revelation—the *epiphany*, as it would have been called—of this divine child. Socrates, in one of his conversations recorded by Plato, declared that he had experienced the rituals at Eleusis and that it was one of the most illuminating experiences of his career.

As Jane Harrison points out, the birth of the sacred child was a central part of the ritual:

> The birth of such a child was...proclaimed by the hierophant at some moment during the celebration of the mysteries: "Brimo has borne a child Brimos," but such a mystery would scarcely be

FIGURE 119. Epiphany (carved stone relief, sarcophagus, Roman, Italy, date unknown)

represented openly on a vase-painting. A simpler name lies to hand. *The child rises out of a cornucopia, symbol of fertility.* He *is* the fruits of the earth. He is solemnly presented to Athena because Eleusis gave to Athens her corn and her mysteries.[7]

This vase (Fig. 120) shows the cast of characters associated with the opera of the Eleusinian mysteries. At the bottom center is the Goddess Earth holding the cornucopia, just as the Earth contains the silos, while out of the cornucopia comes the little boy, the young Dionysus. This is the fruit, the child, but the child is associated with the spiritual birth as well—the virgin birth. Virgin birth has nothing to do with the biological problem: it is the birth of the spiritual life in the individual. When it is read concretely as a biological or historical event, the whole symbol is thrown off center.

The child is reaching toward Athena, the goddess-patroness of the city of Athens. From Eleusis the Earth brings forth the message, and the people of Athens receive it. Above them in the strange little two-wheeled winged chariot is Triptolemus, the youth to whom Demeter and Persephone commit the grain so that he may bring it to all the world. And so this story is associated with two fertilities: the physical food of our physical life and the spiritual food of our spiritual

FIGURE 120. Birth of a divine child at Eleusis (red-figure vase, Classical, Greece, fifth century B.C.)

life—and the gift of wheat and the gift of spiritual exaltation both
come from the Goddess.

THE ABDUCTION OF PERSEPHONE

Another myth central to the Eleusinian mysteries was the Abduction
of Persephone.[8]

The story is that she was out gathering flowers and the god of
the underworld, Hades or Plutus (he's called Plutus in the rites and
Hades in the literature), comes out of a cave and ravishes her to the
underworld. According to a number of versions, the Earth opened up,
and not only did Hades come out and steal Persephone, but a herd of
pigs went down into the hole after them.

Well, just as Isis went in quest of the dead Osiris, so Demeter now
goes in quest for Persephone. The mother begins seeking her daughter, but she finds that the girl's footprints have been wiped out by the
hoofprints of a herd of pigs.

Here we have one of Harrison's pictures of a pig offering in relation to Persephone (Fig. 121). The torches on the right belong to
Persephone as queen of the underworld. The question is, was Persephone herself the pig? Remember the Goddess-as-pig from 5000 B.C.
with the labyrinth of the underworld (Fig. 22)? Sir James Frazer, in
The Golden Bough, wrote about Persephone and Demeter having originally been pig goddesses—and he wrote that perhaps seventy years
before these figures were found!

From that same period from Serbia comes the figure of the twin
goddess (Fig. 9). What we have in the later Classical times is a continuation, sophistication, and beautification of the cults of enormous
antiquity.

So we go from life to death, we go from one mother to another,
from Demeter to Persephone. The meaning of this is that there is no
death. The life that lives in our body is of the eternal life.

So all along we have the two goddesses, and Demeter is going in
search of her daughter. In the legend she comes to a well in the village
of Eleusis. There she is supposed to have sat, disconsolate, mourning
her missing child.

People come and try to console Demeter as she weeps by the well,
but she is beyond consolation and cannot be made even to smile.
All the Olympian gods try to comfort her, but she refuses all solace,

FIGURE 121. Pig sacrifice (red-figure vase, Classical, Greece, c. fifth century B.C.)

until along comes bawdy old Baubo, who puts on an obscene, comical dance and Demeter cannot help but laugh.

Now, this role of the obscene is very interesting—it represents the breaking of the rules of decorum and a shattering of one's commitments and attitudes. In the Classical theater presentations there were three tragedies and usually one comedy. The comedy gives another perspective and it releases you from the tragic, and this is what we have here. Remember in Goethe's *Faust* the Walpurgisnacht line— *"Die alte Baubo kommt allein / Sie reitet auf einem Mutterschwein"* ("Old Baubo comes alone, riding in on the back of a mother pig.")[9]

Here is the same scene as depicted in the Homeric Hymns:

> *But Demeter*
> *who brings the seasons,*
> *whose gifts are so brilliant,*
> *did not want to sit down*
> *on such a splendid couch,*
> *but waited,*
> *in silence,*

FIGURE 122. Demeter and Persephone on the Parthenon (carved stone relief, Classical, Greece, c. 447 B.C.)

FIGURE 123. The well at Eleusis (stonework, Archaic, Greece, c. sixth century B.C.)

her lovely eyes thrust downward,
until
the perceptive Iambe
brought her a chair,
over which she threw
a silver fleece.
Then the goddess sat down
and drew down her veil
with her hands.
And for a long time
she sat on this chair
grieving
and silent,
without embracing anyone
with a word
or an act.
Without smiling,
without eating food
or drink,
she sat there,
wasting away with longing
for her daughter
in her low dress,
until
the perceptive Iambe,
with jokes
and with much clowning around
forced
this sacred lady to smile,
to laugh,
and to
cheer up her spirits.
It was she too
who later pleased her
in angry moments.[10]

This motif is associated with a goddess in Japan as well. The central figure in Japan's Shintō pantheon, Amaterasu is the lovely young sun goddess, and of course the world depends on her shining. On one occasion, she and her ladies were insulted by her brother, and Amaterasu withdrew in indignation into a mountain cave and closed the rock door behind her, so the whole world was dark.

The deities asked one another, "How do we get her back?"

FIGURE 124. Baubo (terra-cotta, Classical, Greece, c. fifth century B.C.)

FIGURE 125. Amaterasu emerging from the cave (woodcut print, Edo period, Japan, nineteenth century A.D.)

Then they thought of a wonderful idea: they'd have a wild party outside the rock door. Amaterasu would hear all the noise and want to know what was going on. They had an uproarious time, and again, one of the goddesses did a bawdy, obscene dance with comic gesturing. All the gods began roaring with laughter.

Little Amaterasu in her cave began to wonder what was going on out there. She opened the door a little bit to peek, and the gods said, "Well, we've got somebody out here that leaves you in the shade," and they held up a mirror so that what she saw was herself.

In curiosity out she came, and two great, strong gods pulled the door back and drew a rope behind her, which is like the rainbow in the Bible tradition: it means the Sun Goddess will never retreat again and the world will never suffer the deluge of darkness again. You will find that rope in Shintō shrines to this day, and it represents exactly this: that the Goddess will never withdraw. And the red disk on the Japanese flag? That is Amaterasu's mirror.

On the so-called Veil of Despoina (Fig. 126) we find curious, comic animal forms, human forms wearing animal masks, and they are all doing a wild dance. Down in the Peloponnese we find Kore dancers of a wild kind associated with the Virgin Goddess Despoina. (Kore, you will remember, was the Peloponnesian name for the Virgin Goddess known in other parts of Greece as Artemis or Persephone.) On the veil, we see her dancing alongside these masked figures.

FIGURE 126. Veil of Despoina (drawing of carved stone relief, Classical, Greece, c. fourth century B.C.)

This is reminiscent of the animal-headed figures one finds in the tantric Buddhist traditions, the dakini, the space fairies, and it suggests too the idea of a carnival. Carnival is that period of no law that comes between the time of the two eons.

There are 365 days in a year, but the round number for the conventional year is 360 days. Thus, there are just as many days of the year as there are degrees in a circle, so the circle of time and the circle of space have the same order. However, between the end of the 360 and the beginning of the next 360, there is a lapse of five days and these are the days of carnival. This is the period of outbreak, of obscenity, of the smashing of law so that the fecundation, the new generation of the new eon takes place, and that's what this obscene dance motif represents in association with the legend of the quest for Persephone. These are the five days when the world of comely law no longer exists and there is room for play, the obscene moment, and the laugh.

If you take life absolutely seriously, you must realize there's the counter-play to it, that the world of law is simply an optional world. When you do something you create a pattern that excludes other possibilities, and there comes a time for opening up to all possibility and the creative act.

Actually, everybody who has ever done creative work of any kind knows this moment. You make your plans in terms of what the mind can think of, and if you hold to those plans you're going to have a dry, dead piece of work. What you have to do is open out underneath into chaos, and then a new thing comes, and if you bring your critical faculty down too early you're going to kill it.

There's a beautiful letter that Schiller wrote to a young author who was having the trouble that's known as writer's block. This young writer had oh, so much to say, but he couldn't write. This is a normal situation. Schiller said simply, "Your problem is that you're bringing the critical factor into play before you have let the lyric factor work."

Look what happens to us in our schools: we learn to criticize Milton and Shakespeare and Goethe and everybody else, and then the teacher says, "Now do some creative work." You sit down and this bit of spilth begins coming out and you think, *Oh, my God!* That's nothing. Of course you can't write like Shakespeare, but you can write like you, perhaps, if you let yourself go.

And so it is here: the moment of chaos, the moment of breaking all rules, the moment of *Who cares what they think?* has to come, and then to smash the new generation. That's what's associated with this carnival motif.

By such means is the goddess relieved, brought back life through laughter. This is the *anodos*, or return of the goddess (Fig. 127). The seed that was stored in the realm of Plutus for the dry summer now comes up as the wealth of life in the fall sowing. In this vase, Persephone is surrounded by erotes and satyrs, phallic and vegetative figures. Dionysus holds his thyrsus in hand, so the Dionysian association is very intimately connected with the Eleusinian mythology.

FIGURE 127. The *anodos* of Kore/Persephone (red-figure krater, Classical, Greece, c. fifth century B.C.)

The tale of another emerging maiden might surprise you (Fig. 128). The name above her head on the right is Pandora; she represents the energy of life that comes with woman.

About this image, Harrison tells us:

> At a first glance, when we see the splendid figure rising from the ground with outstretched arms, the man with the hammer and Hermes attendant, we think that we have the familiar scene of the rising of Kore or Ge. As such, had no inscriptions existed, the design would certainly have been interpreted. But, as it happens, each figure is carefully inscribed. To the left Zeus, next to him Hermes, next Epimetheus, and last, not Ge or Kore, but Pandora. Over Pandora, to greet her uprising, hovers a Love-god with a fillet in his outstretched hands. Pandora rises from the earth; she is the Earth, giver of all gifts.[11]

FIGURE 128. Pandora rising from the Earth (red-figure amphora, Classical, Greece, c. fifth century B.C.)

Pandora is another inflection of the idea of the woman who brings bounty into the world. The later, smart aleck, masculine-inflected story of Pandora—the notion that every woman brings with her a box of troubles—is simply another way of saying that all life is sorrowful. Of course, trouble comes with life; as soon as you have movement in time, you have sorrows and disasters. Where there is bounty, there is suffering.

Epimetheus (hindsight), Hermes, Zeus, and Eros are the principal powers attending the emergence here.

The image on this *lekythos* (Fig. 129) states the theme explicitly: the satyrs are pounding and tilling the Earth. Earth must be hurt and broken so that life may come. Life is pain. Just so, Christ comes to share the cross that we're all nailed to in the world of time. Now, when the Earth is tilled to bring up its fruit, it is hurt, punished. And so in the mysteries there were whippings, and this was why.

There are two pictures of a Dionysian initiation ritual shown at the Villa of Mysteries in Pompeii (first century B.C.) that give us a notion of what the mysteries were about. In the first (Fig. 130), the young initiate kneels, placing her head in the lap of an older woman, who is looking toward the angel with a raised whip. The nude dancer is holding cymbals or castanets. The woman standing in front of her in a dark gown holds the thyrsus, or staff.

FIGURE 129. The Earth Goddess emerging in pain (black-figure *lekythos*, Classical, Greece, fifth century B.C.)

In the second (Fig. 131), a young man undergoing initiation is looking into a metal bowl that has a mirror surface inside, and behind him the assistant is holding up a mask of an aged face, wrinkled and horrible. The concavity of this bowl has been mathematically studied, and what has been found is that anyone looking in at this point would see not his own face, but the mask held back and behind.

The young man looks into the bowl, which is concave, expecting to see his own face appear in the polished surface, but what he sees is the reflection of the mask—this is an initiatory shock. What he sees is not himself as he is today but as he will become what the American Indians call the *long body*—that is to say, the body of his whole life, not just a cross-section of it that is here this morning.

Our passage along the field of time is simply an experience of one cross-section of that long body after another. We try to hold onto this cross-section, but what we're initiated to here is the true body— it's right there, and all we have to do is experience a length of it. Our life is one body, from conception to death, and that is what we must learn, the totality of it.

So what the candidate gets here is a terrific expansion suddenly of the concept of *Who am I?* He realizes that he is not just this youngster

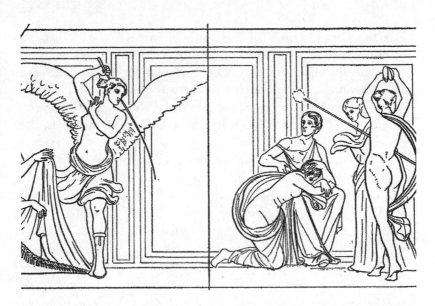

FIGURE 130. A young female initiate being whipped (fresco, Roman, Italy, first century A.D.)

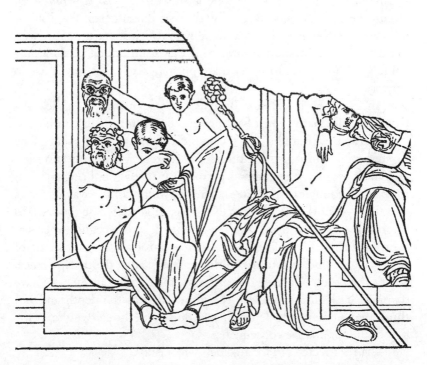

FIGURE 131. Seeing the long body (fresco, Roman, Italy, first century A.D.)

of the moment, but the man of an entire lifetime. And with that you can understand why the secret of the mysteries had to be kept. Suppose before the initiation this young fellow met one of his friends who had already undergone the ceremony and was told about the bowl and the mask, what you might call the gimmick. What would happen to the initiation? Nothing. It would have been killed. And this is why not betraying the secret is so important.

The character of initiation is shock, so that one never forgets it. Jacob Epstein, the great English sculptor, made this point—every work of art must be a shock. It must not be something where you say, "Oh, gee, is it like this?" or "Does it belong to such-and-such a school?" or something like that. It must be a shock. The shock puts a frame around it, and the frame gives you the initial, unique, timeless experience of that piece, not that piece in relation to other times, objects, or concepts. The whole sense of the aesthetic experience is that it is an experience in and of itself, not related to something else. Consequently, portrait painting can be so clumsy. The definition of a portrait is *a picture with something wrong around the mouth*. You look at it and say, "Well, that doesn't look like Bill"— and so you've ruined the picture. But if you just see a picture as a picture—not as a picture of something that's somewhere else—it may come as a shock, and in order that you may see it that way it has to surprise.

An initiation is a shock. Birth is a shock; *rebirth* is a shock. All that is transformative must be experienced as if for the first time.

And so this youth has the shock of discovering his long body. The mysteries have to do with shifting the center of your concentration and focus from the ephemeral personality to the enduring form of forms that you're experiencing normally, simply in the way of forms and that you now experience as the forms. If you become too fixed to the form, the body drops off. The problem is to recognize the relationship of the play of this permanence through the inflections of time so you come back to the world again after that depth experience. That's the point. We have to experience the depth, but then we have to move back into time with the knowledge of the depth and not think that we're in the depth. If you do live as though you're in the depth, inflation is the consequence.

The resurrected virgin: a golden wheat stalk.

Much of what we know about the mystery cults comes from the writings of Christian apologians who were disparaging them. Clement of Alexandria said, in effect, "What an absurdity. Just imagine a ritual that culminates in the experience of seeing a grain of wheat elevated!" Well, the culminating moment in the Catholic Mass consists in seeing a little wafer of wheat elevated; it's not whether it's wheat in the

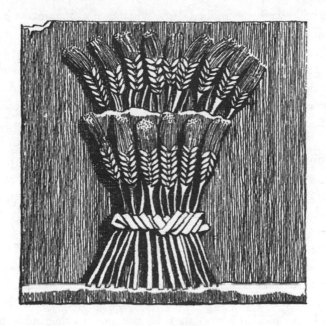

FIGURE 132. The reborn goddess as a sheaf of wheat (carved marble relief, Classical, Greece. c. fifth century B.C.)

form of a wafer or grain or gold that matters, but rather what it symbolizes: the food of our spiritual life, the spiritual food that throws off death.

As we've seen, in all planting and agricultural societies the food that we eat is the divine life itself—this is the basic planting culture myth as it occurs in Melanesia and in many other highly developed areas. The myth is this: in the primary time, there was no separation of sexes, there was no birth, there was no death, and there was a kind of permanent present. At a certain time in this time-which-is-no-time, a murder was committed. One of the beings was killed, cut up, and buried, and from the buried parts came forth the food plants on which the people lived. At that very moment, the sexes were distinguished and, in balance with the death that had come there was generation and birth. So the world begins with a murder, the world of time begins with death, because time is death. Without time everything lasts forever, but time is death and the breaking of the form makes possible the coming of a form, and this is what is presented in this story.

So what we eat is a killed deity, whether it's an animal we're killing and eating or a plant we're picking. The sense of saying grace before meals has been reduced to thanking God for giving you the food, but the real grace should be thanking God for *being* the food. That's the sense of the communion in the Christian Church, where what you eat *is* God—Jesus, who gave his life that we might live.

That's the sense of all these mysteries; our life lives on life. Do you say, "Yes" to that, or do you say, "Gosh, I was hoping our life was something other than that"? This is a mystery of affirmation of the things *as they are*, and all that is symbolized in the holding up of the stalk of grain. The various baskets used in the rituals were apparently ways of rendering this shock of a realization: the long body of your total life, the food that you eat as the divine being, yourself as food.

The Taittirīya Upaniṣad, as I've quoted above, cries, "Oh, wonderful, oh wonderful, oh wonderful. I am food, I am food, I am food, I am a food eater, I am a food eater, I am a food eater...! He who knows this shines like the sun."[12] The goal of the mystery is not to withhold the food that you are from the mouths that are waiting to consume you, but to welcome the consummation.

DIONYSUS AND THE FEMININE DIVINE

In these images (Figs. 133 and 134), Triptolemus with the wheat takes the form of an old man—the youth/old man motif—who is being guided in his chariot by Hermes. On the other side of the same vase is Dionysus in the carriage led by a satyr with the wine cup and vase. Notice the grain in the hand of Triptolemus and the wine in the hand of Dionysus. In the Roman Catholic Mass there is the wafer and the wine; it is a continuation of this Classical mystery cult, with the same message being brought to the initiate.

In the mysteries of Dionysus what is strikingly emphatic is the accent on the obscenity, the torture, and the destructive aspects. Dionysus was born of Semele, but not *quite* born of Semele. Zeus, in one of his philandering affairs, had begotten Dionysus on the mortal woman

FIGURE 133.
Triptolemus in his
miraculous chariot
with Hermes
(black-figure vase,
Archaic, Greece,
sixth century B.C.)

FIGURE 134.
Dionysus in his
miraculous
chariot with
Silenus (black-
figure vase, archaic,
Greece, sixth
century B.C.)

Semele. This lady had the indiscretion to boast of this event to Hera,
known for her jealous rages. This time Hera used guile instead of
power to exact her revenge, and insinuated to Semele that she had not
experienced Zeus in his full majesty and taunted her about this.

So when Zeus next approached Semele, she charged him with
not having shown himself to her as he had to Hera, and though he
warned her against it, she insisted, saying he had promised to give her
anything she wanted. Well, Zeus uncloaked his full divinity and that
was the end of poor Semele: she was incinerated. The moral here is

that you mustn't invoke more of the deity than you are prepared to encounter.

Since Zeus was concerned for the fetus in her womb that was to be Dionysus, he tucked it into his thigh, thereby making Dionysus the twice-born—once from the mother's womb, and once from the male womb of Zeus's thigh. The sense of male initiations is, as we have seen, that you get your physical life from your mother, while you get your spiritual culture life, your life as it shall be lived in your society, from your father. So all the imagery of the male initiation is of the male womb and the male birth: giving birth to a civilized creature, not simply a little nature phenomenon.

After Dionysus was born Hermes received the child and turned him over to the nymphs to be nurtured and educated. The relationship

FIGURE 135. Dionysus on the pirate ship (black-figure krater, Classical, Greece, 330 B.C.)

of these two gods is important: Hermes guides souls to the knowledge of eternal life by way of intellectual initiation, while Dionysus represents sudden inspiration, the energy of life pouring through time and throwing off old forms to make new life.

The story goes that one day Dionysus was standing on a promontory over the Mediterranean when a pirate ship came past, and the pirates said, "Oh, let's grab that young man and sell him off as a slave."

Dionysus let himself be captured and when he was well aboard and they were well out in to the Mediterranean, he let forth a leopard roar and vines began growing up all through the boat of the mast, over the oarlocks, over everything, and in terror the pirates jumped overboard and became dolphins (Fig. 135).

Dionysus becomes the god associated with the religious ecstasy in Athens and other Greek cities. The male-oriented Indo-European mythology, with its authoritarianism and suppression of women, had become the cultural standard by the late Bronze Age, and then comes in Dionysus, and with him the outburst of energy in the mode of experience that had been associated with the Goddess cults. The maenads, the women who participate in his rites, were carried away in

FIGURE 136. Maenad dancing in ecstasy (red-figure kylix, Classical, Greece, c. 480 B.C.)

rapture, intoxicated by the wine of Dionysus, tearing animals apart and dancing wild dances. The leopard that had been, as we've seen, associated with the Goddess, becomes Dionysus's totem, while his thyrsus represents the vegetal sap, or energy of life.

In *The Bacchae*, Euripides tells the story of King Pentheus, who was simply indignant that his own mother was out there in the hills raging around with these wild, ecstatic women.

So he goes out to spy on them in the hills at night to see what they're doing, even though he has been warned to stay away.

And in a wild moment, not recognizing him, they tear him apart. Pentheus's own mother takes his head off and sticks it on a pole and goes screaming in rapture, with her son's head pouring blood onto her hands.

FIGURE 137. The death of Pentheus (red-figure kylix, Classical, Greece, c. 480 B.C.)

Now, what does all this mean?

The two great deities in this context are Apollo and Dionysus. I've mentioned the exploration of these two deities by Frederich Nietzsche in *The Birth of Tragedy*. Nietzsche points out that Apollo represents the lord of light, the *principio individuationis*, the individuated world illuminated by the light of the sun, in which view each of us is different from the other, and the differences are what are charming, interesting, and important here. So in this world we see the differences illuminated by the light of Apollo, and Apollonian art accents the differences and gives a sense of joy in beholding them. The Dionysian world, on the other hand, represents the thrust of time that destroys all things and brings forth all things. It is the generative power, thrust out of darkness.

Now, in our art, in our living, we can so accent the light that we lose touch with the dark energy and dynamism of the time factor within us, and then we become stilted, dry, dead. In contrast to that then we may feel exaltation, the breakthrough of excitement and the vitality of transformation. The problem of life and of art is to balance these two. It's Nietzsche's contention, and there's something to be said for it, that in the Greek patriarchal systems of the tenth, ninth, and eighth centuries B.C., the accent was too strongly on the light side, and that it was the women principally who felt the need to participate in a regenerative aspect, so this desire breaks through in wild excess. Any deity, any power that has been repressed is in danger of breaking forth with excessive force.

Nietzsche sees sculpture as the prime art of the delight in form, and music as the prime art of the movement in time and flow. Music without form is simply noise, and sculpture without the fluency of new inspiration is dead academic stuff. Greek tragedy, he argues, is the prime representation of the interplay of Apollo and Dionysus. The characters on the stage represent the forms that aren't to be broken and the choral group is not individuated, everyone moving as in a parade, which is a great Dionysian moment. Moving in rhythm with one another rather than as individuated entities, they represent the Dionysian factor. The rapture of the tragedy is the rapture of seeing the form broken for a flowing through of the radiance of the transcendent light.

Art holds the mirror up to nature. The mirror motif is very important and through all these forms, which are simply reflected in the mirror, something beyond the form speaks. There's a Tibetan meditation called "the mirror meditation," in which one looks at the mirror and sees oneself in the mirror and then smashes the mirror and knows that nothing has happened. One's body is as where the mirror reflects of one's eternal aspect.

In this vase (Fig. 138), we see Dionysus, riding the full power of this mother energy of destruction and creation symbolized by the leopard. He is riding—but not many of us can ride with cool calm on this energy. That would be the divine summation or apogee of the mystery, to live with a godlike composure on the full rush of the energy of life without being torn to pieces.

The worship of Dionysius is a resurgence of the mysteries that

FIGURE 138. The procession of Dionysus (red-figure vase, Classical, Greece, c. 370–360 B.C.)

were already known in the Greek world, where they were enacted in a calm, decent, harmonious way. However, when a power of the psyche is suppressed, and it then breaks forth, the breaking forth is always overenergetic. It comes out with terrific force—and that must be allowed to happen. This power has to come through and be allowed to work itself out and settle down again.

We've seen the lovely little statue from Knossos (Fig. 30): the Goddess holding serpents in each of her hands, while on her head we see a panther. The panther represents the solar power, the eternal life disengaged from the field of time. Time is the field of birth and death, light and darkness, right and wrong, the pairs of opposites. Adam and Eve ate of the fruit of the knowledge of the pairs of opposites and were pitched into the field of time. Whereas they had been in the garden as one with God and each other, they now were separated from God, and distinguished as male and female. So the serpents represent the energy of life in the field of time, while the panther represents the eternal, solar principal, disengaged from the field of time: absolute, single consciousness. The Goddess spans both realms of experience.

Now, this beautiful and illuminating ceramic piece (Fig. 139) shows dramatically the theme of initiation. It's a red-figured ceramic kylix that very clearly shows the initiation of a young man by a nymph—the woman as initiator. The important thing about the Goddess is not whether women sat on thrones and ruled in a matriarchal social structure; it is whether the quality of Woman, the being of Woman, the sense of Woman was understood, known, and respected.

FIGURE 139. Thetis and Peleus (red-figure kylix, Classical, Greece, fifth century B.C.)

Under the serpent is the name Thetis, and at the end of the scabbard of the youth's sword is the name Peleus. These two are the mother and father of Achilles. In other words, this is a marriage scene—marriage as an initiation of the male into what life is about, not what the mind can conceive it to be.

Now, in the old, masculine literary tradition, the story is told in this way roughly: Thetis was a beautiful sea nymph with whom Zeus fell in love. When he heard, however, Prometheus's prophecy that Thetis's son was going to be more powerful and greater than his father, Zeus thought it better to turn away and he saw to it that the nymph should marry a human husband. So the tale goes that when Peleus went to take her in marriage, she avoided him in what is known as a transformation flight. She transformed herself into a serpent, into a lion, into water, and into fire, but he mastered her in all these guises.

However, that's not what we see here at all. This is from the earlier tradition of the Mother Goddess that lies outside the spheres of the political influence of Athens and the masculine tradition. We recognize the animals as the same ones that the goddess of Crete was holding: in her hands are the serpents, with a panther or lion on her head. We know exactly who she is, and we see her illuminating him.

This is the sense of the mystery initiation; this is what the Goddess does. What happens to him? The serpent on the right is opening the inner eye, the eye of inner vision, mystic vision. The serpent under his ear is opening the ear to the song of the spheres, the mystery song of the universe. The serpent at his heel is biting the Achilles tendon—that is the bite of death, death to ego and rational consciousness, and an opening of the transcendent. The opening would be to the knowledge of the energy and life that the lion represents.

Read in totality, this image symbolizes the major, mystical realization.

If you're living your life thinking, "Am I going to die and do I wish to live on?" you are living in terms of your rational consciousness and of an identification of yourself with your phenomenal personality. You're hoping to maintain your separate existence, and the whole world is singing this song to you, death and desire.

If, on the other hand, you accept death—that is to say, you are willing to die to your continuity in life as a separate personality and really die to it, I say really assimilate death, take the serpent poison into yourself and digest it—the world sings a new song and it's that of the world, not that of the world in relation to your durability or fame or whatnot.

The Buddhists speak of the eight winds of karma. When one is blown about by these, one is trapped in ego consciousness. Ego is not to be eliminated—*elimination* of ego is one of the great yogic mistakes—the ego is to be *related*. The ego function is what puts you in touch with the world as it is and with yourself as you are, but it must be related as well to the mystical realization. The eight karmic winds are desire for pleasure and fear of pain, the desire for wealth and fear of loss, the desire for praise and fear of blame, and desire for fame and fear of disgrace. If you are moved by these, then you are thinking and acting in terms of your ego, not in terms of the universal principles.

So the minute the bite has been assimilated, the inner ear opens and the inner eye opens, and that's what Thetis is giving Peleus. The next thing to look at are those hands, and there you see the yin and yang relationship. His hands are in the yin-yang posture: the two together, good and evil together.

Two points of view prevail in religious thinking: one is the ethical—being good against being evil—while the other is about transcending the pairs of opposites, going beyond good and evil and recognizing that you and the world are manifestations of these two powers in relationship. Peleus has broken through into this realization.

This krater (Fig. 140) shows Dionysus and and his mother, Semele, as the same age, in their eternal aspect, the male and the female, the mother and her child, but the child as her consort as well. Between them is the chalice of his wine—God's blood in the later Mass. The posture of the hands is a very interesting one: it's a mudra, a symbolic

FIGURE 140. Dionysus and Semele (krater, Archaic, Greece, c. 550 B.C.)

posture that is used in Hindu meditation that conveys the power and vitality of consciousness in the world. This is the counterpart of Christ's coronation of the Virgin in heaven, the timeless world of the relationship of the mother to that whom she brings forth as her child.

Unearthed in the year 1837 near the town of Pietroasa, in the area of Buzau, Romania, this Orphic bowl [Fig. 141] had been buried with twenty-one other precious pieces, possibly at the time of the Huns. Taken to Moscow during the First World War for protection from

FIGURE 141. The Pietroasa bowl (cast gold, Hellenistic, Romania, third or fourth century B.C.)

FIGURE 142. Central figure of the Pietroasa bowl (cast gold, Hellenistic Romania, third or fourth century B.C.)

the Germans, the whole collection was melted down for its gold by the Communists. Fortunately, however, during the winter of 1867–1868 it had been on loan for six months in England, where it had been photographed and galvanoplastically reproduced.[13]

In the center sits the goddess Demeter on the mystery basket (Fig. 142), and in her hand is the cup, which might be thought as the grail or the chalice of the blood of Dionysus with the mark of the vine. There are sixteen figures around her, and by following them we can follow the mystery journey stage by stage.[14]

The inner circle around the goddess shows the condition of the mind of the prisoner who has not been initiated. Still in the sleep of life, all he sees is dog-eat-rabbit. All is sorrowful, life lives on life: lions eating gazelles, leopards eating gazelles, gazelles eating plants, dog-eat-dog. Woe! Life is something that should not have been! But if we have undergone the initiation and realize the play of eternal forms through the temporal inflections, we experience the radiance through the sorrow.

Then the song is sung, like Orpheus who when slain by the maenads after his failure to bring back Eurydice from Hades. His head goes floating down the river still singing and ends on the isle of Lesbos, the isle of lyric poetry.

You always have to behead yourself and let the head sing and to forget your earthly life. But if you are initiated you know that this is just the superficial display of a harmony. As Goethe says, "All rests well in God, the Lord."[15]

All struggle, all fighting rests well in the divine. So if you can get rid of the fear and the desire and get into the posture of ecstasy, of aesthetic arrest, the world will sing. It is *here*. As the Thomas Gospel tells us, "The Kingdom of the Father is spread upon the earth, and men do not see it."[16] We don't see it because we're afraid and we're full of desires, but eliminate those, and we'll see.

So this is the condition of the dreamer, and roundabout we see the way of initiation, the way to get past it, to realize your androgyny in the metaphysical sense, and your immortality along with your mortality. Realize that, and you realize that you're okay—and so is the world.

FIGURE 143. Mary, *vièrge ouvrante* (carved ivory, Gothic style, France, date unknown)

CHAPTER 8

·

Amor

The Feminine in European Romance[1]

I WAS AT A CONFERENCE in Japan back in 1957 with Mitch Ayadi and Joe Kitagawa, two major scholars on comparative religions at the University of Chicago. Both Mitch and Joe were in Japan with their wives, while I was solo, and we were going to travel together from Osaka to Kobe by train. Those Japanese trains are precisely on time; if they're two seconds late, there will be a public announcement of apology.

The train came into the station, and the doors opened. We were walking toward the train. The two wives were walking ahead; Joe, Mitch, and I were next; and behind us was the porter with the luggage. The train came in, the doors opened, the two wives went in, the doors closed, and the train was on the way to Kobe.

Well, our first impulse was to laugh, and then we realized, *Good god!* These girls don't know how to speak Japanese! There were three stations in Kobe, and we spent the evening looking for these lost wives. And the porter said to Joe, "That never happens to Japanese wives; they walk behind us."

This made me think of the words that end Goethe's *Faust*—and this is going to be one of my great themes: *"Das Ewig-Weibliche, / Zieht uns hinan"* ("The eternal female draws us on").[2] Well, they drew us on that evening, all right, as we tried to find those two women.

All these stories about relationship of male to female appear in little customs that we take for granted, but they represent deep relationships that go way, way back. Now, in speaking about the female in the West, I'm interested in presenting two completely contrary traditions that coincide in our contemporary inheritance. One is what I would call the European tradition: *"Das Ewig-Weibliche, / Zieht uns hinan."* There the female has been a fundamental figure since at least 25,000 B.C. The Paleolithic caves and those little Venus figurines date from the first appearance of Homo sapiens in Europe.

About 10,000 B.C. we begin to have the signs of agriculture and of the domestication of animals. We're moving now from hunting and gathering to settled agricultural communities. The community enlarges gradually, and certain centers become important trading towns; these then develop into cities. The first cities in the whole history of the world emerge in Mesopotamia and shortly later in the Nile Valley during the fourth millennium B.C. That's some five thousand years after the first appearances of agriculture. Now, the span between 10,000 and 4000 B.C. is the Neolithic, the New Stone Age, and the principal deity there is the Goddess. The woman gives birth and nourishment as Mother Nature does, and her magic and Earth's magic are the same; that profound association is fundamental.

The arts of agriculture diffused and spread from certain centers where the Goddess was dominant, springing from three main centers. One was Southwest Asia and Southeast Europe; another is Southeast Asia in the Thailand area; and another is over in in Mexico and Central America. In other parts of the world—not in the fertile river valleys but in the great plains where the hunters had been—animal domestication becomes more important than plant domestication, and there you had herding tribes. There, the male deities were the most important and for the most part the goddesses appear as consorts of the male.

In the agricultural systems, on the other hand, the Goddess is what counts. She's it. She's not only the creator of the universe, she *is* the universe and we are her children. As one comes from the mother and is of the mother's body and substance, so are we from the universe.

In India, where the female principle has been terribly important and is dominant to this day, there was an episode of male dominance with the Aryan invasions in the second millennium B.C. But then within six or seven hundred years the goddess came back, and Kālī was *it*. This goddess came in then in the very great story called the *Devī Mahātmya*, the Great Praise of the Goddess. All the gods, her children, have been impotent in the slaying of a monster called the Monster Buffalo. Unable to do anything, they all stand in a circle and give their powers back to the place from which it came, and a great

FIGURE 144. Kālī astride Śiva (gouache on paper, India, date unknown)

dark cloud emerges and out of this cloud comes the beautiful form of a goddess with eighteen arms, each arm holding one of the powers of the gods, and she goes and slays the monster.

This is the reply to Marduk, who slew the goddess of the abyss, Tiamat, and thought the power was his.

Here, when the gods find they are impotent, they have to give the power back to where it ultimately came from: to the female principle. She is the power of life, which lives in us in both its natural and in its so-called supernatural aspects. And in the Greek world we have the rise, then, of the mystery cults, the goddess Demeter, Persephone, and in Egypt, Isis, Nephthys. These are the guides to rebirth, and it's their symbology that comes in the symbol of the Virgin Mother as the Madonna.

However, what you find in the more sophisticated mythological imagery of the Upaniṣads, which represent a synthesis of the two positions, is that the creative deity is himself the universe. There is a marvelous passage in the Bṛhadāraṇyaka Upaniṣad, which dates to about the ninth century B.C., where the divine self, *brahman*, the primordial energy of which we all are manifestations, said to itself, "*ātman*," ("I"). Now it's neither male or female, it's an it. And no sooner did it say "I" than it was afraid. It was afraid that it would be killed. And then it reasoned, thinking, "Of what should I be afraid since there's nothing here but myself?" No sooner did it allay its fear that way when it thought, "I wish there were someone else here." These are the two prime drives of life: fear and desire. Filled with the desire that there should be something there beside itself, it swelled to the size of a male and female embracing, and then split in half. Then the male begot on the female the world, and he first united with her in anthropomorphic human form, and she thought, "How can he unite with me who am of his substance?" She turned herself into a mare, and he into a stallion, and he united with her. She turned herself into a cow and he into a bull, and so on down to the ants. And then he looked around and said, "I have poured forth all this; I am this."

Now, the sense is there that we are one with the deity. This is in the mood you might say of Mother Goddess thinking, whereas anyone who says, "I and the Father are one" in our tradition gets crucified. Jesus was crucified for saying that, and then the same thing happened in Islam to the mystic al-Hallaj nine hundred years later. To claim identity with the divine is blasphemy here.

So we've got two quite contrary traditions. One is fixed on the visible world and its separate forms, so that when you say "I" what you're thinking of is your separate form as distinct from others. And the other mythology is interested in a transpersonal perspective, in which it recognizes that we are all of the one life, we are all of the one consciousness. We are specifications individually of that which is transcendent of individuations, and yet we are individuals also.

One of the problems in mythology, in religion, is to experience this opening to others as being one with yourself, what we call compassion, *Mitleid* (literally the German for "suffering with")—and with that goes understanding, with that goes identification, and against that, then, is a separate soul that is in our Orthodox tradition created, and yet is eternal. This is logically absurd, but that's what you've got, an individual created as a separate entity.

During the fourth, third, second, and first millennia B.C. we have invasions from the herding people into the planting areas. In the Western world there are two orders of invading people. One order are the Semitic sheep- and goat-herding people, and they are based largely in the Syro-Arabian desert, and it's from there that they come as Bedouins, as freebooters, as pillagers, plunderers, and conquerors. Read the Book of Judges, read the Book of Joshua, and your hair will stand on end—these are not the chapters I usually recommend. Just read the taking of Jericho, for example: "Kill everything in the city," is the order that is given by the same God who a couple of months earlier had said, "Thou shalt not kill." You can work this one out in your own mind.

During the same period, the so-called Aryans or Indo-Europeans were coming from the north into Central Europe, south into Italy, Greece, Persia, and India, and west into Britain and Ireland. All the languages of Europe spoken today except Basque come from this Indo-European heritage. The farthest northwest are the Celtic languages of Ireland, the Isle of Man, Scotland, Wales, and formally of France. The main Celtic invasions began around 1000 B.C., about the same time that what is called the Hallstatt culture moved into Central Europe.

When Caesar conquered Gaul and entered Britain in 50 B.C. or so, it was the Celtic people who inhabited what is now France and the British Isles. Rome conquered and dominated the area from about 50 B.C. until around A.D. 450. By that time, the soldiers were complaining about the weight of their backpacks and how many miles they had to walk a day, and everything was falling apart. The Roman Empire had overextended itself and so began to withdraw. The Danube marked the northeastern border of the empire, and northwestward of there you have another set of Indo-European people, the Germans. To the east the Persians were pressing in, so Rome was collapsing, and they withdrew from England.

However, the Roman armies had been protecting Britain from invasion. As soon as the Roman armies withdrew, the Celts who had been there before began raiding in from Scotland and Ireland. The word *Scot* really means "raider" and refers principally to the Irish. At the same time, German raiders swept in from the northeast. These were what we call the English: the Anglo-Saxons and Jutes, who came in from what is now Denmark. They conquered the territory that Rome had held, which came to be called England, but the territory that Rome had not entered, namely Scotland, Wales, and Ireland, the English didn't enter either.

Now, this is an important thing to bear in mind when we're

thinking of the history of the mythologies in Europe. Our popular notion of English history begins with the period of Rome's withdrawal and the English entry into the British Isles, but before that there were the Celts. The Celts themselves had been invaders, and before them were the great old Neolithic and Bronze Age people, the planting people who left great megalithic monuments throughout Ireland dating back to as early as 2500 B.C.

In the Celtic world, the mythology of the Mother Goddess was dominant. Then, when the Germanic warrior people came in, the gods of the old Celtic people retreated into fairy hills.

Most of the fairy tales of Europe originate from the Celtic tradition. Now, there are lots of fairy hills in Ireland and one of the things about a fairy hill is that it's invisible and nobody knows it's there, and another remarkable thing about fairy hills is that you can walk in what you think is a straight line but you will have walked around a fairy hill—it is that inaccessible. Yet this fairy world is just one small dimension deeper than the visible world; it's everywhere. The fairies are the inhabiting nature powers, and the reason they are so fascinating and enchanting is that their nature and your unconscious nature, your deep nature, are the same. The fairies are representatives of that permanent energy consciousness that underlies all the phenomenal forms of life. This is Mother Goddess stuff.

In the Middle Ages, particularly in the twelfth and thirteenth centuries, there was a great resurgence of Celtic thinking in Europe, and its principal manifestation was in the Arthurian romances. The romances of Arthur and the Grail are all Celtic themes, and they go way, way back.

The thirteenth century was the century of the Virgin. The Goddess comes back into the Christian, anti-Goddess tradition by way of Mary, Mother of God, and there has been, particularly in Catholicism, a steady magnification of the Virgin from the fifth century A.D. to the present.

One of the great problems for St. Paul was whether Christianity was something for the Gentiles as well as for the Hebrews, and he opted for the Gentiles. One of his companions was a Greek, St. Luke, and it's in the Luke Gospel that the image of the virgin birth appears. You won't find it in the books of Matthew, Mark, or John, who were all Jews; it's in the Gospel According to Luke, the Greek. There's no such thing as a virgin birth, at least overtly, in the Hebrew tradition, as this is an idea totally repulsive to it. Now, when you think of

Sarah giving birth to Isaac when she was about 108 years old ("Sarah laughed"),[3] mythologically speaking, that's a virgin birth. Read carefully the birth of Samson—but Samson wasn't a Jew, he was a Philistine, which is to say, an Indo-European. The story of his birth is very close to a virgin birth story, but really, the virgin birth does not belong to the Old Testament tradition.

What the virgin birth represents is the birth of the spiritual life in the human animal. It has nothing to do mythologically with a biological anomaly. In the Indian *kuṇḍalinī* system the first three cakras are our animal zeal to life, animal erotics, and animal aggression. Then at the level of the heart there is the birth of a purely human intention, a purely human realization of a possible spiritual life which then puts the others in secondary place. The symbol in the *kuṇḍalinī* system for this *cakra* is a male and female organ in conjunction—an upward-facing and a downward-facing triangle. At this level the spiritual life is generated, and that is the meaning of the virgin birth.

The virgin birth appears in practically every tradition in the world. American Indian myths are full of virgin births. Quetzalcoatl was born of a virgin, he created human beings, and he died and was resurrected, and one of the prime symbols of Quetzalcoatl was the cross.[4] When the Roman Catholic Spaniards entered Mexico they didn't know what to think of this. They had two explanations. One was that St. Thomas, the apostle to the Indies, had reached America and had taught the doctrine of Christ. Being so far from Rome and the authority of Rome, however, the doctrine deteriorated in America into this monstrous thing called Aztec Quetzalcoatl. The other explanation they had was that the devil was throwing up mockeries of their own traditions in order to frustrate the mission. In either case, they recognized that this was the same god in a different local form.

Gods represent mystical principles, possibilities of human experience, and they take different forms in different cultures according to the environment, history, and requirements of the culture as inflections of spiritual life. Just as the human form itself is inflected in various ways in various parts of the world, so also are the myths that represent the invisible ranges of the psyche inflected. One more point: when you have a culture like the cultures of the invaders, the accent is more on the culture than on nature. When you have a Goddess mythology, it's Mother Nature that we hear of, and this Mother Nature mythology is deep—it's universal.

As I've pointed out, a warrior people fighting for its existence against others accents the special forms of that society and its way of life, and so you have a social rather than a nature accent, and this can go so far that it amounts to an attempted abolition of nature, and that's what you get in the Old Testament. Read again Exodus, Leviticus, Numbers, Deutoronomy: laws, laws, laws. How to part your hair, how to blow your nose, what to eat and what not to eat. It has nothing to do with nature; it has to do with what we do that holds us together. We can't associate with anybody else, and so we don't get mixed up with anybody else. Food laws, whether they are for the Brahmins or the Jews, are isolating—that's what they're there for. Just read them over; they don't make sense in any other terms.

Now, the nature mythologies and the societal mythologies are in conflict with each other: the God mythologies accent the social and the Goddess mythologies accent the nature aspects. In the biblical case, the patriarchs came in with the social accent: everybody else is abominable and should be wiped out, along with their gods. As Second Kings 5:15 admonishes, "There is no God in all the earth but in Israel." Period. From a human standpoint this is an outrageous statement. The Goddess, on the other hand, is in everybody, in every place, and *is* every place; the business of recognizing her there is the business of this mythology. So you can see why the God mythology was so violently against her: she represented nature, and nature is fallen in the biblically based traditions. Nature fell in the Garden and every natural impulse is sinful unless it has either been circumcised or baptized away. That's rooted in our culture.

That's a historical background for the feminine divine in Western Europe. In the early Paleolithic the Goddess is associated with the dwelling sites, while the male shamans and the male rites are associated with the great caves and the paintings. It's interesting that the female form appears in plastic forms and the male forms appear in painted forms. Painting is analytical, sculpture is synthetic—two totally different mental and emotional attitudes.

Then we have the emergence of agriculture, and here the Goddess, who had belonged in the domestic sites, becomes the dominant deity, because the main source of the food is now domestic and not from a hunt. We've got a settled community where our food supply is grown. The first tillers of the soil were women, and if you study planting people today, you will see that the men do the heavy work preparing the ground, but the women plant the seeds. It's their magic. However, when the plow was invented and you had something that simulated by analogy sexual intercourse with the plowing of the Mother Earth, then the men took over the work in agriculture, but the Goddess remained the principal figure. We have this agriculture system going right up into Europe with the Old Bronze Age, whose signs we can still find at Newgrange in Ireland (c. 2500 B.C.) and Stonehenge in England (1700 or 1800 B.C.).

FIGURE 145. Spirals at Newgrange (carved stone, Neolithic, Ireland, c. 2500 B.C.)

Then in come the raiding Indo-European warrior people. In the British Isles, the first wave to arrive was the Celts.

Now, a typical Celtic story is of a warrior who follows a deer into the forest. The deer disappears into a hill and the deer is the Goddess. She is the queen of the hill and he goes by magic into the hill and becomes her lover and protector. He stays with her what he thinks is perhaps six months or a year and then he says, "I'd like to go back to see how my friends are."

She tries to dissuade him, but he keeps asking and so she says, "Well, okay. You can go. But don't get off the horse." She gives him permission and he rides off.

And when he leaves the hill, everything's changed. "My God, three hundred years have passed!" There's nobody around who was there when he had been. He is in that wonderful place of nature that is beyond time. The entry into the eternal hill, a fairy hill, is a passage into the realm of the unconscious where the tick of time is not heard. It is where you dream your mother and father are still alive and telling you what to do, and the dead are all there—you are outside the field of time.

So this warrior goes riding on, and then he drops his glove. Not thinking, he stoops over to pick it up, but when he touches the Earth he dissolves into a little pile of ashes.

It's an old Celtic theme, and it's an old Japanese theme also. It's interesting that the great creative period in pre-Buddhist Japan before the sixth century A.D. is the same period as pre-Christian Celtic Europe. Many themes run back and forth.

Then this socially oriented mythology from the Near East is brought into Europe as Christianity, and that overlies the native nature-oriented mythology. The mythology of the Bible has nothing whatsoever to do with the European experience. It's pasted on top of what was already there. It was brought in by force of arms and maintained by terrific authority, and the crisis period comes at the end of the fourth century A.D. It's at this time that Theodosius the Great declared that no religion but the Christian religion would be tolerated in the Roman Empire, and no variety of Christianity except that of the Byzantine throne. Immediately people begin burying things to protect them from the vandalism of the early Christians—and the vandalism of the early Christians was utterly incredible. When you voyage in the Eastern Mediterranean lands of Greece, Syria, and Egypt and see the beautiful monuments that have been deliberately destroyed, you can't believe the amount of energy that went into destroying them. The Acropolis and the other great temples—those things didn't fall apart. They were knocked down by vandals. They represented the beauty of the Goddess. "Thou shalt not have a graven image."

But not just works of the pagans were attacked. The prelates had decided which books in the Bible were canonical, and any others were to be burned. This is when the Nag Hammadi Coptic scrolls were buried, the Thomas Gospel and the rest.

The biblical and Goddess traditions were radically against each other, and while the biblical has remained the authorized tradition, there has been in European culture this waterway of the living Mother Earth flowing underneath. In the Old Testament we read in early Genesis, "Remember thou art dust and to dust thou shalt return."[5] Well, the Earth is not dust, the Earth is life, vital, and this intrusive god who comes in late, wanting to take everything over to himself, he denigrates the Earth itself and calls it dust? What he tells you there is, "You really are your mother's child and you'll go back to her. She's nothing but dust, however." Similarly, you read in Genesis 1:1, "When God created, the breath (or spirit) of the Lord brooded over the waters." It doesn't say he created the waters. The waters are the Goddess—she was there first.

Turn to Proverbs and there she comes back as the wisdom goddess Sophia, and she says, "When he prepared the heavens, I *was* there."[6] She says it. What you have is the same old mythology that the Babylonians and the Sumerians had of two powers, the female power and the male power in tension, relationship, and creative co-action. But what happened in the Bible was that the male power was anthropomorphized in the form of a man and the female power was reduced to an elemental condition—just water. It says, "God's breath brooded over the waters."[7] It doesn't say the waters of the Goddess, it just says the waters. She's screened out, but she always comes back.

It is very interesting the way the male tries to take over when he comes in. He'll tell you, "This is God," but your heart knows, "No, it isn't, it's Mother." As I like to ask, who wants Abraham's bosom?

So in our tradition we have a deceptive overlay, but in that overlay itself are clues to an original Mother Goddess mythology, because the mythology of Genesis up to chapter 11 is old Sumerian nature mythology: the mythology of the flood, the mythology of the tower, the mythology of the creative being who splits in two—Adam with Eve, his rib (or as Joyce calls her, the "cutlet-sized consort"). The whole thing is Mother Goddess taking over.

One of the most interesting Mother Goddess motifs is found in the story of Cain and Abel. Samuel Noah Kramer is a principal translator of Sumerian texts and he has translated a very interesting text from about 2000 B.C. in which a herder and an agriculturalist are competing for the favor of a goddess.[8] The agriculturalist says, "Oh, well, I'll give you wheat and make you bread and all that."

The shepherd says, "Oh, I'll give you cheese and milk and all that."

The Goddess says, "I'll take the agriculturalist."

Next comes Genesis out of the Yahwist tradition, and it dates from about 800 B.C. Here you have Cain and Abel competing for the grace of a male deity, and he chooses the shepherd. Why? Well, weren't these Israelites themselves shepherds? Didn't they come into the city world, and wasn't Cain the one who founded cities?

One can see throughout the biblical mythologies how the role that is properly and naturally and obviously that of a female is taken over by the male.

When we turn to the main mythologies of Europe, we find four perfectly good, solid human mythologies all linked to nature: the Celtic, the Germanic, the Italic of Italy and Rome, and the Greek. These were mature mythologies, all of them Goddess-based, and you can go from one to the other and locate the counterparts—the Three Fates and the Norns. The Fates guide us, just as "The eternal female draws us on." So we read from Seneca, *"Ducunt volentem fata, / nolentem trahunt"* ("The Fates guide those who will; those who won't they drag").[9] It's good guidance: it's the guidance of your nature. Your mind, however, can put you in conflict with your nature—and the Goddess is the one who represents that nature.

Virgin Mary

Out of the sheer male cult of the Old Testament, we have the Gospel of Luke, where the Virgin conceives the Christ of God.

In A.D. 431, the Council of Ephesus, Artemis's city, declared Mary to be truly Theotokos, the Mother of God. By the time we get to the thirteenth century, all the cathedrals are built in her name. She is the mediator because one cannot approach God directly—and that certainly is a truth. The only god you can approach is the god you can conceive of, and who can conceive of God? So you approach God through the Mother, through the source of your human nature, and

FIGURE 146. Mary enthroned, with Christ on her lap, at Chartres Cathedral (carved stone, Gothic, France, twelfth century A.D.)

she pleads for you. She is not *worshipped* but *venerated*; she is almost a goddess, she doesn't quite get there, but she does now receive the title *co-savior*.

You can find her on the west portal of Chartres Cathedral in the role of Isis or of Cybele, as the throne of Imperato, of the Lord of the World, the Christ. It is she who gives him to the world, just as Māyā gives all the forms and names to the world. All the gods derive from the mother: She's the Mother of Form; She's the Mother of Names. Beyond her is transcendence and consequently she represents that which is transcendent, as well as what is potential, what is in the future; she is the source and the end. This is the worship-as-veneration of the female power in the Western world.

The Court of Love

The Arthurian Legends are a way in which Europe in the Middle Ages tried to assimilate and bring together these two completely contrary mythologies, philosophies, and ways of thinking about life. The Celtic culture was very strong in Europe; the big Celtic period was from 1000 b.c., with a high moment around 500 b.c., when the Celts almost captured Rome. According to legend, Rome was saved by the noise that the geese in the temple of Juno made as the Celts were trying to scale the Capitoline Hill.

Then the Roman conquest of Britain simply put an overlay of Classical mythology on top of the Celtic and, as we saw earlier, there was no problem uniting the two. These same gods are the gods who then appear in the European fairy tales that begin coming through in the eleventh through the thirteenth centuries.

The Romans retreated from England around a.d. 445, and the Anglo-Saxons invaded. The British kings in the south of England were assisted in their defense by a character named Arthur or Artus (his name comes from the same root as Artemis), who is described in the chronicles of Gildas[10] and Nennius[11] of the sixth and eighth centuries as *dux bellorum* ("a leader in war"). Arthur was probably a native Roman-trained officer, and he was a very important figure, apparently, in the defense of Britain. Twelve battles are attributed to Arthur (twelve telling us that he had already become a sun god), and the number of people whom he killed in each battle was enormous.

Finally in one battle he was killed, and the Angles and Saxons took over what's now called England.

Celtic refugees left southern England and fled to France across the channel to Brittany, which became the center of those people. In Brittany developed what is known as the Hope of the Bretons: namely, that Arthur one day would return and win back for them their land, Great Britain.

So Brittany is one of the big centers for the generation of Arthurian traditions. It begins with an oral tradition about the return of Arthur, and where would he meanwhile have been living? He would have been living in one of three places. First, there were the great burial mounds, and sleeping in one of these would be Arthur.

The second great tradition was that he was waiting on Avalon, a fairy land in the western seas to which he was transported by three fairy queens at the time of his death and where he has slept through the ages. Times have passed, but there he is, in one of those fairy hills, or fairy isles from which he will return. And the word *Avalon* is related to the word *apples*. It is the land of the golden apples, the Hesperides, out beyond the known world. This is a Greek idea but also a Celtic one. Here again these two traditions come together: we have the European fairy land where the hero dwells and what he thinks are a couple of years are actually hundreds of years, and he will come back then to save us.

A third idea was that he was in the Antipodes. In the Middle Ages, despite what people say about the world having thought to be flat, it was believed that the world was a sphere, and that all the land was in the Northern Hemisphere while the Southern Hemisphere was all water. And down there at the bottom of the sphere, for example, were the Antipodes, the land below or beyond the oceans where Arthur might be dwelling.

In Dante's *Divine Comedy*, Virgil leads the poet through the Inferno to the island of Purgatory on the far side of the world. When Columbus first approached the South American mainland and saw the mighty Orinoco River, he was convinced that he was seeing one of the four rivers that the Bible tells us flowed from Eden, which would have been at the peak of Mount Purgatory.

So we have this mythological theme of Arthur about to come back: the once and future king. Then we have the breakthrough into literature with Geoffrey of Monmouth's *History of the Kings of Britain*, and there you find a lot of familiar stories. Shakespeare took some of his themes from this: *King Lear*, for instance, with its fairy-tale division of the kingdom, and *Cymbeline*. At the end, we have the story of the battle for Britain and Arthur's life, only in this version he's a king.

The warrior helping to defend kings has himself become in the folk memory a great king. And this first recorded story tells of Arthur, king of a little British empire, who is challenged by Rome. When he goes to conquer Rome with his army, he receives news that his nephew Mordred is conniving with Authur's wife, Guinevere, to take the throne, and so he returns for his final battle. Guinevere in this case is simply an ambitious and unappreciated wife; you have none of the later romance in this early telling.

This is the story of Arthur as it was known in Anglo-Saxon Britain. In A.D. 1066 the Normans from France conquered Britain and took over, so you have the Celts who were conquered by the English, and the English who were conquered by the Normans. For the next couple of centuries nobody of any aristocratic character would speak English. The gentry were all speaking French, while the English were out in the yard taking care of the animals. When the meat is on the table, we call it veal, or *veau*, the French word. When it's out in the yard, it's a calf, the English word. The English tended the sheep, while the Normans ate the mutton (*mouton*), and so forth.

So here's what we have: the Celts, the English, and the Normans, all stuck together on this little island. There were no television sets in those days, so what do you do with a long evening? They would invite bards to come in and entertain; typically they were Celtic bards who would come and sing in Norman French to the high society of the castles. This wonderful combination of the Norman French and the Celts brings forth a whole literature of Celtic myth tales, with Celtic heroes and heroines all dressed in medieval costumes and professing to be good Christians, but enacting old, old stories.

The Norman courts included not only England but most of France; it was Joan of Arc who released France, you might say, from this Anglo-Norman supervision in the fifteenth century. At this early time, however, there was another wonderful lady, Eleanor of Aquitaine (1122–1204), who was the hereditary ruler in her own right of the southwestern part of France, the wife of two kings, the mother of three kings, and the grandmother of everybody of any royal pretentions in the following generations. She married Louis VII, king of France, went with him on crusade, and probably became bored with him, and so one morning when the king woke up, Eleanor wasn't there. By the way, you think women are coming into their own only now, but they were in their own in the Middle Ages—those girls knew how to take care of themselves.

Eleanor had ridden off to marry another king entirely: Henry II, Plantagenet king of England, and she brought with her a good part of France. She was the mother of Henry's sons, King Richard the Lion-hearted and King John, and of Louis's children, most notably Marie de Champagne.

Marie de Champagne (1145–1198) was another remarkable woman. She became the queen regent of France from 1181 to 1187, and her court was the heart of the rebirth of humanism that gave rise to the Renaissance. Marie's court poet was Chrétien de Troyes, and it is to him that the earliest versions of most of the Arthurian romances can be attributed.

Now, the medieval poets never claimed to invent their stories; they always cited the source (*matière*), and what they did was reinterpret, amplify, and further develop a traditional theme (*san*). The stories that Chrétien developed between about 1165 and 1195 constitute, in many ways, the bibliography of the Arthurian romances. He wrote the earliest recorded telling of *Tristan and Iseult*. This has been lost, but other writers picked up the same story, as it is one of the dominant themes of the Middle Ages.

The story of Tristan is of choosing love over marriage. Marriage in the Middle Ages—as in most of history—was a socially arranged affair wherein the family would make the arrangements for political or financial reasons. In twelfth-century France, there was a protest against this; the protest was enunciated by the troubadours and the whole tradition of *Amor*. If you spell *Amor* backward you get *Roma*; *Roma* means the Church and the sacrament of marriage, and *Amor* means the awakening of the heart. The poets or troubadours of southern France were writing in a language called Provençal, and this is the world from which Eleanor of Aquitaine came—her grandfather, William X of Aquitaine, was the very first troubadour.

The psychological question of great concern was this: What is love? What is *Amor*? Up to that time we had in the Christian West only two ideas of amorous relationship: one was lust, which I define as the zeal of the organs for each other, which has very little to do with who the carrier is, so it's impersonal; and then, contrary to that, you have *agapē*, or spiritual love—"Love thy neighbor as thyself"[12]—and again, this is impersonal.

However, the great characteristic of Europe is recognition of personality, of the individual. There is no culture in the world with a tradition of portrait art comparable to that of the West—think of Rembrandt. There is a deep meaning in the individual. *Amor* has to do with *personal* love—the meeting of the eyes. The marvelous Provençal poet Girhault de Borneilh wrote a definition of love that holds for the whole troubadour tradition. It's written, of course, from the standpoint of the lover, and the lover is always the male and the beloved is the female:

> *The eyes are scouts of the heart.*
> *The eyes go forth to find an image to recommend to the heart.*
> *And if it is a gentle heart, then Amor, love, is born.*[13]

A gentle heart—this is the key word: *gentle*. In another trend of this period it was the *noble* heart, usually associated with warrior deeds. The gentle heart is the heart that is capable of love and not simply of lust. This is a fine definition: *Amor*, love, comes from the meeting of the eyes.

The great tale of *Amor* is the tale of Tristan and Iseult. Though we know that Chrétien wrote a version of this tale, it has not come down to us, and so the greatest of the existing versions was written by Gottfried von Strassburg in the very early thirteenth century.

Tristan was a young orphan who was born in Brittany, the place from which this whole tradition emerges. An enormously talented youth, he could speak no end of languages, play no end of musical instruments, and he knew how to butcher game—he knew everything. Tristan goes to serve his uncle King Mark in Cornwall.

There is an interesting aspect to these Arthurian stories: it is always the nephew and the uncle, the mother's brother: the matrilineal line. You've got Tristan and Mark, Arthur and Mordred, and so forth.

When Tristan arrives he learns that a warrior has arrived from Ireland to collect tribute from the Cornish people because the Irish king had conquered Cornwall. The tribute consisted of youths and maidens to be brought to Ireland to serve in the Irish court, and the people didn't want their children to go. Tristan said to his uncle Mark, "Let me take care of this. I'll go and meet him in single combat, defeat him, and then there will no more tribute." This is a deliberate echo of the story of Theseus and the Minotaur, an intentional restating of ancient Classical motifs.

Morholt, the Irish champion, has a sword that has been anointed with poison by the queen of Ireland, who is named Iseult—and whose daughter is also named Iseult. This is a common trope in courtly love: poison on the sword. The combat takes place and Morholt's sword comes down on Tristan's thigh and cuts it, and the poison is introduced. Tristan's sword comes down on Morholt's helmet, cuts right through, and smashes Morholt's skull, killing him, but a little chink of Tristan's sword is left in Morholt's head.

The tribute is finished, and Morholt is brought back to Ireland. Now, his little niece Iseult, the daughter of Queen Iseult, loved her uncle and when the chink was extracted from Morholt's head she kept it as a memorial in her little treasure box.

Back in Cornwall Tristan's poisoned wound begins to stink and nobody can bear it, and he says to Mark, "Put me in a little boat, and the boat will carry me by magic to the very place where the healing will be attended to"—the healing has to be accomplished by the one who injured him.

In *Amor*, the love wound—the sickness no doctors can cure—can be cured only by the one who issued the wound: namely, the one you fell in love with. This is a replay of the poison-in-the-sword motif.

So Tristan sails off in the boat and it carries him indeed to Ireland, to the court of the very person whose poison is killing him. He is playing the harp out in the little boat, feeling very sick, as he sails into Dublin Harbor. The people ashore go out and hear this youth play—this is Orpheus. They bring him ashore and lo and behold, they carry him to be cured by the very queen who poisoned him.

For some reason the queen doesn't know that this man is the one who killed her brother Morholt. Of course, our hero had changed his name and called himself Tantrist (French: "too sad") instead of Tristan, so how could she know who he was? So she works to cure him, as she is a compassionate woman. When the wound no longer stinks, she invites her daughter, Iseult, in to hear this wonderful harpist, and when the daughter enters, Tristan plays more marvelously than he's ever played in his life. In other words, he's fallen in love—only he doesn't know it yet. This is the mystery of this whole tale: he doesn't know it.

Finally Tristan is cured, and he goes back to Cornwall. He's so excited about this wonderful girl that he talks her up to his uncle and says, "You ought to marry her!" Can you beat it? He's so innocent of his own emotions that he thinks his uncle should marry this girl.

Well, everybody thinks his uncle should get married anyhow because they need a queen, so they send Tristan back—with his name still twisted around—to fetch this girl. Well, he arrives back in Ireland to find that there is a dragon making it tough for people. And the king has said, "Whosoever kills this dragon shall have Iseult in marriage."

Well, of course, Tristan rides out to kill the dragon. There is also, however, a seneschal, a sort of courtier who isn't capable of killing dragons, but he wants very much to marry Iseult. So whenever he gets a notion of somebody going out to kill that dragon, he trails along.

When Tristan has slain the dragon, he opens its mouth, cuts out its tongue as proof of his deed, sticks the tongue in his shirt, and walks away.

The seneschal comes afterward and cuts off the dragon's head, then brings the head to court to claim Iseult.

Poor Tristan. One thing you should never do with a dragon's tongue is stick it in your shirt—because it's poisonous. So while he is walking away with the dragon's tongue in his shirt, Tristan faints and falls into a pool, and the only part of him sticking out is his nose, so he's breathing all right.

Iseult and her mother happen to be out for a stroll along the pool, and as they stroll along, they look and say, "There's somebody down there!" So they pull Tristan out—for some reason they don't even recognize that he is Tantrist, the one who was there before—and take him to court once again to heal him.

They put him in the bathtub to heal him. In the meanwhile, Iseult is fooling around with Tristan's equipment in his room when she pulls his sword out of its sheath, and lo and behold, "My gosh, there's a nick in this sword!" So she goes to her little treasure box and there is this missing piece. She sees that it fits, and oh, she loved her uncle! So she takes this heavy sword and goes in to kill Tristan in the bathtub.

He looks up and says, "Hold on. You knock me out and that seneschal dope gets you."

Iseult has to admit that this is a good point. In the meantime, the sword is getting kind of heavy, so that is the end of that.

Once Tristan has once again been healed, he is brought to court with the big question: Who gets Iseult? The first claim is made by this chap the seneschal, who comes in with the dragon's head, which looks very conclusive.

Tristan, however, has only to say, "Open its mouth and let's see what's missing there."

No tongue. And where is the missing part?

"It's here!" says Tristan, holding out the tongue, and so he got Iseult.

This stupid little boy, he still wants to bring her back to uncle Mark. So her mother, the one who prepared the poison that brought this whole thing about, prepares a love potion for Iseult to deliver to Mark so that the two will have a love marriage.

Now, this is a great problem theologically and in every other way. In any case, the queen puts the potion and her daughter into the keeping of young Iseult's faithful nursemaid, Brangaene.

Well, Brangaene doesn't pay very close attention. On the way back, Tristan and Iseult, both about fifteen years old, each take a sip of the love draught, thinking it is wine. Suddenly the couple becomes aware of the love that has been gradually growing in their hearts.

When Brangaene learns what happened, she is appalled. This is a wonderful moment: she goes to Tristan and says, "You have drunk your death!"

And Tristan answers, "I don't know what you mean. If by death you mean this pain of love, that is my life."

This is the essential idea of *Amor*, experiencing the pain. The essence of life is pain, all life is suffering. In Japan in almost the same period Lady Murasaki writes *The Tale of Genji*, and you have this love play of the cloud gallants and the flower maidens—they're experiencing in a very sensitive way the Buddha's wisdom, that all life is suffering, and the suffering of love is the suffering of life and where your pain is, there is your life.

Tristan continues, "If by this love, this agony of love, you mean my death, that is my life. If by my death you mean the punishment that will be ours when discovered in adultery, I accept that." This is pushing right through the pair of opposites of life and death, and this is where love is: the pain pushed through. And then he finishes, "And if by death you mean eternal death in Hell, eternally I accept that too."[14]

Now, that's a big, big statement, and this is the spirit of *Amor* in the Middle Ages. You can't call it just an aristocratic game, and it wasn't just a love affair. It was a mission transcendent of all the values of this world and a pitch into eternity. When Dante was going through the stages of hell, the first and least horrendous was that of the carnal lovers. Among them were Tristan and Iseult and Lancelot and Guinevere, all the great lovers of all time. And he recognizes one couple, Paolo and Francesca, and like a good sociologist he calls Francesca down and asks, "How did you get into this condition?"

In the most poignant lines in the whole poem, she answers, "We were reading the book of Guinevere and Lancelot. And when we came to the meeting of their eyes, we looked at each other and read no more in the book that day."[15] There they are in what looks like hell to us, but the wonderful, wise miracle man, William Blake, said in his book of aphorisms, *The Marriage of Heaven and Hell*, "I was walking among the fires of hell, delighted with the enjoyments of Genius; which to Angels look like torment and insanity."[16] I think that's the answer. So what Tristan accepted was the fire of this agony that is love for eternity, and that will be his life in eternity.

Then comes the whole story of their deception of Tristan's uncle, King Mark. From the troubadour standpoint Mark has no right to Iseult. He has never seen her, she has never seen him, there has been no meeting of the eyes, there is no love—there can't be *Amor*. There might be great kindness and compassion but not this thing called love. And so when Tristan and Iseult are at court, and Mark discovers their love, he can't bring himself to have them killed. He loves them both, so he says, "Get out of my sight, go into the woods."

And next you have the great story of the forest years of Tristan and Iseult. They enter a cave that has an inscription over it—"The Cave for Lovers." That cave was carved and furnished in the period before the Christians came: it was a Celtic mystery cave furnished as a darling little chapel. And at the place where the altar would have been there is a crystalline bed, and the sacrament of that chapel is the sacrament of love. This appears first in Gottfried of Strassburg's version of the story. He invented this little chapel.

Now, in the chapel's roof were two little windows to let the sunlight in. One day Tristan hears hunting horns in the distance—it is King Mark out on a hunt. And Tristan thinks, "Lest Mark discover the cave and peer down and see Iseult and myself here in bed together, I will put my sword between us."

This is the great mistake. This is placing honor over love, and that is a crucial theme in medieval *Amor*. In medieval German it's *ere* ("honor") and *minna* ("love"). The German troubadours were called *minnesingers. Ere* was pitted against *minna*, and *ere* won, so Tristan lay the sword between them.

Mark looks down indeed and sees the two with the sword between and says, "I have been misinformed. I've misjudged them." And so he invites them back to court.

Of course, Tristan and Iseult can't help themselves; they are caught again, and this time things are serious. Iseult is required to endure a trial in which she has to go across a river, take a vow that she has never slept with anyone but her husband, and then hold in her hand a red-hot iron. If she tells the truth, her hand will not be burned, but if she has not told the truth she will be burned by this red-hot iron.

Well, they work it out. Tristan gets a job as a ferryman and disguises himself. She gets in the boat, he paddles across, and when he lifts her out, he falls down on top of her. "Oh! Sorry."

Cleaned off, she goes and takes the vow, saying, "I have never lain with any man but my husband—and the ferryman who just fell on me." So her hand is not burned.

Tristan is exiled nonetheless, and he goes back to Brittany whence he came. When in Brittany he happens to hear the name Iseult—it is the name of a lovely young woman there—and he falls in love with her because of her name.

He marries Iseult of the White Hands, the third Iseult (after the queen and Tristan's beloved). But he can't sleep with her because she wasn't *his* Iseult; his *Amor* keeps him away from this.

One day, Tristan's dissatisfied wife goes out riding with her brother, Sir Kahedin, when her horse steps into a puddle. The water splashes up onto her thigh, and she says to her brother, "The water is bolder than Tristan."

Kahedin asks, "What's this?"

So she tells him.

Outraged, Kahedin goes to Tristan and charges him with gross dereliction of duty, and Tristan confesses his love for Iseult—*his* Iseult.

"Perfectly understandable," says Kahedin. "Sure."

Later on Tristan is sore wounded in a battle. He lies dying, and the only one who can possibly cure him is the other Iseult, *his* Iseult—she was, after all, the one who dealt Tristan the death wound. So Kahedin goes to fetch Tristan's Iseult to cure him, and if she agrees to come he will return with a white sail. If she refuses, he will return with a black sail—here you get the echo of the Theseus story.

Well, Kahedin returns with Iseult with a white sail flying, but the jealous wife, Iseult of the White Hands, tells Tristan the sail is black, and Tristan dies of grief.

That is a good love story, with all the poignancy and drama. But it's serious—the pain and the possibility of hell.

So this tension between marriage and love was a problem at the end of the twelfth century. How do you put these things together?

Chrétien of Troyes did the first-known *Tristan*; his second work was *Erec*. The ladies of the court had not really been happy about the story of Tristan and Iseult because the consummation of their love took place out in the forest. The ladies wanted it to be in the court—where it would refine the court. So *Erec* is a story of married love, and it's a good, typical male problem.

Erec is a real champion warrior who falls in love with Enid. He is so in love with her that he falls out of training and is no longer a great warrior. Then he realizes, "I've lost my whole character through this!" So he rejects Enid and rides out on his own adventure on his great charger, but she trots along after him on her palfrey, a light woman's horse. She is true to him throughout all this rejection, and finally through this loyalty to him when he has rejected her, he regains both his warrior character and his wife as a loyal supporter.

Well, the ladies weren't awfully excited about that story either.

The next one is one of the strangest stories, called *Cligès*. This is a story of a lover who proposes himself to his beloved—but she is married and will have nothing to do with him. She will not commit adultery—until her husband dies. So they contrive to kill him.

Many of the commentators for some reason call this a moral solution. Evidently the solution wasn't very satisfying, as you don't hear much about *Cligès*; nobody's ever tried that one again.

Next comes the Lancelot and Guinevere story called *The Knight of the Cart*. This is Chrétien's great story, and it's really beautiful. The beauty of it is that Arthur recognizes that Lancelot and Guinevere are in love, and he understands what love is, he values and appreciates it. He is not the French cuckold, what in Provençal is called *le jaloux*, the jealous one.

Now, a very interesting episode gives this romance its title.

Guinevere has been abducted. Lancelot starts out to recover her, but he rides his horse to death. There he is, walking along in a heavy suit of armor and not getting anywhere very fast, when a cart rolls up slowly and passes him.

It would be utterly dishonorable for a knight in his armor to ride in a cart, because carts were used for carrying criminals to execution, carrying manure, carrying animals, and all sorts of things. No knight would ride in a cart.

When the cart passes Lancelot, however, he thinks, "If I were in that, I'd get to Guinevere faster. But honor..."

For three steps he hesitates—and then gets in the cart, his first trial of honor against love.

One of the trials he has to endure before getting to Guinevere is a motif known as the Trial of the Perilous Bed. The knight in full armor comes into a naked marble room. In the middle of it is a bed on rollers. The adventure is to rest quietly on that bed.

So Lancelot approaches the bed and the bed shies away. He approaches it again, but again the bed shies away. Finally, he has to make a running jump in full armor with shield and everything else and land on that bed. He achieves this—but as soon as he hits the bed, it starts bucking around like a western bronco, bumping against the walls and everything else. When it finally settles down, a lion comes in. Well, Lancelot manages to take care of the lion, but he is sorely injured.

Now the ladies of the castle come down, wondering what has happened to the hero down here. They revive him, and then he goes on to the next adventure.

My friend Heinrich Zimmer years ago asked, "What is the meaning of the perilous bed? What can that possibly be?" And I think he came up with the right answer. He said, "It is metaphorical of the male experience of the female temperament. You can't understand what the hell's going on there," as he said, "but be patient and it will settle down and all the joys of beautiful womanhood will be yours."

I had an experience with the perilous bed when I was doing a book on Hindu art—editing one of Zimmer's unfinished books after he had died—and I had collected all the pictures I needed except three or four.

Now, I had known Ananda K. Coomaraswamy, who was at that time the leading authority on these matters, but he had just died. I knew that the pictures that I wanted were in his collection up in Boston and that his widow would have them. So I phoned her up and asked if I had come up to look through the doctor's collection to find these three pictures that I needed.

It was a very hot day in Boston, but I thought it would take me
only about a half hour to go through these files.

"Oh," she said, "come on up." So I went up. "Joe, here's the
room, there are the files."

I'd just opened the shelves when in she came and said, "So, Joe,
it's kind of hot, don't you think you want a lemonade or something
like that?"

"Okay." I didn't at all but didn't want to appear rude.

So we had lemonade and had a nice long talk, and then she went
off and I was just about getting into it again when it was dinnertime.
So off we go to dinner and again we talked. I come back again, I was
poking around in the files, when she said, "You know, Joe, it'd be
perfectly all right, you can sleep on that couch over there, really, it'd
be perfectly all right."

I said to myself, "This is the perilous bed, and I'm going to hang
on here."

Three days. The pictures are in the book, I got them, but I tell
you, that was the Trial of the Perilous Bed.

Lancelot's next trial is what's called the Sword Bridge. This is
an archetypal motif in many mythologies from the Hindus to the
Eskimo. A chasm has to be crossed on a sword bridge, and the hero
is to go across that bridge. The meaning of this in troubadour terms
is that, when you're following the way of *Amor* instead of the way of
society, you are following what's known as the Left-Hand Path.

The Right-Hand Path is the path that stays inside the rules, that
keeps to the social norms. The Left-Hand Path, on the other hand,
is the way of great danger and the way of passion, and there's nothing more destructive to a life course than passion. This is the lesson:
on the way of the Sword Bridge you must keep your mind on *Amor*,
not passion, or the slightest step off or the slightest quiver of fear will
throw you into a torrent that will carry you all way down. This is the
lesson of the Left-Hand Path and of *Amor*.

Lancelot crosses the Sword Bridge, overthrows the guards of the
castle where Guinevere is being imprisoned, and comes to receive the
greeting of his queen.

She is as cold as ice.

Why?

He hesitated for three steps before getting on that cart.

The rules of love, they really are severe. If you're giving up every-thing for something, then *give up everything for something* and stay with it with your mind on where you're going.

These are wonderful lessons for people who are off on the Left-Hand Path—and that's the path to be on if you want to have a spiri-tual instead of a nice sociological life.

Another of Chrétien's stories is quite wonderful: *Yvain.* Very briefly, it is the story of finding your soul bride and then being recalled to society and losing her, then having to go back to find her and unite the two worlds, the world of love and the world of society. This was a problem that was very acute in those times, and is still acute for us now: how to integrate our *Amor* with our responsibilities.

THE RENAISSANCE OF THE GODDESS

In the fifteenth century, at the height of the Italian Renaissance—the time of Cosimo de' Medici, patron of philosophers and artists—there came to Florence a Byzantine priest with a copy of a manuscript in Greek known as the *Corpus Hermeticum.* These were hermetic writ-ings of the late Classical period that exactly paralleled the dawn of Christianity: the first three centuries A.D.

Cosimo asked Marsilio Ficino to translate this Greek text into Latin, and the minute it became known to the philosophers and artists of Florence, there was an enormous outburst of symbolic art. What the Florentines recognized was that the symbology of the Christian tradition and the symbology of the Classical, hermetic tradition were the same, but in two different renditions, one concretizing the sym-bols and the other opening them to their meanings.

Botticelli is simply alive with all this. And in his paintings Titian represents Classical figures and Christian figures, all carrying the same message. The great art of this time comes out of that realization, and this is the great end to excluding Christianity from the world context and from religious revelation.

These two traditions coming together—the Classical and the Christian—is the inspiration that informs the Renaissance from the fifteenth century into the Baroque.

According to a legend preserved in Aeschylus's *Prometheus Bound,* the tormented nymph Io, when released from Argus by Hermes, fled,

FIGURE 147. *Isis with Hermes Trismegistus and Moses* (fresco, Renaissance, Vatican, 1493)

in the form of a cow, to Egypt; and there, according to a later legend, recovering her human form, gave birth to a son identified as Serapis, and Io became known as the goddess Isis. The Umbrian master Pinturicchio (1454–1513) gives us a Renaissance version of her rescue, painted in 1493 on a wall of the so-called Borgia Chambers of the Vatican for the Borgia Pope Alexander VI (Fig. 147).

Pinturicchio shows the rescued nymph, now as Isis, teaching, with Hermes Trismegistus at her right hand and Moses at her left. The statement implied there is that the two variant traditions are two ways of rendering a great, ageless tradition, both issuing from the mouth and the body of the Goddess. This is the biggest statement you can make of the Goddess, and here we have it in the Vatican—that the one teaching is shared by the Hebrew prophets and Greek sages, derived, moreover, not from Moses's God,[17] but from that goddess of whom we read in the words of her most famous initiate, Lucius Apuleius (born c. A.D. 125):

> I am she that is the natural mother of all things, mistress and governess of all the elements, the initial progeny of worlds, chief of the powers divine, queen of all that are in hell, the principal of them that dwell in heaven, manifested alone and under one form of all the gods and goddesses. At my will the planets of the sky, the wholesome winds of the seas, and the lamentable silences of hell are disposed; my name, my divinity is adored throughout the world, in divers manners, in variable customs, and by many names.
>
> For the Phrygians that are the first of all men call me the Mother of the gods of Pessinus; the Athenians, which are spring from their own soil, Cecropian Minerva; the Cyprians, which are girt about the sea, Paphian Venus; the Cretans, which bear arrows, Dictynian Diana; the Sicilians, which speak three tongues, infernal Proserpine; the Eleusians their ancient goddess Ceres; some Juno, others Bellona, others Hecate, others Ramnusie, and principally both sort of the Ethiopians, which dwell in the Orient and are enlightened by the morning rays of the sun; and the Egyptians, which are excellent in all kind of ancient doctrine, and y their proper ceremonies accustomed to worship me, do call me by my true name, Queen Isis. [18]

FIGURE 148. Orpheus the savior (carved stone, late Roman, Italy, third century A.D.)

Down in the early Christian catacombs in Rome is a carving (Fig. 148). Where you would have expected to see the figure of Christ, you see the figure of Orpheus. Orpheus the fisher echoes Christ's admonition, "I'll make you fishers of men." Orpheus is playing his lyre here—that is to say, the harmonious music of the spheres. We see that lion and lamb lie down together as if to say that the lion is going to eat the lamb, all right, but that it's okay—they are all participating in this harmonious round of the universe; the way of nature has not and will not be changed, but one can understand what lies behind them. So there's Orpheus in the center, harmonizing nature.

And round about are scenes from the Old and the New Testament. There is the ram, which had been the sacrificial animal of the Jews, and the bull, which had been the pagan sacrificial animal. It is a completely syncretic image showing the conjunction of pagan, Old Testament, and New Testament figures: Moses drawing water from the rock, Jesus resurrecting Lazarus, David about to slay the giant Goliath, and Daniel in the lion's den, not afraid of the lion's mouth. The message is the realization that these different testaments are but local transformations of one great spiritual message.

FIGURE 149. Serpent Bowl (carved alabaster, provenance unknown, second or third century A.D.)

Here (Fig. 149) is another bowl from the same period as the
Pietroasa bowl. The sixteen people are naked, just as the Graces are,
before the golden, winged serpent of Hermes, the lord who guides
dead souls to immortality. The cult of nakedness associated with the
paradisal experience of having left the ways of the world behind date
very far back.

The lower part of the bowl shows the cycles of the spheres, so
these people are in the realm of the Muses and the light of Apollo. We
can see the guardians of the four directions, and there are the same
number of columns here as there are days in a month. So outside is the
bowl of time, but within is eternity. The women are standing in that
posture of the Venus de' Medici, but whereas the Venus de' Medici is
turned in a coy gesture of shielding the breasts and the genitals, here
she is pointing to them as representing power, and the man is standing
with hand on breast and an attitude of veneration before the serpent.

FIGURE 150. Eucharistic bowl (carved stone, Byzantine, Greece, thirteenth
century A.D.)

From the Mt. Athos monastery in Greece we have again sixteen surrounding figures in the center (Fig. 150). Here, instead of the grail maiden with the chalice, we have Mary herself with the child in her arms—this is the way they're rendered in the Byzantine world. The child is here at the breast of the Virgin but looking outward, with the angels scattering incense. She is like the throne of Isis, and he like the pharaoh: a great image of woman supporting the universe.

FIGURE 151. Orpheos Bakkikos crucified (cylinder seal, Byzantine, Greece, c. 300 A.D.)

The pagan and Christian material is combined on this small piece (Fig. 151), labeled Orpheos Bakkikos. Here we see Orpheus crucified, with the crescent moon above and the seven stars of the heavenly stages above him.

> The seven stars represent the Pleiades, known to antiquity as the Lyre of Orpheus, and the cross suggests, besides the Christian cross, the chief stars of the constellation Orion, know also as that of Dionysus. The crescent is of the ever-waning and -waxing moon, which is three days dark as Christ was three days in the tomb.[19]

FIGURE 152. Crucifixion (print, Germany, c. 1495–1498)

Then we come to Albrecht Dürer's representation of the crucifixion (Fig. 152), in which the sun and moon have come together. This
is a restatement of the theme that I brought up of the two conscious-
nesses: lunar consciousness engaged in the field of time and space, and
solar consciousness disengaged are the same consciousness.

When you realize this, you can ask yourself, "Who am I?" and the answer is not "I am this vehicle, the body," but rather, "I am consciousness." And when you do shift to solar consciousness, you can let your body go with gratitude. So Christ lets his body go and he goes to the Father. Father and Son are analogous to the fifteenth night of the moon when the sun is setting and the moon rising at precisely the same moment and they look at each other across the world, after which the moon declines only to be born again.

The water of immortal life comes forth from the pierced side of the one who has given his body, and the skull of the old Adam is washed in the blood of the Savior and so is redeemed. Dürer brings together the old Adam, the new Adam, the water of immortal life, and the lunar and solar calendars in one symbolic image.

That, ultimately, is the story of the mysteries, which have come into the Christian tradition from the old pagan system. It is my thought that Christianity is far more Greek than Hebrew. The whole theme of the virgin birth is alien to traditional Judaism; it is absolutely native to the Classical tradition. The dove comes to Mary, the swan comes to Leda, and the birth of the Christ or the birth of Helen—the most beautiful and glorious representation of the human body and spirit the world has ever seen—this is all one great mythology and the Gnostic and hermetic thinkers of the early Christian era understood that and expressed that in these bowls and mosaics.

Going back at least nine thousand years to the early agriculture of the Near East and Old Europe, we have a tradition of the power of the Goddess and of her child who dies and is resurrected—namely, it is we who come from her, go back to her, and rest well in her. This tradition was carried through the cults of ancient Mesopotamia, Egypt, and down into the Classical world, before finally delivering the message into Christian teaching.

In 1493 a man named Franchinus Gaffurius published in a book titled *Practica Musicae* this drawing (Fig. 153), which tells us the whole classical iconographic story of the transformation of the soul and the stages of illumination.[20]

Apollo is seated at the top and the three Graces are dancing beside him. In his hand is the lyre that plays the song of the universe, and beside that is that vessel of abundance. The inscription over Apollo's head says, "The energy of the Apollonian mind moves everywhere through the muses." That is the energy of the illuminated mind. The Muses are the inspirers of spiritual knowledge, and the source of their

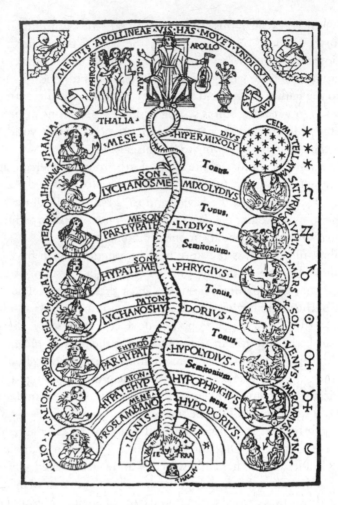

FIGURE 153. *Practica Musicae* (printed book, Renaissance, Italy, 1496)

energy is the Graces. The Graces are naked because nakedness represents disengagement from the limitations of the clothing of time and space, but the Muses who represent the message of this naked truth in the world, they are clothed in the forms of the world. In the field of time the mystery is clothed, while in the eternal sphere it is unclothed.

The Graces are three aspects of Aphrodite; she's the prime goddess related to Apollo—his *śakti*—and the Graces are her inflection as the moving powers of the energy of the world. Euphrosyne is the Grace representing the joy of the radiance that flows out to the world through the qualities of the nine Muses. Aglaea, whose name means "splendor," represents the energy returning to the deity. Thalia, whose names means "abundance," unites the two. This is the process of rendering into the world the radiance of the Apollonian consciousness.

The central figure is the great serpent whose tail is Cerberus, the three-headed dog who guards the underworld. Thalia is also the name of the ninth Muse, so she is both below Cerberus's head and she is also the central Grace above. Her name is Silent Thalia when she is under the threshold of the Earth. Why is she not heard? She is not heard because we are afraid of the three heads of the dog who is the same as the three beasts that threatened Dante when he stood on the path of the dark wood in the middle of his life. The head in the center is that of a lion, and that means the fire of the sun—the threatening fire of today, the present, and the fear of yielding ourselves to the present. Are you going to try to hang onto what you have been, or are you going to let today burn you into something else?

You are living the present in terms of the past, and the adventure consists in throwing yourself open and becoming vulnerable to what this moment has in store for you in the way of shattering what you thought you were and bringing forth what you might be. You can't accept the bite of death and so you're not hearing the song of the universe, and that is why Thalia is silent. The head on the lion's right is of a wolf, and he represents the fear of the passage of time. The future takes away what you've got. Dante translates it as *abaras*, that which takes away what you've got while you are trying to hold on to it, and thereby not giving yourself up to the future. In fear of that experience, one holds back, and the wolf represents fear.

The animal on the right is the head of the dog, which represents desire and the hope for the future. Anyone who is hanging on to his ego is hanging on out of fear and desire, and the goal of this initiation is to cancel out both of those. What binds us is the present, past, and future and so we're bound to the ego. This is the image of that snake biting Peleus's Achilles tendon (Fig. 139): "Let the serpent of death bite your heel, do hear the song of the universe and then the Muses sing." When you have died to your ego and rational consciousness, there opens the intuition, that is to say, you hear the song of the Muse and this is the female power again.

The story that I shared from the Bṛhadāraṇyaka Upaniṣad tells how *brahman*, the Universal Self, had not known of itself. It simply was. As soon as it said "I" (*ātman*), it felt fear. With the birth of ego you have fear, the wolf.

Still, *ātman* reasoned, "Of what should I be afraid since there is no one or no thing around but myself?" Then, however, immediately it thought of its solitude. It wished there was someone else there, and so it was filled with desire, and that is the dog. As soon as there is ego, there is fear and desire.

When the Buddha sat under the tree of the immovable spot he was tempted by the three daughters of the god of lust, Lord Kāma, and their names were Desire, Fulfillment, and Regret. Since he had not identified himself with ego but with the consciousness that informed not only himself but also those three, he was unmoved. Then he was tempted to fear by the army of the Lord Māra or Death, and again he was unmoved, and so he did not hold his ego and passed to the realization of his eternal life.

Insofar as we are bound to ego, we are bound down below the heads of Cerberus, and we do not hear the voice of the eternal life and the consciousness of the universe.

When you have put your head in the mouth of the lion you hear the song of nature. So Thalia is the Muse of bucolic poetry, the poetry of the nature world around you, the sheep and the lion and the trees and the grasses and the mountains.

There is a wonderful passage in Knud Rasmussen's[21] book about the Eskimo and the shamans whom he met. One shaman, an old man named Najagneq, admitted that he had invented a number of trick devices and mythological spooks to frighten his neighbors off and keep them safely at bay.

Rasmussen asked him, "Are there any of these spooks that you pretend to master? Is there any one that you really believe in?"

And Najagneq said, "Yes, a power that we call Sila, one that cannot be explained in so many words: a very strong spirit, the upholder of the universe, of the weather, in fact of all life on Earth—so mighty that his speech to man comes not through ordinary words but through storms, snowfall, rain showers, the tempests of the sea, all the forces that man fears, or through sunshine, calm seas, or small, innocent, playing children who understand nothing. When times are good, Sila has nothing to say to humankind. He has disappeared into his infinite nothingness and stays away as long as people do not abuse life but have respect for their daily food. No one has ever seen Sila. His place of sojourn is so mysterious that he is with us and infinitely far away at the same time."

"The inhabitant or soul of the universe," Najagneq continued, "is never seen; its voice alone is heard. All we know is that it has a gentle voice, like a woman, a voice so fine and gentle that even children cannot become afraid. And what it says is: *Sila ersinarsinivdluge,* 'Be not afraid of the universe.' "[22]

Each of nine Muses is associated with one of the celestial and earthly spheres as registered in the Ptolemaic system. Just as Dante did when he left the Earth to fly to the moon, one must move through the spheres of the earthly elements of earth, water, air, and fire to come to the first Muse and the celestial body of the moon. Selene, the moon, is associated with the art of Clio, the muse of history and historical writing. The moon is the planet that moves the tides of life, the tides of the ocean, and the tides of the menstrual cycle and is consequently the power that informs history. The arrow held by Selene in the sphere of the moon is held down, pointing us to the Earth and its history, while the caduceus of Hermes points upward, directing us to spiritual heights.

Mercury (Hermes) translates the experience of phenomenality into the experience of the radiance of the eternal principle, and this is the art of Calliope, the Muse of epic poetry, which translates history into myth. In epic poetry history is transformed into revelation, history becomes legend. The Earth, the moon, and Mercury respectively represent the pastoral voice of the planet, the voice of history, and then the recognition of a spiritual principle within those. They are the first of the three celestial triads.

The next triad consists of Venus, the sun, and Mars. The Muse of Venus (Aphrodite) is Terpsichore, the Muse of the dance. Recall Aphrodite's lovers Ares and Hermes, war and love: this is the tragic center. The Muse of the sun is Melpomene, the muse of tragedy, and tragic poetry. Through tragedy we shatter the ego and go through to rapture. What is tragedy but the shattering of the main characters in the drama? And the rapture of tragedy is the release from bondage to the historic personality. The Muse of Mars (Ares) is Erato and her art is erotic poetry. This second triad is the transition through the sun door into the high sphere of purely spiritual experience. In this triad we have the dance of tragedy, the erotic aspects, and the tragic moment itself.

With that we are released from bondage to matter and Earth,

and we come to the highest triad: Jupiter (Zeus), the lord governing the world, Saturn (Kronos), the one who cuts off entirely, lifting us through asceticism to the highest sphere, and then the sphere of the fixed stars, which represent orderly, unchanging stability. We come to Zeus, the lord of the gods, and the Muse here is Euterpe, the muse of flute song. That to me was the most surprising mystery, the lovely purity of the flute tone. It is a pure, limpid thing, and here we are in this realm of purity of this kind. When we come to Kronos, we find Polyhymnia, the muse of choral sacred song. Kronos, Lord of Time, is the lord of asceticism, and with his sickle he cuts you off altogether; just as, lower down, the sun cuts you off from the earthly concerns, Kronos cuts you off even from the eternal. Cast your mind to the ultimate transcendent through Polyhymnia, the Muse of sacred choral song.

Last comes the ultimate emporium, the heaven of the fixed stars, and here we find Urania, the Muse of astronomy. You can see an increase in the spiritual and decrease in the weight of matter as we ascend.

We are led then to the very feet of the Lord of Light—Phoebus Apollo—whose energy informs the Graces. Euphrosyne, rapture, sends the energy down; Aglaea, splendor, brings the energy back; and Thalia, abundance, unites the two.

When translated into Christian theology, the Graces and their three powers become masculine: God the Father, God the Son, and God the Holy Spirit: the Father who embraces the Son and the Holy Spirit, the Son who goes in love into the world to share its sufferings and to invoke our participation in his agony so that our minds will be brought into relation to the divine mystery that informs us all, and then the Holy Spirit who carries us back to the Father. The definition of the Trinity is three divine persons in one divine substance, so he becomes the substance of life.

In the Graces, we have the opposite, moving aspect representing the female dynamic, counterpart to the Indian *śakti*, which pours its rhythm into us through the poetry of the Muses—and the basic energy for it all is Apollo, the Lord of Light. The scale shown in Gaffurius's image represent the notes of what is known as the conjoined tetrachord—what we would call the A minor scale: Hypodorian, Hypophrygian, Hypolydian, Dorian, Phrygian, Lydian, Mixolydian, and Hypomixolydian, and these are the Greek names for the notes.

So much for Apollo—the radiance of the god shines primarily

through the Graces, and they are rendered through the inspiration of the arts, which cannot be received until you have canceled ego by putting your head into the mouth of the lion.

LIFT-OFF

Now, this twelfth-through-fifteenth-century flowering really marks the birth of the modern mind-set, with its accent on the individual as a peculiar, special person. For centuries, this mind-set has opened up the hero journey, first to men, and now to women as well. Each woman has the opportunity, for the first time, to find her own path, to take on her own role—not simply as Woman, but as *this* woman, *this* personality. In the past, women have been bound simply to biological, social tasks; they were pregnant most of the time and they had to take care of the children. They also had the enormous social tasks of supporting the household and preparing the food, and the clothing, and everything.

That's no longer what women have to deal with. They are released to develop individually, personally, as men have been released for many centuries, and it's that release of the personality that had put men in the dominant position—not the muscles or anything of the kind. Men were simply no longer bound back as irrevocably to the nature roles.

I think now, with Nora (the protagonist of Ibsen's drama *The Doll's House*) having closed the door, it's the personality of the individual woman that is going to find itself, and the roles will no longer simply be the classic ones.

I taught at a women's college for nearly four decades, and as I said to my students, all I can tell you about mythology is what men have said and have experienced, and now women have to tell us from their point of view what the possibilities of the feminine future are. And it is a future—it's as though the lift-off has taken place, it really has, there's no doubt about it. And it's been one of my great pleasures teaching at Sarah Lawrence all these years instead of teaching a classroom of anonymities, to have had these person-to-person conferences with one woman after another. The sense of individuality that I got from that is something that makes all this general talk about women and men mean nothing to me at all. There is something that the world hasn't really recognized yet in the female, something that we are wait-ing now to see.

To repeat once more Goethe's old line, "The eternal feminine is what draws us on." Having been drawn on for thirty-eight years, I watch it go on its own and I go back into an observant rather than a teaching role, watching the marvel of this ascent into heaven of the Goddess.

Foreword to Marija Gimbutas's *The Language of the Goddess*[1]

As JEAN-FRANÇOIS CHAMPOLLION, a century and a half ago, through his decipherment of the Rosetta Stone, was able to establish a glossary of hieroglyphic signs to serve as keys to the whole great treasury of Egyptian religious thought from c. 3200 B.C. to the period of the Ptolemies, so in her assemblage, classification, and descriptive interpretation of some two thousand symbolic artifacts from the earliest Neolithic village sites of Europe, c. 7000 to 3500 B.C., Marija Gimbutas has been able, not only to prepare a fundamental glossary of pictorial motifs as keys to the mythology of that otherwise undocumented era, but also to establish on the basis of these interpreted signs the main lines and themes of a religion in veneration, both of the universe as the living body of a Goddess-Mother Creator, and of all the living things within it as partaking of her divinity—a religion, one immediately perceives, which is in contrast to that of Genesis 3:19, where Adam is told by his Father-Creator: "In the sweat of your face you shall eat bread till you return to the ground, for out of it you were taken; you are dust, and to dust you shall return." In this earlier mythology, the earth out of which all these creatures have been born is not dust but alive, as the Goddess-Creator herself.

In the library of European scholarship the first recognition of such a matristic order of thought and life antecedent to and underlying the historical forms of both Europe and the Near East appeared in 1861 in Johann Jakob Bachofen's *Das Mutterrecht,* (*The Mother Right*) where it was shown that in the codes of Roman Law vestigial features can be recognized of a matrilineal order of inheritance. Ten years earlier, in America, Lewis H. Morgan had published in *The League of the Ho-dé-no-sau-nee, or Iroquois,* a two-volume report of a society in which such a principle of "Mother Right" was still recognized; and in a systematic review, subsequently, of kinship systems throughout America and Asia, he had demonstrated an all but worldwide distribution of such a pre-patriarchal order of communal life. Bachofen's recognition, around 1871, of the relevance of Morgan's work to his own marked a breakthrough from an exclusively European to a planetary understanding of this sociological phenomenon. There is to be recognized in Marija Gimbutas's reconstruction of the "Language of the Goddess" a far broader range of historical significance, therefore, than that merely of Old Europe, from the Atlantic to the Dnieper, c. 7000–3500 B.C.

Moreover, in contrast to the mythologies of the cattle-herding Indo-European tribes that, wave upon wave, from the fourth millennium B.C. over-ran the territories of Old Europe and whose male-dominated pantheons reflected the social ideals, laws, and political aims of the ethnic units to which they appertained, the iconography of the Great Goddess arose in reflection and veneration of the laws of Nature, Gimbutas's lexicon of the pictorial script of that primordial attempt on humanity's part to understand and live in harmony with the beauty and wonder of Creation adumbrates in archetypal symbolic terms a philosophy of human life that is in every aspect contrary to the manipulated systems that in the West have prevailed in historic times.

One cannot but feel that in the appearance of this volume at just this turn of the century there is an evident relevance to the universally recognized need in our time for a general transformation of consciousness. The message here is of an actual age of harmony and peace in accord with the creative energies of nature which for a spell of some four thousand prehistoric years anteceded the five thousand of what James Joyce has termed the "nightmare" (of contending tribal and national interests) from which it is now certainly time for this planet to wake.

Goddess Studies

ESSENTIAL READING

THIS BRIEF LIST IS COMPOSED OF VOLUMES that I consider critical
sources for the study of goddess traditions in the fields of mythology and depth psychology. The works listed below are all scholarly
in their voice, ranging from archaeology to classical studies, cultural
history, mythology, depth psychology, and women's studies—all oriented toward Goddess studies. A few of these authors Campbell himself relied on, as the reader will see in the endnotes of this volume,
whereas the others I believe would have been in Campbell's library
had he lived long enough to read their work.

—Safron Rossi, PhD

Baring, Anne, and Jules Cashford. *The Myth of the Goddess: Evolution
of an Image.* London: Arkana, 1993.
A synthesis of archaeology, art history, religious studies,
and depth psychology, this is an excellent and encompassing
introduction to the history and mythology of goddesses.

Dexter, Miriam Robbins. *Whence the Goddesses: A Source Book.* New
York: Teachers College Press, Columbia University, 1990.
This study explores the history of goddesses from ancient
Europe and the Near East through mythology and religious
cult practices. Through excellent primary-source translations
of the mythographic material, the author gives a rich and
deep comparative and historical reading of goddesses from
Indo-European cultures.

Downing, Christine. *The Goddess: Mythological Images of the Feminine.* Bloomington, Indiana: Author's Choice Press, 2007.

A contemporary depth-psychological and feminist meditation on the Greek goddesses in relationship to the author's life, this volume provides both rigorous and deep readings of mythological, cultural, and religious material.

Gimbutas, Marija. *The Language of the Goddess.* San Francisco, California: Harper & Row, 1989.

Gimbutas's work was revolutionary to archaeology and cultural history, and Campbell relied almost entirely on her work for the series of lectures that comprise the chapters in this volume that deal with the Paleolithic and Neolithic eras. Her work, which she dubbed archaeomythology, focused on Neolithic Old Europe, which was one of the cultures that predated the incursion of Indo-European peoples and languages into Europe. This heavily illustrated book, for which Campbell wrote the foreword, is an analysis of the symbols and figurines of Neolithic Old Europe in the context of their revealing the mythology of the Great Goddess and an egalitarian social structure.

Harrison, Jane Ellen. *Prolegomena to the Study of Greek Religion.* Cambridge, England: The University Press, 1903; Princeton, New Jersey: Princeton University Press, 1991.

This was an important volume in Campbell's studies of the Greek mythological tradition. Harrison was one of the earliest scholars of pre-Olympian Greek religion and mythology, and this volume continues to be critical in understanding both the history of goddesses in Greek mythology and in archaic Greek religious life.

Kerényi, Carl. *The Gods of the Greeks.* London: Thames and Hudson, 2002.

Campbell relied on this esteemed and important classicist's work, which covered a broad area of Greek culture, history, and mythology. This book is an elegant retelling of many Greek myths, serving as an excellent initial source, with primary-source citations for further research.

Kinsley, David. *The Goddesses' Mirror.* Albany, New York: State University of New York Press, 1989.

A scholarly study of goddesses of the East (India and East Asia) and West (West Asia and Europe). The author explores the importance of goddesses through their cultural context, and through their presence in both elite and popular sources of religious tradition.

Monaghan, Patricia, editor. *Goddesses in World Culture.* Santa Barbara, California: Praeger, 2010.

This three-volume set of essays by various scholars gathers the mythologies and religious traditions of more than a hundred goddesses throughout world cultures.

Monaghan, Patricia, editor. *Encyclopedia of Goddesses and Heroines.* Novato, California: New World Library, 2014.

The forthcoming abridged edition of Monaghan's three-volume set.

Paris, Ginette. *Pagan Meditations.* Dallas: Spring Publications, 1989.

Drawing on Classical studies, depth psychology, and contemporary cultural concerns, including feminism, this book explores the traditions and myths of Artemis, Aphrodite, and Hestia. Using the archetypal psychological perspective of inquiry, the author shows how these goddesses live on in our psyches, individually and collectively.

Endnotes

[Editor's comments are placed within brackets. References to Campbell's works are given in short form for simplicity: full reference may be found in "A Joseph Campbell Bibliography" following.]

INTRODUCTION

1   [Originally published in *Parabola* 5. November, 1980.]
2   William Shakespeare, *Macbeth*, I.5, l. 41.
3   Colin Turnbull, *The Forest People: A Study of the Pygmies of the Congo* (New York: Anchor Books, 1962).
4   [The exploration of these agricultural centers and their mythologies is the central theme of Campbell's *Historical Atlas of World Mythology*, vol. 2, *The Way of the Seeded Earth*.]
5   Chāndogya Upaniṣad 5.3–10.
6   See Leonard William King, *Chronicles Concerning Early Babylonian Kings*, (London, 1907), vol. 2, pp. 87–91.
7   *Enuma elish*, tablets I to VI.57, found at www.sacred-texts.com/ane /enuma.htm.
8   Sigmund Freud, *Moses and Monotheism* (New York: Alfred A. Knopf, 1939), pp. 111ff.

CHAPTER 1

1   [This chapter is based primarily on a one-day lecture of a longer symposium entitled "Myths and Mysteries of the Great Goddess" that Campbell gave at La Casa de Maria in Santa Barbara, California, on April 6, 1983; this lecture is entitled "The Goddess in the Neolithic Age" (L1153). All lecture numbers in these notes correspond to archival records maintained by the Joseph Campbell Foundation (jcf.org). Recordings and transcripts are maintained at Opus

Archives (opusarchives.org). Notes marked—as this one is—in brackets are comments by the editor. Reference notations are not so marked.]

2 Leo Frobenius, *Atlantis*, vol. 1, *Volksmärchen der Kabylen* (Jena: Eugen Diederich, 1921), pp. 14–15.

3 [See Campbell, *Historical Alas of World Mythology*, vol. 1, pt. 1, pp. 51–79.]

4 [See Campbell "Renewal Myths and Rites," *The Mythic Dimension*.]

5 Alexander Marshack, *The Roots of Civilization* (New York: McGraw-Hill, 1972), p. 283.

6 Marija Gimbutas, *The Language of the Goddess* (San Francisco: Harper & Row, 1989), p. 141.

7 Gimbutas, *Goddesses and Gods of Old Europe, 6500–3500 B.C.: Myths and Cult Images* (Berkeley and Los Angeles: University of California Press, 1982), p. 201.

8 [See Campbell, "Renewal Myths and Rites," *The Mythic Dimension*.]

9 Chāndogya Upaniṣad, VI.8.7.

10 Henri Frankfort, Mrs. H.A. Frankfort, John A. Wilson, and Thorkild Jacobsen, *Before Philosophy: The Intellectual Adventure of Ancient Man* (New York: Penguin, 1960).

11 Julius Caesar, *The Gallic Wars*, trans. W.A. McDevitte and W.S. Bohn (New York: Harper & Brothers, 1869), found at classics.mit.edu/Caesar/gallic.html.

12 Arthur Schopenhauer, *Über die Grundlage der Moral*, 1841, found at archive.org/details/basisofmorality00schoiala. [The title Campbell gives is his own translation from the German; this essay is known more commonly in English as "On the Basis of Morality."]

13 Epistle to the Galatians, 2:20.

14 Daisetz Teitaro Suzuki, *The Zen Doctrine of No-Mind: The Significance of the Sutra of Hui-Neng* (York Beach, ME: Red Wheel/Weiser, 1972), p. 94.

CHAPTER 2

1 [This chapter is based on a lecture entitled "The Goddess in the Neolithic Age" (L1153) that Campbell delivered in 1983 at La Casa de Maria during a symposium titled "Myths and Mysteries of the Great Goddess" (see note 1, chap. 1); on two lectures from a symposium titled "Classical Mysteries of the Great Goddess 1 and 2" delivered on January 15, 1982, at the Theater of the Open Eye in New York City (L756–757); a lecture titled "Imagery of the Mother Goddess" delivered August 13, 1976, at the Theater of the Open Eye in New York City (L601); a lecture titled "The Mythic Goddess" delivered May 18, 1972 (L445); and transcript notes from an unknown, perhaps unrecorded lecture from the Campbell archival collection titled "Joseph Campbell: The Goddess Lecture/Abadie."]

2 [See Campbell, *Atlas*, vol. 2, for further discussion of these agricultural centers and diffusion.]

3 Carl O. Sauer, *Agricultural Origins and Dispersals* (New York: The American Geographical Society, 1952).

4 James Mellaart, *Çatal Hüyük: A Neolithic Town in Anatolia.* (New York: McGraw-Hill, 1967).

5 Ignace J. Gelb and Burkhart Kienast, *Die altakkadischen Königsinschriften des*

dritten Jahrtausends v.Chr. (Freiburger altorientalische Studien 7. Wiesbaden: Steiner, 1990).

6   Dante Alighieri, *La Divina Commedia: Paradiso,* translated by Allen Mandel-baum (New York: Alfred A. Knopf, 1995), canto 33, ll. 1–21.

7   [For mythologies of sun goddesses, see Patricia Monaghan *O Mother Sun!: A New View of the Cosmic Feminine* (Freedom, CA: The Crossing Press, 1994).]

8   Campbell, *The Mythic Image,* p. 40.

9   [See Campbell, *Myths of Light,* for more discussion of these figures.]

10   Gimbutas, *Language of the Goddess,* p. 187.

11   Taittirīya Upaniṣad, 3:10:6, found at en.wikisource.org/wiki/Taittiriya _Upanishad.

12   Jane Harrison, *Prolegomena to the Study of Greek Religion* (Princeton, NJ: Princeton University Press, 1991); see chapter 1: "Olympian and Chthonic Ritual."

13   Gimbutas, *Goddesses and Gods,* p. 17.

14   ["Riane Eisler in *The Chalice and the Blade* (1987) proposes the term *gylany: gy* from woman and *an* from *Andros* for man with the letter *l* standing for the linking of both halves of humanity—for a social structure where both sexes were equal" (Gimbutas, *Language of the Goddess,* p. xx).]

15   Ibid.

16   [Quoted in Joachim Gasquet, *Cézanne: A Memoir with Conversations* (London: Thames and Hudson, 1991).]

17   Gimbutas, *Goddesses and Gods,* p. 211.

18   James George Frazer, *The Golden Bough* (New York: Simon & Schuster, 1996), pp. 543–44.

19   [For more on the myth of Hainuwele, see Campbell, *The Masks of God: Oriental Mythology,* pp. 173–76.]

20   J. D. S. Pendlebury, *A Handbook to the Palace of Minos at Knossos* (London: Max Parrish, 1954), p. 26.

21   Anne Baring and Jules Cashford, *The Myth of the Goddess: Evolution of an Image* (New York: Penguin, 1993), p. 127.

22   Baring and Cashford, *Myth of the Goddess,* p. 112.

23   Bhagavad Gīta, 2:22.

24   John G. Neihardt, *Black Elk Speaks* (Albany, New York: State University of New York Press, 2008), p. 33.

25   Françoise Hudry: *Liber Viginti Quattuor Philosophorum* (Turnhout, Belgium: Brepols 1997), 7.1–2. [*Liber viginti quattuor philosophorum,* ascribed to Hermes Trismegistus, is composed of twenty-four definitions of the nature of God; Campbell here translates the second: *"Deus est sphaera infinita cuius centrum est ubique, circumferentia nusquam."*]

26   William Shakespeare, *Hamlet,* act 3, scene 2, l. 22.

CHAPTER 3

1   [This chapter is based primarily on a lecture delivered during a two-day sym-posium titled "Classical Mysteries of the Great Goddess" delivered on January 15, 1982 (L757); and a lecture titled "The Indo-European Goddess" delivered during a three-day symposium from April 4 to 8, 1983 (L1155).]

2   *Kalidasa, Shakuntala and Other Works*, translated by Arthur W. Ryder (New York: E. P. Dutton & Co.; London: J. M. Dent and Sons, 1914, found at www.sacred-texts.com/hin/sha/index.htm.

3   Sir William Jones, "The Third Anniversary Discourse, on the Hindus," 1786, found at www.utexas.edu/cola/centers/lrc/books/readT.htm.

4   [Campbell said "where the Iron Curtain *falls*" since he died two years before the dissolution of the Soviet Union and the Warsaw Pact in 1989.]

5   Gimbutas, *The Kurgan Culture and the Indo-Europeanization of Europe: Selected Articles from 1952 to 1993*, Miriam Robbins Dexter and Karlene Jones-Bley, editors (Washington, D.C.: Institute for the Study of Man, 1997), p. 89–90.

6   [See Campbell, *The Masks of God: Primitive Mythology*, pp. 405ff.]

7   [See, for example, John Bintliff, *The Complete Archaeology of Greece: From Hunter-Gatherers to the 20th Century A.D.* (Chichester, England: John Wiley and Sons, 2003), p. 200.]

8   Gimbutas, *Goddesses and Gods*, p. 238.

CHAPTER 4

1   [This chapter is based on a lecture titled "The Goddess in Crete and Sumer" delivered during a three-day symposium from April 4 to 8, 1983 (L1154); a lecture titled "The Mythic Goddess" delivered May 18, 1972 (L445); and a transcript of an unrecorded lecture entitled "Great Goddess" delivered April 21, 1983, at the New School for Social Research in New York City.]

2   [See Campbell, "The Mystery Number of the Goddess," *The Mythic Dimension*, where he explores the development of numerical thought and its cosmological implications in various mythologies in greater detail.]

3   P. Delougaz, "A Short Investigation of the Temple at Al-'Ubaid." (*Iraq* 5, 1938), pp. 1–11.

4   [See Harriet Crawford, *Sumer and Sumerians*, 2nd ed. (Cambridge, England: Cambridge University Press, 2004), p. 80. She writes, "Of the three examples currently known to us two are dedicated to goddesses, the one at al-Hiba to Inanna and that at al-Ubaid to Ninhursag. It has been suggested that the oval shape was specific to female deities. The best preserved of these is the Temple Oval at Khafaje (Delougaz 1940)."]

5   Baring and Cashford, *Myth of the Goddess*, p. 190.

6   Diane Wolkstein and Samuel Noah Kramer, *Inanna: Queen of Heaven and Earth* (New York: Harper & Row, 1983), p. 146.

7   [According to André Parrot, whom Campbell quotes in *The Mythic Image* in reference to an extended drawing of the Warka vase, the theme is of the cult of the goddess Innin. (p. 83) Innin is thought to be another Sumerian variation of Inanna, derived from an earlier form *Nin-ana* ("the lady of the heaven"). Gelb (1960), however, disagrees and claims that *Innin* is the oldest root of the name and a separate goddess. I. J. Gelb, "The Name of the Goddess Innin" *Journal of Near Eastern Studies* 19, no. 2 (Chicago, IL: University of Chicago Press, April, 1960), pp. 72–79.]

8   Sir Leonard Woolley, *Ur of the Chaldees* (Quebec, Canada: InExile Publications, 2012).

ENDNOTES 275

9   [See Campbell, *Atlas*, vol. 2, pt. 1, p. 80.]
10 [See Campbell, *Hero with a Thousand Faces*, pp. 87–89, 185–86.]
11 Wolkstein and Kramer, *Inanna*, p. 127
12 [Tiamat is a primordial Goddess in Babylonian mythology. In the Babylonian creation epic *Enûma Eliš*, she gives birth to the first generation of gods. See Stephanie Dalley, *Myths from Mesopotamia* (Oxford, England: Oxford University Press, 1989) and *Enûma Eliš: The Epic of Creation*, translated by L.W. King (London: Luzac and Co., 1902), found at sacred-texts.com/ane/enuma.htm.]
13 Shakespeare, *Hamlet*, act 1, scene 2, l. 129. [The word given here as *sullied* has also been read as *solid*; as with the following lines in the soliloquy, Hamlet (like Shakespeare) seems to be indulging in word-play.]
14 [See Campbell, *Mythic Image*, p.23.]
15 [See Serge Sauneron, *The Priests of Ancient Egypt*, translated by David Lorton (Ithaca, NY: Cornell University Press, 2000).]

CHAPTER 5

1   [This chapter is based primarily on a lecture that Campbell delivered during a two-day symposium titled "Classical Mysteries of the Great Goddess IV" on January 16, 1982 at the Theater of the Open Eye in New York City (L759); a lecture titled "Building of Deities: Greek Pantheon" delivered on August 14, 1976, at the Theater of the Open Eye in New York City (L605); and on transcript notes from an unknown, perhaps unrecorded, lecture from the Campbell archival collection titled "Joseph Campbell: The Goddess Lecture/Abadie."]
2   Johann Wolfgang von Goethe, *Faust*, pt. 2, ll.12104–12105.
3   Bṛhadāraṇyaka Upaniṣad, 1.4.6.
4   E.A. Wallis Budge, *The Papyrus of Ani*, book 10, "The Chapter of the Deification of the Members," (New York: Putnam, 1913), found at archive.org/details /papyrusofanireproibudg.
5   *Papyrus of Nesbeni*, chapter 64, "Chapter of the Coming Forth by Day in a Single Chapter" (London: British Museum Press, 2002) ll. 2–3.
6   [For a thorough exploration of the mathematical and mythological permutations of the numbers 432 and 9, see Campbell, "The Mystery Number of the Goddess," *Mythic Dimension*.]
7   Martin P. Nilsson, *A History of Greek Religion*, translated by F.J. Fielden (New York: W.W. Norton & Co., 1964), pp. 28–29.
8   *The Homeric Hymns*, translated by Charles Boer (Putnam, CT: Spring Publications, 2003), pp. 4–6.
9   *The Hymns of Orpheus*, "Orphic Hymn I to Prothyraeia," translated by Thomas Taylor (Philadelphia: University of Pennsylvania Press, 1999), found at http://www.theoi.com/Text/OrphicHymns1.html#1.
10 Baring and Cashford, *Myth of the Goddess*, p. 322
11 S. Giedion, *The Eternal Present: The Beginnings of Art* (Oxford, England: Oxford University Press, 1962), pp. 212–20.
12 *Homeric Hymns*, p. 182.
13 Nilsson, *Greek Folk Religion* (Philadelphia: University of Pennsylvania Press, 1972), p. 79.

14   The Archive for Research in Archetypal Symbolism, commentary on record
      3Pa.063, found at www.aras.org.

15   Campbell, *Mythic Image*, p. 287.

16   Carl Kerényi, *Asklepios: Archetypal Image of the Physician's Existence*, translated
      by Ralph Manheim, translator, Bollingen Series LXV.3 (New York: Pantheon
      Books, 1959), p.50. [Quoted in Campbell, *Mythic Image* p. 287.]

17   [See Joseph Fontenrose, *The Delphic Oracle, Its Responses and Operations, with
      a Catalogue of Responses* (Berkeley and Los Angeles: University of California
      Press, 1981).]

18   [Campbell is paraphrasing Martin Buber, *I and Thou*, translated by Ronald
      Gregory Smith (New York: Scribner, 2000).]

19   Friedrich Nietzsche, *The Birth of Tragedy*, translated by Shaun Whiteside
      (London, England: Penguin Books, 2003). [Campbell is giving a redaction of
      Nietzsche's thesis.]

20   Goethe, *Faust*, pt. 2, l. 6272.

21   *Homeric Hymns*, p. 87.

22   "The Homeric Hymn 5 to Aphrodite," translated by H. G. Evelyn-White,
      Homeric Hymns (Cambridge, Massachusetts: Harvard University Press, 1998),
      p. 421.

23   Harrison, *Prolegomena*, p. 315–316.

24   Baring and Cashford, *Myth of the Goddess*, p. 313

25   *Homeric Hymns*, pp. 60–61.

26   *Homeric Hymns*, pp. 137–38.

CHAPTER 6

1   [This chapter is based on a lecture entitled "The Mythic Goddess" delivered on
      May 18, 1972 (L445); on a lecture from a symposium titled "Classical Myster-
      ies of the Great Goddess I" delivered on January 15, 1982, at the Theater of the
      Open Eye in New York City (L756); and on a lecture titled "Imagery of the
      Mother Goddess" delivered on August 13, 1976, at the Theater of the Open
      Eye in New York City (L601).]

2   Samuel Butler, *The Authoress of the Odyssey* (Ithaca, NY: Cornell University
      Press, 2009).

3   Harrison, *Prolegomena*, p. 293.

4   Harrison, *Prolegomena*, p. 294.

5   Goethe, p. 152.

6   Nietzsche, *Also Sprach Zarathustra*, "Auf den glückseligen Inseln," 1883,
      found at www.zeno.org/Philosophie/M/Nietzsche,+Friedrich/Also+sprach
      +Zarathustra/Zweiter+Teil.+Also+sprach+Zarathustra/Auf+den+glückseligen
      +Inseln.

7   Bhagavad Gītā, 2:2.

8   Bhagavad Gītā, 2:23.

9   Aeschylus, *The Eumenides*, translated by Robert Fagles (New York: Penguin,
      1977), pp. 232–33.

10   Harrison, *Prolegomena*, p. 216.

11   Harrison, *Prolegomena*, p. 214.

12   [See Xenophon, *Anabasis*, 7.8, found at www.fordham.edu/halsall/ancient
      /xenophon-anabasis.asp.]
13   Homer, *The Odyssey*, translated by Robert Fagles (New York: Penguin Classics,
      1996) 10.428–40.
14   Frank Budgen, *James Joyce and the Making of Ulysses* (Oxford, England: Oxford
      University Press, 1972), p. 17.

Chapter 7

1   [This chapter is based on a lecture entitled "The Mythic Goddess" delivered on
      May 18, 1972 (L445); on a lecture from a symposium titled "Classical Myster-
      ies of the Great Goddess I" delivered on January 15, 1982, at the Theater of the
      Open Eye in New York City (L756); and on a lecture titled "Imagery of the
      Mother Goddess" delivered on August 13, 1976, at the Theater of the Open
      Eye in New York City (L601).]
2   Thomas Gospel, 1.108; translated by Guillaumont, Puech, Quispel, Till, and
      abd al Masih, *The Gospel According to Thomas: Coptic Text Established and
      Translated* (New York: Harper & Row, 1959).
3   First Book of Kings, 11:5.
4   Book of Genesis, 3:22–24.
5   [See Kerényi, *Eleusis: Archetypal Image of Mother and Daughter,* translated by
      Ralph Manheim (Princeton, NJ: Princeton University Press).]
6   Kerényi, *Eleusis*, pp.54–55.
7   Harrison, *Prolegomena*, p. 525.
8.   [The canonical myth of Demeter and Persephone is recounted in the
      "Homeric Hymn to Demeter." See translations by Charles Boer or H. G.
      Evelyn-White.]
9   Goethe, *Faust*, ll. 3962–63.
10   *Homeric Hymns*, pp. 161–62.
11   Harrison, *Prolegomena*, pp. 280–81.
12   Taittirīya Upaniṣad, 10:6.
13   Campbell, *The Mythic Image*, p. 388.
14   [Sequence of Pietroasa bowl: Figure 1 is in the short jacket holding a net with
      a fishing pole in his left hand. This is Orpheus, known as Orpheus the Fisher.
      Orpheus is said to be the savior just as Christ, and what he fishes out of the
      water is us, we are the fish, and he brings us up from the abyss of the uncon-
      scious to the light of human consciousness. When Jesus called the fishermen to
      become his apostles and said, "I will make you fishers of men," he was actually
      using this Orphic image of men as fish. Lost in the waters of dream and our
      unilluminated lives as a fish, unconscious of our true humanity, we are brought
      to the surface by the fisherman, the fisher king.
           Figure 3 is the initiate entering the gate. He takes from a basket on the
      head of a door guardian a pinecone. On his shoulder is the raven of death,
      so this is a man in the world of birth and death, now entering the sanctuary
      of initiation, and he's holding in his hand the torch of the underworld. The
      pinecone taken from the door guardian with the sacred basket calls attention
      to the importance not of the cone, the outer form, but of the seeds that are in

it. What is important, the vehicle or what the vehicle carries? Is it the body or
the consciousness that is within the body? What is important about you and
me is not the vehicle but the spirit that is carried by this vehicle of our lives.
The function of the ritual is to disengage our consciousness from identification
with the vehicle to identification with the spirit. Having taken the cone from
the head of the door guardian, the candidate comes under the guidance of a
female figure holding a little basket or bucket of ambrosia. She is the guide
into the mysteries and brings the candidate to the sanctuary of the two goddesses. Demeter is seated with the raven of death on her shoulder. She is the
goddess of the telluric world of the seed, the cycle of birth and death. Down
in the underground with the torch in hand is Persephone, who represents the
enduring eternal fires of the life of the abyss. We do not know what the actual
candidate's initiatory experience would have been, but we do know who the
goddesses are and therefore the myth. The initiate goes from the lesson and
knowledge of Demeter, the mother of our life to that of Persephone, Queen
of the Underworld, the mother who receives us in our death. At the conclusion of that experience we are shown representations of his spiritual state. The
candidate is now bearded, he has matured in his consciousness, and the raven
of death is behind him. He is now the one who has been initiated, and the
goddess Fortuna, figure 8 with the cornucopia, gives him blessing.

The second initiation is represented in figures 9 and 10. Figure 10 is
Hades or Plutus, and in his hand is an enormous cornucopia. He is seated
and beneath him is a kind of crocodile, which is an appropriate representation
of the powers of the abyssal world. The candidate now has the palm of the
pilgrim in his hand. In his right hand is an object that has been identified by
scholars as a poppy, the dream plant that gives visions. Now, what is this initiation going to be? This is the ultimate abyss of life. When the candidate comes
out from Hades's realm he is holding an empty bowl, the wings of the spirit are
on his head, and he has a female body. In other words, he is in the character of
the androgyne. The figure who represents this mystery is in woman's clothing,
but it is Heracles. The initiation that we are undergoing is that of the transcendent mystery. We've gone through the preliminaries of the timely world
and timeless world. Now we come to the transcendent mystery about ourselves
and that is, in one aspect, the androgyne. Although in our historical character
we are either male or female, in our eternal character we have transcended
polarity; we are in essence aspects of an androgyne power. Just as Circe the pig
goddess introduced Odysseus to the androgyne motif of Tiresias, so here it is
the two pig goddesses, Demeter and Persephone, who introduce our candidate
to the androgyne mystery. The other mystery that is to be realized is represented in Castor and Pollux, the twins who are not quite twins. Their mother
conceived Pollux as a god and Castor as a human, and so we are to realize that
each of us is not only mortal but also immortal. In our mortal character we are
either male or female, and in our immortal character we are the androgyne.
This is the deep initiation of this mystery, our immortality and our androgyny
in our eternal aspect. We have to distinguish between the mystical and the
secular aspects of our lives. In our mystical sense, we are both, and we are also
both mortal and immortal. The candidate passes the abyss of Plutus/Hades and

comes to the realization of his androgyny and of his duality. Castor, the mortal twin, has the raven of death on his shoulder, and now the initiate is approaching the threshold of return. Past the figures of Castor and Pollux, the candidate is represented again with a full bowl. Our candidate, now fulfilled, moves back into the field of history as one side of the pair of opposites, the side of mortal life, knowing that the immortal life is also a part of him, as well as the female principle, though not manifest in the phenomenal field. His bowl is now full of the fruit of the initiation, and the female guide brings him to the throne of Apollo. Apollo is the lord of light, the light of consciousness, and his hand is the lyre of the music of the spheres and he sits with a deer at his feet.]

15 [See Campbell, *Hero with a Thousand Faces*, pp. 59-60.]

16 Thomas Gospel, 1.113.

CHAPTER 8

1 [This chapter is based on a series of lectures entitled "The Feminine in European Myth and Romance I, II, III" delivered on April 5, 1986 (L919-921); on two lectures titled "The Great Goddess I and II" delivered on November 13, 1982 (L836-837); and on a transcript of an unrecorded lecture entitled "Great Goddess" delivered on April 21, 1983, at the New School for Social Research in New York City.]

2 Goethe, *Faust*, ll. 12110-111.

3 Genesis, 18:12.

4 [Quetzalcoatl is a Mesoamerican Aztec god often depicted as a feathered serpent. See Campbell, *Hero With a Thousand Faces*, pp. 307-8.]

5 Genesis, 3:19.

6 The Book of Proverbs, 8:27.

7 Genesis, 1:2.

8 Samuel Noah Kramer, *Sumerian Mythology: A Study of Spiritual and Literary Achievement in the Third Millennium B.C.* (Philadelphia: University of Pennsylvania Press, 1998).

9 Seneca, *Epistulae morales ad Lucilium* 107.11, found at en.wikisource.org /wiki/Moral_letters_to_Lucilius/Letter_107.

10 Gildas, *De Excidio et Conquestu Britanniae* ("On the Ruin of Britain"), sixth century A.D., found at http://www.gutenberg.org/ebooks/1949.

11 Nennius, *Historia Brittonum* ("History of the Britons"), eighth century A.D., found at http://www.fordham.edu/halsall/basis/nennius-full.asp.

12 The Gospel According to Mark 12:31; the Gospel According to Matthew 22:39.

13 Girhault de Borneilh, *"Tam cum los oills el cor...,"* from John Rutherford, *The Troubadours: Their Loves and Their Lyrics* (London: Smith and Elder, 1873; General Books, 2010), pp. 34-35.

14 Campbell's translation of Gottfried von Strassberg, *Tristan und Iseult*, ll. 12495-502.

15 Campbell's translation of Dante, *La Divina Commedia: Inferno*, canto 5, ll. 115-42.

16 William Blake, *The Marriage of Heaven and Hell*, "A Memorable Fancy."

17 [Discussion of Isis Borgia image taken from file in Opus Archives Joseph

Campbell Collection, image box 178. Folder titled "Isis Instructing Hermes and Moses."]

18   Apuleius, *The Golden Ass*, translated by W. Adlington (New York: The Modern Library, 1928), book 11.

19   Campbell, *The Masks of God: Creative Mythology*, p. 24.

20   [See Edgar Wind, *Pagan Mysteries in the Renaissance* (New Haven: Yale University Press, 1958), appendix 6: "Gaffurius on the Harmony of the Spheres."]

21   [See Campbell, *Myths to Live By*, chapter 10: "Schizophrenia: the Inward Journey."]

22   Knud Rasmussen, *Across Arctic America* (New York and London: G. P. Putnam's Sons, 1927; University of Alaska, 1999), pp. 82–86; and H. Osterman, *The Alaskan Eskimos, as Described in the Posthumous Notes of Dr. Knud Rasmussen*. Report of the Fifth Thule Expedition 1921–24. vol. 10, no. 3 (Copenhagen: Nordisk Forlag, 1952), pp. 97–99.

Appendix

1   [Originally published in Gimbutas, *The Language of the Goddess* (New York: Harper and Row, 1989). Campbell wrote this shortly before his death in 1987.]

PERMISSION ACKNOWLEDGMENTS

———•———

Grateful acknowledgment is made to the following rights holders.

Archaeological Museum of Piraeus, Greece: Figures 66, 88
Archaeological Museum of Volos, Greece: Figure 16
Robin Baring after Peter Levi, *Atlas of the Greek World*: Figure 133
Brooklyn Museum, Brooklyn, NY: Figure 54
Joseph Campbell, editor, *Papers from the Eranos Yearbooks: Eranos 2. The
    Mysteries*: Figures 141, 142, 149
O. G. S. Crawford, *The Eye Goddess*: Figure 48; Map 4
Marija Gimbutas, *The Civilization of the Goddess*: Figure 21
———, *The Gods and Goddesses of Old Europe*: Figures 20, 23; Map 1
———, *The Kurgan Culture and the Indo-Europeanization of Europe*: Map 3
Tim Hallford: Figure 145
Iraq Museum, Baghdad: Figures 47, 52
Koszta József Múzeum, Szentes, Hungary: Figure 17
Sasha Kudler: Figures 36, 79, 82
M. E. L. Mallowan and Cruikshank Rose, "Excavations at Tall Arpachiyah,"
    Iraq 2: Figure 39
James Mellaart, *Çatal Hüyük*: Figures 8, 9, 10, 12, 13, 14, 15
Musée d'Acquitaine, Bourdeaux, France: Figure 6
Musée de l'Homme, Paris, France: Figure 2
National Archaeological Museum, Bucharest, Romania: Figures 18, 22
Naples National Archaeological Museum, Italy: Figure 11
Naples National Archaeological Museum, Italy / Bridgeman Art Library:
    Figures 87, 100, 101

Royal Museums of Fine Arts of Belgium, Brussels: Figure 116
Städtischen Museum Engen, Germany: Figure 4
Tornyai Janos Museum, Hódemzövásárhely, Hungary: Figure 80
University of Belgrade, Serbia: Figure 19
University of Pennsylvania Museum of Archaeology and Anthropology,
    Philadelphia / Bridgeman Art Library: Figure 50
Walters Art Museum, Baltimore, MD: Figures 32, 38

The following are used through a Creative Commons license:
Peréz Guillén @ flickr.com: Figure 58
Ricardo Liberato (liber) @ flickr.com: Figure 57
Steve Swayne (serendigity) @ flickr.com: Figure 27
Alisa Triolo @ flickr.com: Figure 75

The following were created by or for Joseph Campbell and Joseph
    Campbell Foundation: Figures 3, 5, 7, 24, 25, 26, 29, 30, 31, 34, 37, 43, 44,
    45, 46, 51, 55, 56, 65, 71, 73, 74, 77, 78, 81, 83, 84, 89, 90, 92, 93, 96, 97,
    106, 107, 108, 111, 114, 115, 125, 127, 135, 137, 138, 144, 147, 148, 150, 151

Image research intern: Jordan Chavez

Joseph Campbell Foundation wishes to acknowledge the invaluable
assistance of the volunteers of the Opus Archives and Research Center
(opusarchives.org).

A JOSEPH CAMPBELL BIBLIOGRAPHY

━━━━━━━●━━━━━━━

Following are the major books authored and edited by Joseph Campbell. Each entry gives bibliographic data concerning the first edition or, if applicable, the original date of publication along with the bibliographic data for the edition published by New World Library as part of the Collected Works of Joseph Campbell. For information concerning all other editions, please refer to the Complete Works of Joseph Campbell on the Joseph Campbell Foundation website (www.jcf.org).

AUTHOR

Where the Two Came to Their Father: A Navaho War Ceremonial Given by Jeff King. Bollingen Series I. With Maud Oakes and Jeff King. Richmond, VA: Old Dominion Foundation, 1943.

A Skeleton Key to Finnegans Wake: Unlocking James Joyce's Masterwork. With Henry Morton Robinson. 1944. Second edition, Novato, CA: New World Library, 2005.*

The Hero with a Thousand Faces. Bollingen Series xvii. 1949. Third edition, Novato, CA: New World Library, 2008.*

The Masks of God, 4 vols. New York: Viking Press, 1959–1968. Vol. 1, *Primitive Mythology,* 1959. Vol. 2, *Oriental Mythology,* 1962. Vol. 3, *Occidental Mythology,* 1964. Vol. 4, *Creative Mythology,* 1968.

The Flight of the Wild Gander: Explorations in the Mythological Dimension— Selected Essays 1944–1968. 1969. Third edition, Novato, CA: New World Library, 2002.*

Myths to Live By. 1972. Ebook edition, San Anselmo, CA: Joseph Campbell Foundation, 2011.

The Mythic Image. Bollingen Series c. Princeton, NJ: Princeton University Press, 1974.

The Inner Reaches of Outer Space: Metaphor as Myth and as Religion. 1986. Reprint, Novato, CA: New World Library, 2002.*

The Historical Atlas of World Mythology:

Vol. 1, *The Way of the Animal Powers.* New York: Alfred van der Marck Editions, 1983. Reprint in 2 pts. Part 1, *Mythologies of the Primitive Hunters and Gatherers.* New York: Alfred van der Marck Editions, 1988. Part 2, *Mythologies of the Great Hunt.* New York: Alfred van der Marck Editions, 1988.

Vol. 2, *The Way of the Seeded Earth,* 3 pts. Part 1, *The Sacrifice.* New York: Alfred van der Marck Editions, 1988. Part 2, *Mythologies of the Primitive Planters: The Northern Americas.* New York: Harper & Row Perennial Library, 1989. Part 3, *Mythologies of the Primitive Planters: The Middle and Southern Americas.* New York: Harper & Row Perennial Library, 1989.

The Power of Myth. With Bill Moyers. Edited by Betty Sue Flowers. New York: Doubleday, 1988.

Transformations of Myth Through Time. New York: Harper & Row, 1990.

The Hero's Journey: Joseph Campbell on His Life and Work. Edited by Phil Cousineau. 1990. Reprint, Novato, CA: New World Library, 2003.*

Reflections on the Art of Living: A Joseph Campbell Companion. Edited by Diane K. Osbon. New York: HarperCollins, 1991.

Mythic Worlds, Modern Words: On the Art of James Joyce. Edited by Edmund L. Epstein. 1993. Second edition, Novato, CA: New World Library, 2003.*

Baksheesh & Brahman: Asian Journals—India. Edited by Robin Larsen, Stephen Larsen, and Antony Van Couvering. 1995. Second edition, Novato, CA: New World Library, 2002.* [Reissued in paperback, together with *Sake & Satori,* in 2017; see *Asian Journals* entry below.]

The Mythic Dimension: Selected Essays 1959–1987. Edited by Antony Van Couvering. 1997. Second edition, Novato, CA: New World Library, 2007.*

Thou Art That. Edited by Eugene Kennedy. Novato, CA: New World Library, 2001.*

Sake & Satori: Asian Journals—Japan. Edited by David Kudler. Novato, CA: New World Library, 2002.* [Reissued in paperback, together with *Baksheesh & Brahman,* in 2017; see *Asian Journals* entry below.]

Myths of Light. Edited by David Kudler. Novato, CA: New World Library, 2003.*

Pathways to Bliss: Mythology and Personal Transformation. Edited by David Kudler. Novato, CA: New World Library, 2004.*

Mythic Imagination: Collected Short Fiction. Novato, CA: New World Library, 2012.*

Goddesses: Mysteries of the Feminine Divine. Edited by Safron Rossi. Novato, CA: New World Library, 2013.*

Romance of the Grail: The Magic and Mystery of Arthurian Myth. Edited by Evans Lansing Smith. Novato, CA: New World Library, 2015.*

Asian Journals: India and Japan. Combined paperback reissue of *Baksheesh & Brahman* and *Sake & Satori.* Book I: *Baksheesh & Brahman*—edited by Robin Larsen, Stephen Larsen, and Antony Van Couvering; book II: *Sake & Satori*—edited by David Kudler. Novato, CA: New World Library, 2017.*

The Ecstasy of Being: Mythology and Dance. Edited by Nancy Allison, CMA. Novato, CA: New World Library, 2017.*

* Published by New World Library as part of the Collected Works of Joseph Campbell.

EDITOR

Books edited and completed from the posthuma of Heinrich Zimmer:

Myths and Symbols in Indian Art and Civilization. Bollingen Series vi. New York: Pantheon, 1946.

The King and the Corpse. Bollingen Series xi. New York: Pantheon, 1948.

Philosophies of India. Bollingen Series xxvi. New York: Pantheon, 1951.

The Art of Indian Asia. Bollingen Series xxxix, 2 vols. New York: Pantheon, 1955.

Other books edited:

The Portable Arabian Nights. New York: Viking Press, 1951.

Papers from the Eranos Yearbooks. Bollingen Series xxx, 6 vols. Edited with R. F. C. Hull and Olga Froebe-Kapteyn. Translated by Ralph Manheim. Princeton: Princeton University Press, 1954–1969.

Myth, Dreams and Religion: Eleven Visions of Connection. New York: E. P. Dutton, 1970.

The Portable Jung. By C. G. Jung. Translated by R. F. C. Hull. New York: Viking Press, 1971.

My Life and Lives. By Rato Khyongla Nawang Losang. New York: E. P. Dutton, 1977.

INDEX

ABOUT THE AUTHOR

JOSEPH CAMPBELL was an American author and teacher best known for his work in the field of comparative mythology. He was born in New York City in 1904, and in early childhood became interested in mythology. He loved to read books about American Indian cultures and frequently visited the American Museum of Natural History in New York, where he was fascinated by the museum's collection of totem poles. Campbell was educated at Columbia University, where he specialized in medieval literature, and, after earning a master's degree, continued his studies at universities in Paris and Munich. While abroad he was influenced by the art of Pablo Picasso and Henri Matisse, the novels of James Joyce and Thomas Mann, and the psychological studies of Sigmund Freud and Carl Jung. These encounters led to Campbell's theory that all myths and epics are linked in the human psyche, and that they are cultural manifestations of the universal need to explain social, cosmological, and spiritual realities.

After a period in California, where he encountered John Steinbeck and the biologist Ed Ricketts, Campbell taught at the Canterbury School, and then, in 1934, joined the literature department at Sarah Lawrence College, a post he retained for many years. During the 1940s and '50s, he helped Swami Nikhilananda to translate the Upaniṣads and *The Gospel of Sri Ramakrishna*. He also edited works by the German scholar Heinrich Zimmer on Indian art, myths, and philosophy. In 1944, with Henry Morton Robinson, Campbell published *A Skeleton Key to Finnegans Wake*. His first original work, *The Hero with a Thousand Faces*, came out in 1949 and was immediately well received; in time, it became acclaimed as a classic. In this study of the "myth of the hero," Campbell asserted that there is a single pattern of heroic journey and that all cultures share this essential pattern in their various heroic myths. In his book he also outlined the basic conditions, stages, and results of the archetypal hero's journey.

Joseph Campbell died in 1987. In 1988 a series of television interviews with Bill Moyers, *The Power of Myth*, introduced Campbell's views to millions of people.

ABOUT THE
JOSEPH CAMPBELL FOUNDATION

———————●———————

THE JOSEPH CAMPBELL FOUNDATION (JCF) is a nonprofit corporation that continues the work of Joseph Campbell, exploring the fields of mythology and comparative religion. The foundation is guided by three principal goals.

First, the foundation preserves, protects, and perpetuates Campbell's pioneering work. This includes cataloging and archiving his works, developing new publications based on his works, directing the sale and distribution of his published works, protecting copyrights to his works, and increasing awareness of his works by making them available in digital formats on JCF's website.

Second, the foundation promotes the study of mythology and comparative religion. This involves implementing and/or supporting diverse mythological education programs, supporting and/or sponsoring events designed to increase public awareness, donating Campbell's archived works (principally to the Joseph Campbell and Marija Gimbutas Archive and Library), and utilizing JCF's website as a forum for relevant cross-cultural dialogue.

Third, the foundation helps individuals enrich their lives by participating in a series of programs, including our global, Internet-based Associates program, our local international network of Mythological Roundtables, and our periodic Joseph Campbell–related events and activities.

www.jcf.org